learn

Office 97

J. David Lifer
Gary L. Margot

que E&T

Learn Office 97

Library of Congress Catalog No: 97-69642

ISBN:1-57576-887-9

01 00 99 98   4 3 2 1

Screens reproduced in this book were created using Collage Plus from Inner Media, Inc., Hollis, NH.

Credits

Publisher:
Robert Linsky

Executive Editor:
Kyle Lewis

Series Editors:
Robert L. Ferrett,
John Preston, Sally Preston

Development Editor:
Custom Editorial Productions

Product Marketing Manager:
Susan L. Kindel

Managing Editor:
Caroline Roop

Team Coordinator:
Angela Denny

Designer:
Louisa Klucznik

Production Team:
Custom Editorial Productions

About the Authors

Dr. Gary L. Margot is an Associate Professor in the College of Business and Economics at Ashland University. He received his B.S. from The Ohio State University in Computer Information Systems, his M.A. from Central Michigan University in Management, and his Ph.D. from The Ohio State University in Business Education with specialization in technology.

Dr. J. David Lifer is an Associate Professor in the College of Business and Economics at Ashland University. He received his A.A.S. from The Ohio State University in production agriculture, his B.S. from Ashland University with a teaching certificate specializing in computer science, business, and biology. He also holds an M.B.A. from Ashland University in Executive Management, and his Ph.D. from The Ohio State University in Business Education with specialization in technology.

Trademark Acknowledgments

All terms mentioned in this book that are known to be trademarks or service marks have been appropriately capitalized. Que Education and Training cannot attest to the accuracy of this information. Use of a term in this book should not be regarded as affecting the validity of any trademark or service mark.

Preface

Que Education and Training is the educational publishing imprint of Macmillan Computer Publishing, the world's leading computer book publisher. Macmillan Computer Publishing books have taught more than 20 million people how to be productive with their computers.

This expertise in producing high-quality computer tutorial and reference books is evident in every Que Education and Training title we publish. The same tried-and-true writing and product-development process that makes Macmillan Computer Publishing books bestsellers is used to ensure that educational materials from Que Education and Training provide the most accurate and up-to-date information. Experienced and respected computer application experts write and review every manuscript to provide class-tested pedagogy. Quality-assurance editors check every keystroke and command in Que Education and Training books to ensure that instructions are clear, accurate, and precise.

Above all, Macmillan Computer Publishing and, in turn, Que Education and Training have years of experience in meeting the learning demands of students across all disciplines.

Philosophy of the Learn Series

The Learn Series has been designed for the student who wants to master the basics of a particular software quickly. The books are very visual in nature because each step is accompanied by a figure that shows the the results of the step. Visual cues are given to the student in the form of highlights and callouts to help direct the student to the location in the window that is being used in a particular step. Explanatory text is minimized in the actual steps, but is included where appropriate in additional pedagogical elements. Every lesson includes reinforcement exercises to immediately give the student a chance to practice the skills that have just been learned.

Structure of a Learn Series Book

Each of the books in the Learn series is structured the same way. The following elements comprise the series:

Introduction

Each book has an introduction. This consists of an introduction to the series (how to use this book) and an introduction to the software.

Lesson introduction

The introduction to each lesson includes a lesson number, title, and a brief introduction to the topics that will be covered in the lesson.

Task introduction

A listing of all tasks included in the lesson are shown on the opening page of each lesson. Each task is explained in a section at the beginning of the task.

Completed project

A screen capture or printout of the results of the lesson is included at the beginning of the lesson to provide an example of what will be accomplished in the lesson.

"Why would I do this?"

At the beginning of each task is a "Why would I do this?" section which is a short explanation of the relevance of the task. The purpose is to help show why this particular element of the software is important and how it can be used effectively.

Figures

Each step has an accompanying figure placed to the right or left of the step. Each figure provides a visual reinforcement of the task at hand, and highlights buttons, menu choices, and other screen elements used in the task.

Pedagogical Elements

Three recurring elements are found in the Preston Ferrett Learn series:

 In Depth: detailed look at a topic or procedure, or another way of doing something.

 Quick Tip: faster or more efficient way of doing something.

 Pothole: area where trouble may be encountered, along with instructions on how to recover from and/or avoid these mistakes.

Glossary

New words or concepts are printed in italics the first time they are encountered. Definitions of these words or phrases are included in the glossary at the back of the book.

End-of-lesson material

The end-of-lesson material consists of Student and Application Exercises. The Student Exercises consist of:

True/False questions There are True/False questions that test the understanding of the new material in the lesson.

Visual Identification A captured screen or screens gauge the familiarity with various screen elements introduced in the lesson.

Matching Matching questions are included to check familiarity with concepts and procedures introduced in the lesson.

The **Application Exercises**, included at the end of each lesson, consist of two to five exercises that provide practice in the skills introduced in the tasks. These exercises generally follow the sequence of the tasks in the lesson. Since each exercise is usually built on the previous exercise, it is a good idea to do them in the order in which they are presented.

Data disks

The data disks contain files for the step-by-step tasks in each lesson.

Annotated Instructor's Edition

If you have adopted this text for use in a college classroom, you will receive, upon request, an Annotated Instructor's Edition (AIE) at no additional charge. The Annotated Instructor's Edition is a comprehensive teaching tool that contains the student text with margin notes and tips for instructors and students. The AIE also contains suggested curriculum guides for courses of varying lengths, answers to the end-of-chapter material, test questions and answers, and Office slides. Data files and solutions for each tutorial and exercise, along with a PowerPoint presentation, are included on disk with the AIE. Please contact your local representative or write to us on school or business letterhead at Macmillan Computer Publishing, 201 West 103rd Street, Indianapolis, IN 46290-1097, Attention: Que Education and Training Sales Support.

Introduction to Office 97

Office 97 is a software suite that combines a number of individual applications into an integrated, full-function software system.

The individual applications that make up Office 97 have similar design features; thus, learning one application makes it easy to master other applications in the suite. In addition, you can integrate objects from one application into a different application to accomplish many kinds of tasks needed to run a home or business. This ability to share information between the various applications is a powerful feature found in Office 97.

Office 97 Professional Edition contains five applications. The first application is Word, a word processing program. Using word processing software allows the user to create, modify, spell check, grammar check, and print a professional-looking document.

The second application is Excel, a spreadsheet program. Spreadsheet software is designed to help you create and analyze financial and statistical data easily. People in business and education use spreadsheets to do "what if" analysis. In today's businesses, spreadsheets have become a standard tool to capture and evaluate relevant business information.

The third application is Access, a relational database program. Databases enable you to store and manage large amounts of information. You can use Access's many features to locate and display data contained in database tables. Access's query feature lets you display only data that meet certain criteria, an important feature when your database contains many records. Access's report feature lets you print data from the database in a number of styles and formats.

The fourth application is PowerPoint, a presentation graphics program. Presentation graphics include slides and overheads you create to support a spoken presentation. PowerPoint software includes major features to help you work with text, clip art, sound, and graphs and charts, all with a few simple keystrokes. You can quickly create, view, modify, print, and show a presentation that will be very professional in its appearance.

The fifth application is Outlook, an integrated information management tool that helps you manage your e-mail, appointments, contacts, and tasks. Outlook enables you to handle the day-to-day information issues while working at your desk, including appointments, special dates such as meetings or birthdays, reminder notes, or finding someone's address.

An important key to reaching the potential of Office 97 is the integration feature for sharing information among the applications. You can integrate a spreadsheet or a chart created in Excel into a Word document. You can place a copy of a letter created in Word into your PowerPoint presentation to make an important point.

Office 97 has many common features used by all five applications. Once you learn how to use the standard features found in one application those features would work the same in the other applications. For example, you check spelling, apply fonts and styles, adjust paragraph alignment, copy and paste, insert clip art, save files, and print using the same commands or toolbar buttons in all applications. Thus, the learning curve for the Office 97 suite is greatly reduced because of this standardization.

The Concept of this Book

This book is designed for people who are new to the Office 97 applications but who also need to know how to use them in real life situations. The authors have combined their many years of business experience and classroom teaching to provide a basic step-by-step approach that leads to the development of skills that are advanced enough to be useful in the workplace. This book is divided into several sections: an overview section that covers Windows and Office basics, a Word section, an Excel section, an Access section, a PowerPoint section, and a section devoted to Outlook. Interspersed between these sections are integration lessons that show you how to use applications together to create integrated documents. If a section includes more than one lesson, the first lesson covers basics and later lessons cover more advanced techniques and features.

To the Student:

Your *Learn* textbook comes with a Learn On-Demand CD-ROM. Learn On-Demand provides you with unique ways to learn and practice the material covered in the book. This CD-ROM can help make your learning experience more enjoyable and help you pass your tests by allowing you to learn in an interactive environment.

Learn On-Demand is available to you through your campus' computer lab or you can install it on your own computer. This section shows you how to install the software on your computer and how to use Learn On-Demand.

System Requirements

The minimum system requirements that you need to install Learn On-Demand are

- An IBM-compatible PC with a minimum of 486SX CPU

- 8MB RAM (16MB recommended)

- Microsoft Windows 95®

- Microsoft Office 97®

- VGA display adapter and monitor (640×480 or better)

- Two-button mouse

- Audio sound card (optional, but recommended)

- 4x speed or faster CD-ROM

If you are taking a course that includes more than one Learn book, you will need additional hard drive space to install the software for those books. The following table will help you determine how much additional hard drive space you need.

FILE TYPES	ESTIMATED HARD DISK SPACE REQUIREMENTS
Learn On-Demand program files	2MB
Application support files	1MB per application
Content files (for example, graphics and lesson files)	3.5MB per lesson
Sound files	20–25MB (optional)

If you would like to access Learn On-Demand's audio, you can choose to run the sound directly from your CD-ROM, which will lower the memory requirements.

If you add new titles to **Learn On-Demand** at a later date, you have the option of specifying the directory\folder where the content will be installed. If you use the existing directory\folder, new content files are added to that directory\folder. If you specify a new directory\folder, the install program determines that a previous installation is present and prompts you to do one of the following: select **Yes** to install all new files and move all old files to the new specified location, select **No** to install all new files to the old location, or select **Cancel** to specify a new location.

Installing Learn On-Demand

CD had virus!

You can install Learn On-Demand in several ways. Note the following install options:

OPTION	DESCRIPTION
Minimal install	Copies the basic program files to your computer but requires the CD for graphics and sound.
Standard install	Copies all program files to your computer but requires the CD for sound.
Full install	Copies all program and sound files to your computer.

If you accept the default directory\folder to install Learn On-Demand, all Learn On-Demand files are placed in \Learn\OnDemand\Learn Office 97. If you choose another location to install Learn On-Demand, all the files are copied to the directory\folder you specify. No files are copied to any other location during the install.

Use the following procedure to install **Learn On-Demand** from the CD-ROM to your hard drive. Place the **Learn On-Demand** CD in the CD-ROM drive.

1 From the taskbar, select the **Start** Menu.

2 Point to **Settings**.

3 Select Control Panel. The Control Panel window opens.

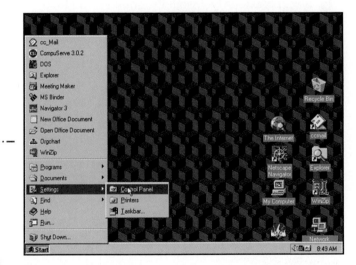

4 Double-click the **Add/Remove Programs** icon. The **Add/Remove Programs** dialog box opens.

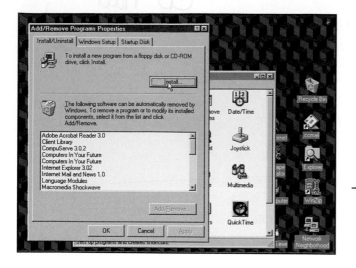

5 Select **Install**. The Install Program From Floppy Disk or CD-ROM dialog box opens.

6 Select **Next** in the Install Program From Floppy Disk or CD-ROM dialog box.

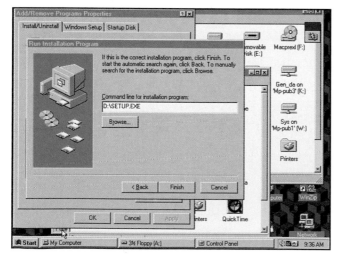

7 If necessary, type **D:\SETUP.EXE. (D:\ represents the CD-ROM drive. Your CD-ROM drive may be different.)** Please verify that the drive letter is correct. The command appears in the **Command line** text box. Select **Finish**. The **Learn On-Demand** Installation program launches.

8 Follow the directions as they appear on your screen. **Learn On-Demand** is installed with the options selected during the installation process. After installation is complete, an item for **Learn On-Demand** appears automatically in the **Programs** submenu. The **Learn On-Demand** shortcut appears in this item's submenu.

Uninstalling Learn On-Demand Titles and Software

Learn On-Demand includes an uninstall program. The uninstall program is included in the **Learn On-Demand** program folder. You can access this folder from the **Start** menu. You can use this program to remove titles from **Learn On-Demand**. The same program can be used to uninstall the **Learn On-Demand** software. **Learn On-Demand** automatically uninstalls when you use **uninst.exe** to remove the final title.

Use the following procedure to uninstall a title from **Learn On-Demand**:

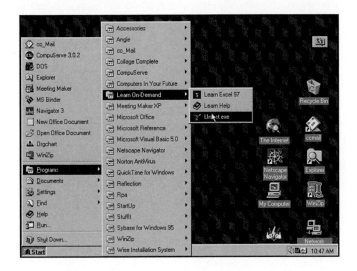

1 Select **Start**.

2 Select **Programs**.

3 Select **Learn On-Demand**.

4 Select **Uninst.exe**.

Starting Learn On-Demand

To start Learn On-Demand:

1 From the taskbar, select the **Start** menu. The **Start** menu appears.

2 Select **Programs**.

The **Programs** menu appears.

3 Select the **Learn On-Demand** program group. The Learn On-Demand submenu appears.

4 Select **Learn Office97**.

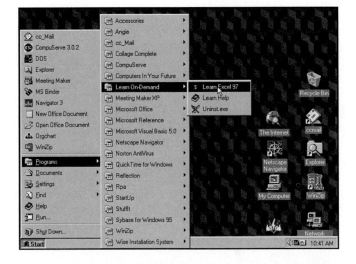

5 The **Learn On-Demand** toolbar floats on the Windows desktop. **Learn On-Demand** is now ready for use. At this point, you need to start **Office**.

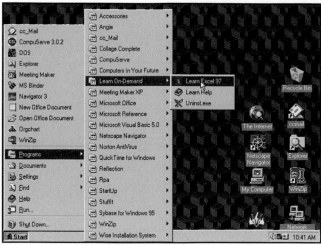

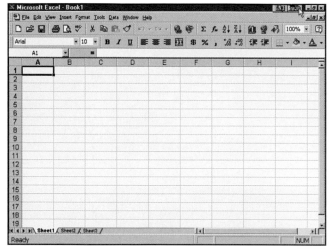

6 The **Learn On-Demand** toolbar appears on the application title bar.

Using Learn On-Demand

Specific tasks in Learn On-Demand are covered in topics. You can learn about a topic by using any of the four **Learn On-Demand** playback modes: **Concept, Concurrent, Teacher**, or **Demo.** These modes are individually covered later in this tutorial.

The **Interactive Training—Lesson Selection** dialog box is the central location from which you can find and view available training modules, lessons, and topics. From this location, you can launch a desired topic in any of **Learn On-Demand**'s training modes. The dialog box contains three tabbed pages: **Contents, Search**, and **Topics for**. The purpose of each page is to help you view and locate training relevant to your specific needs, which are reviewed later in this tutorial.

Click the Teacher button on the application title bar to open **The Interactive Training—Lesson Selection** dialog box. You are now ready to select the desired topic and training mode.

❶ Displays all the modules, lessons, and/or topics available. Click the plus box to expand the listings and click the minus box to contract the listings. A description of each selected topic appears below the list box.

❷ Enables you to quickly locate topics of interest. You can enter a keyword to find all related topics.

❸ Displays only those topics that relate to your working application. A description of each selected topic appears below the list box.

❹ When selected, displays the lessons within the modules.

❺ When selected, groups the topics by lesson. Expanding lessons displays the topics within them.

❻ When selected, displays all available topics.

❼ Provides a description of the key concept of the current topic.

❽ Enables you to learn while you work.

❾ Prompts you to enter mouse clicks or keystrokes as you complete tasks in a simulated environment.

❿ Displays an animated demonstration of the task being completed in a simulated environment.

⓫ Closes the **Interactive Training—Lesson Selection** dialog box and returns you to your application. This button does not close Learn On-Demand. The Learn On-Demand icon still appears on your application title bar.

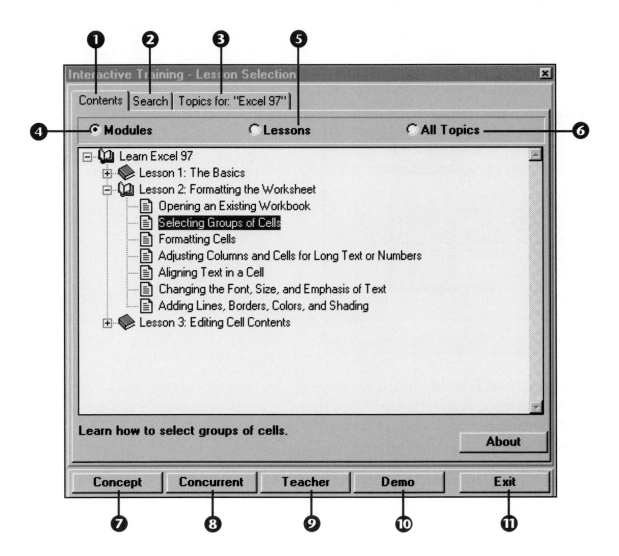

Using Concept Mode

While it is important to learn how to perform a task, it is also important to learn when and why a task is performed. **Learn On-Demand**'s **Concept** mode displays the key concept of a topic to help you gain a better understanding of how the topic relates to everyday uses of the application.

Use the following procedure to learn how to use **Learn On-Demand's Concept** mode:

1 Select a topic describing the task you want to learn how to complete. Click the **Concept button**.

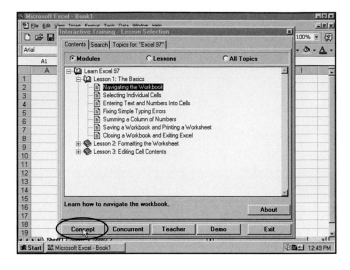

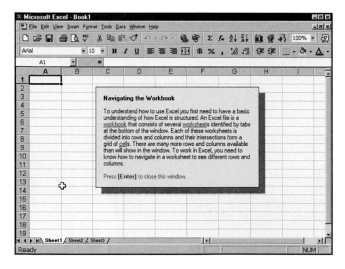

2 **Learn On-Demand** displays the key concept for the topic. When you have finished viewing the topic, click anywhere or press any key. The concept information disappears from your screen.

Using Concurrent Mode

With **Learn On-Demand's Concurrent** mode, you can learn interactively while working with the "live" application and data. This unique mode makes it possible for you to accomplish real tasks with actual data.

When **Concurrent mode** is selected, the **Topic** dialog box opens within the application. This dialog box includes a series of steps that need to be followed in sequence to complete the selected task. As steps are completed, a red check mark appears, indicating that the step has been completed. **IMPORTANT NOTE:** You must follow these steps exactly as directed.

1 Concurrent mode prompts the student with a hotspot around the area of the screen needing action.

2 The hotspot is outlined with a red marquee.

3 The red line drawn from the hotspot to the current step provides easy and clear onscreen directions.

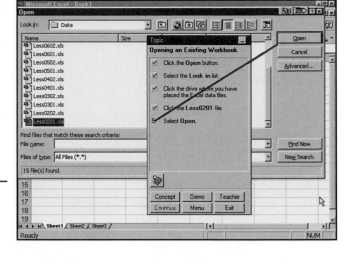

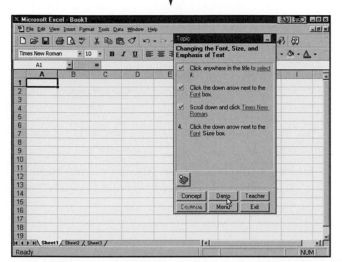

If you need further assistance during your **concurrent** training session, you can switch to another training mode by clicking the **Concept**, **Demo**, or **Teacher** mode button.

Using Teacher Mode

Teacher mode prompts you to enter the necessary mouse clicks or keystrokes to complete tasks in a simulated environment. When you are working in **Teacher** mode, **Learn On-Demand** places a **hotspot** over the location where you need to complete an action. The **hotspot** is outlined with a red marquee. If you make a mistake, **Learn On-Demand** prompts you to try again. Notice that **Teacher** mode provides a simulated environment, so active data and system settings in your application are protected. You can control **Teacher** mode by using the following buttons, which appear at the bottom of the **Teacher** mode screen. Use the following procedure to learn how to complete a task in **Learn On-Demand's Teacher** mode:

Click the **Teacher** button to open the **Interactive Training—Lesson Selection** dialog box, if necessary.

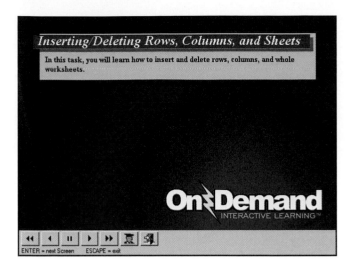

1 Select a topic describing the task you want to learn how to complete. With the topic selected, click the Teacher button.

2 **Learn On-Demand** displays an opening screen with the objective of the topic in Teacher mode.

3 ▶ Click the forward button to begin training. The training for the selected topic appears in **Teacher** mode.

Buttons appear at the bottom of the Topic dialog box.

You can use the buttons, which are described in the following figure, to perform additional Learn On-Demand functions.

❶ Enables you to move to the beginning screen within a topic. (Applicable for multiple-step topics only.)

❷ Enables you to move backward one step at a time.

❸ Pauses **Teacher** mode.

❹ Enables you to move forward one step at a time.

❺ Enables you to move to the last screen within a topic.

❻ Returns you to the **Interactive Training—Lesson Selection** dialog box. From this dialog box, you can select another topic.

❼ Exits **Teacher** mode.

❽ **In Depth:** Detailed look at a topic or procedure or another way of completing a task.

❾ **Quick Tip:** Faster or more efficient way of doing something.

❿ **Pothole:** Area where trouble may be encountered and ways of recovering from mistakes.

⓫ Displays the key concept for the selected topic. Tells you when you would use a software function and why.

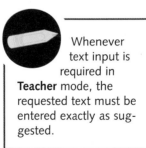 Whenever text input is required in **Teacher** mode, the requested text must be entered exactly as suggested.

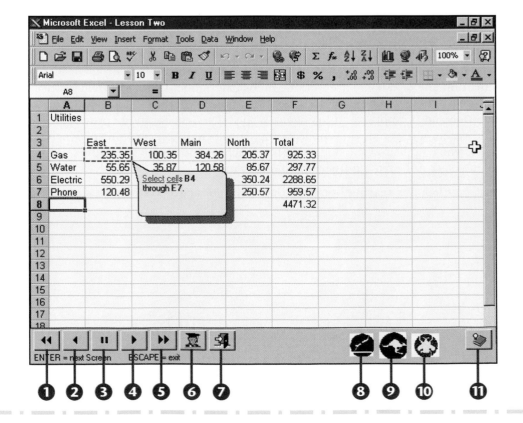

In addition to the buttons, pressing the ⏎Enter key advances Teacher mode one frame at a time. Pressing the Esc key exits Teacher mode.

Using Demo Mode

Demo mode enables you to learn by watching an animated demonstration of operations being performed. All required activities, such as moving the mouse and selecting menu items, are completed automatically.

When you are working in **Demo** mode, you can stop the demonstration at any time by pressing the Esc key. You can also pause the animation by holding the ⬆Shift key. Releasing the ⬆Shift key resumes the demonstration.

Use the following procedure to learn how to complete a task in **Learn On-Demand's Demo** mode:

1 Click the **Teacher** button to open the **Interactive Training—Lesson.**

The **Interactive Training—Lesson Selection** dialog box opens.

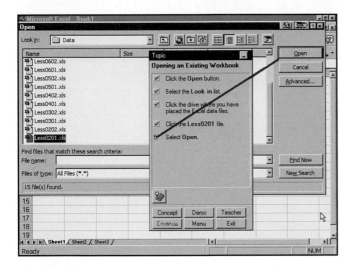

2 Select the topic describing the task you want to learn how to complete. Click the **Demo** button. **Learn On-Demand** displays an animation that demonstrates how to complete the task.

3 You can obtain more information about a topic at any time while using **Demo** mode by pressing the F1 key to display the **Concept** button. Clicking this button once displays conceptual information about the task, and clicking it again removes the information from your screen. Pressing the Esc key removes the button. Depending on the topic being viewed, other buttons may also appear, including the **In Depth**, **Speed**, and/or **Pothole** buttons.

Searching by Topic

After you have started **Learn On-Demand** and are in the application (with your file open) for which you want training, you can select a topic. Simply choose a selection from the list of available modules, lessons, and/or topics from the **Search Tab** in the **Interactive Training—Lesson Selection dialog box.**

1 Click the **Search** tab. The **Search** page appears.

2 Type the keyword **format**.

3 Related keywords of **format** appear in the **Select a keyword from the list box**. Select format from the list.

4 Related topics appear in the **Pick the topic** list box.

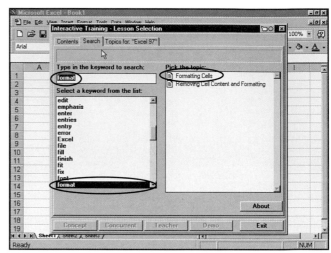

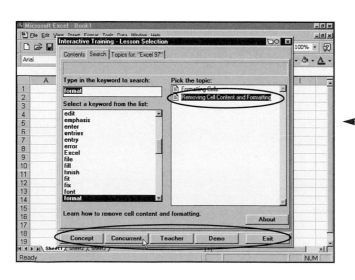

5 Select a topic from the **Pick the topic** frame.

6 Select your desired mode: **Concept**, **Concurrent**, **Teacher**, or **Demo**. Follow the steps as outlined on your screen.

Exiting Learn On-Demand

Use the following procedure to exit **Learn On-Demand:**

1 Click the **Learn On-Demand** button on the application title bar. The **Learn On-Demand** menu appears.

2 Select the **Exit** command. The Learn On-Demand—Exit dialog box opens.

3 Select **Yes**.

Learn On-Demand closes.

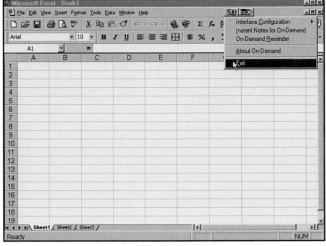

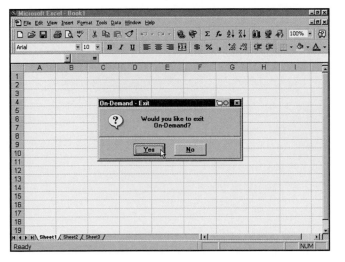

Technical Support

Should you need assistance installing and/or operating **Learn On-Demand**, call Macmillan Technical Support at (317) 581-3833 or send an email to support@mcp.com.

Glossary of Terms

checklist—Steps listed in the Topics dialog box in **Concurrent** mode. To perform the topic, these steps must be followed exactly as they appear.

Concept mode—Learning mode displaying the key concept of a topic. Explains when, where, and why you would use a program's features, as well as any other important conceptual information about a topic.

Concurrent mode—Learning mode enabling you to learn interactively while you work without leaving your "live" application.

content files—Graphics and lesson files associated with Learn On-Demand.

Demo mode—Learning mode enabling you to learn by watching an animated demonstration of operations being performed in a simulated application environment.

hotspot—Area where user input is required.

keyword—A word or phrase used to find a specific training topic. Users enter keywords on the **Search** page in the **Interactive Training—Lesson Selection** dialog box.

reminder—After a period of inactivity, **Learn On-Demand** Reminder displays a message reminding you that **Learn On-Demand** is active.

Teacher mode—Learning mode enabling you to learn interactively by prompting you to enter mouse clicks or keystrokes as you complete tasks in a simulated application environment.

topic—The most specific level of organization within PTS courseware titles. Each topic provides all the information required to complete a specific task within an application.

Table of Contents at a Glance

Table of Contents

Lesson 4: Word 97: The Basics | 46

Lesson 5: Formatting Text in Word 97 | 64

Lesson 6: Special Features in Word 97 | 84

Lesson 7: Excel 97: The Basics — 104

Lesson 8: Special Excel Features — 130

Lesson 9: Excel Charts — 154

Lesson 10: Integrating Word and Excel   172

Lesson 11: Access 97 Basics   182

Lesson 12: Using Filters and Queries   202

Lesson 1
Windows 95 Basics

Introduction

This lesson is designed to introduce you to some of the basic features of Windows 95. It is important for you to understand these features to efficiently use the computer resources. By being exposed to Windows 95, you can make modifications that customize your computer to meet your specific needs.

Visual Summary

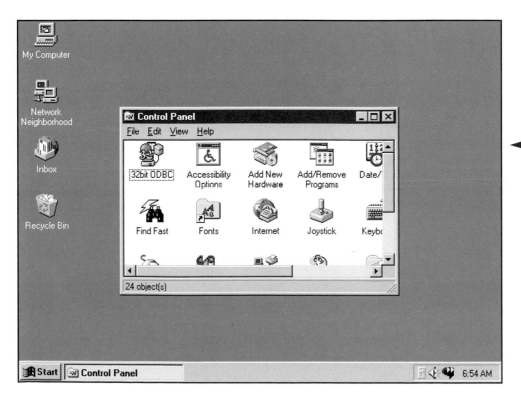

When you have completed this lesson, you will understand how to modify the Windows desktop and work with windows.

Task 1

Starting Windows and Using the Mouse

Why would I do this?

Starting Windows 95 gives you access to Windows' many powerful applications and features. You can work most easily with Windows programs by using a mouse to issue commands and adjust portions of onscreen windows. By using your mouse instead of the keyboard, you decrease the time it takes to accomplish a task.

In this task, you learn how to start Windows and perform basic mouse operations.

Desktop icons   Pointer   Desktop

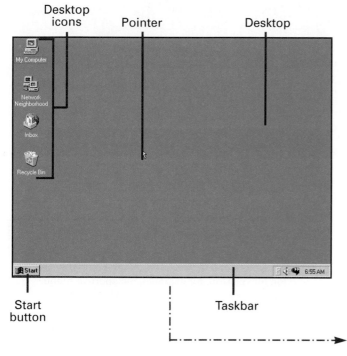

Start button   Taskbar

1 Turn on your computer. After a few moments, Windows 95 starts. The Windows 95 opening screen displays.

In Depth: When you start Windows 95, the screen that displays is called the *desktop*. The desktop is where you work with Windows programs and features. Just as on a real desktop, the Windows 95 desktop has tools you can use to perform a number of tasks. The *desktop icons* vary depending on your computer setup, but all of them give you easy access to a feature or program. The Start button opens the Start menu, from which you can choose applications. The *taskbar* displays the names of all open windows. To move from one application to another, click the taskbar button of the program you want to switch to.

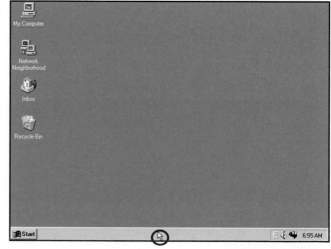

2 Move the mouse on your mouse pad and observe how the pointer moves on the screen. Position the mouse pointer on the taskbar.

In Depth: Before you begin using Windows 95, you should be familiar with basic mouse operations.

Pointing means moving the mouse pointer to a specific location on the screen.

Clicking means pressing the left mouse button one time. Clicking is normally used to select an object.

Double-clicking means pressing the left mouse button two times in quick succession. Double-clicking is often used to open or display an object.

Dragging means pressing and holding the left mouse button while moving the mouse pointer. Dragging is used to move objects from one location to another.

Right-clicking means pressing the right mouse button one time. Right-clicking is normally used to display a shortcut menu.

3 Click the **Start** button to open the Start menu.

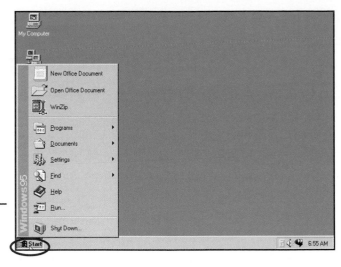

4 Click once on the desktop to close the Start menu. Right-click on the desktop to see a shortcut menu.

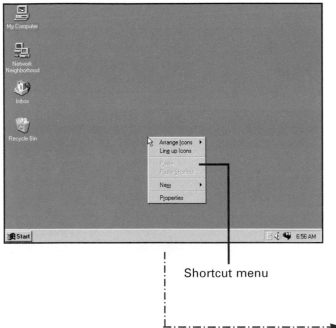

Shortcut menu

In Depth: *Shortcut menus* display options and commands that relate to the location where you right-clicked. When you right-click on the desktop, for example, the shortcut menu gives you access to commands for customizing or working with the desktop.

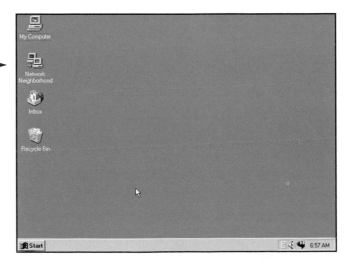

5 Click once on the desktop to close the shortcut menu.

Task 2

Using the Start Button

Why would I do this?

The Start button on the taskbar is the gateway to Windows 95 operations. Clicking the Start button displays the Start menu, from which you can select a number of different options to work with Windows.

In this task, you learn how to access programs using the Start button.

1 Click the **Start** button. The Start menu opens.

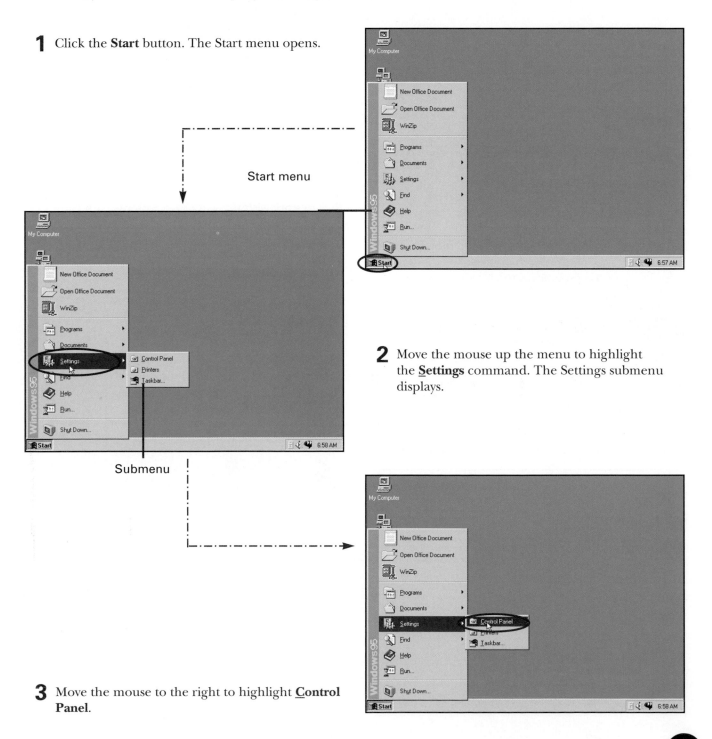

Start menu

Submenu

2 Move the mouse up the menu to highlight the **Settings** command. The Settings submenu displays.

3 Move the mouse to the right to highlight **Control Panel**.

4 Click **Control Panel**. The Control Panel window opens.

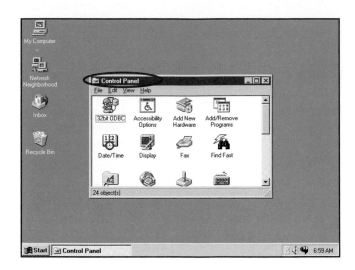

Task 3

Resizing and Moving a Window

Why would I do this?

After a window is open, you can change its size to make it easier to work with the window's contents. You can move a window on the desktop to make it easier to work with another application.

In this task, you learn how to resize and move a window.

1 Position the pointer on the **Maximize** button.

In Depth: You can change the size of a window in one of three ways. The window can be *maximized* so that the window fills the screen. The window can be *minimized* so that it becomes a button on the taskbar. A minimized application is still running and can be activated at any time by clicking its button on the taskbar. Alternatively, the window can be *resized* to change its width or height. After a window has been maximized, the Maximize button changes to the Restore button. The *Restore* button can be used to return the window to its original size.

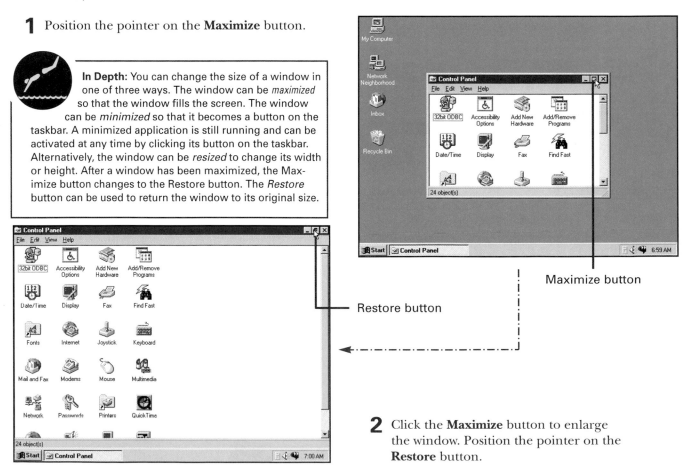

Maximize button

Restore button

2 Click the **Maximize** button to enlarge the window. Position the pointer on the **Restore** button.

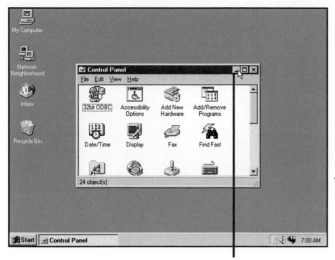

Minimize button

3 Click the **Restore** button to return the window to its previous size. Position the pointer on the **Minimize** button.

4 Click the **Minimize** button to reduce the window to a button on the taskbar.

5 Click the **Control Panel** button on the taskbar to open the Control Panel window. Position the pointer in the lower right-hand corner of the Control Panel. The pointer becomes a two-headed arrow.

6 Hold down the mouse button and drag the sizing corner upward and inward to reduce the size of the window by about two-thirds.

7 Move the window by clicking in the title bar and dragging the window to the center of the desktop.

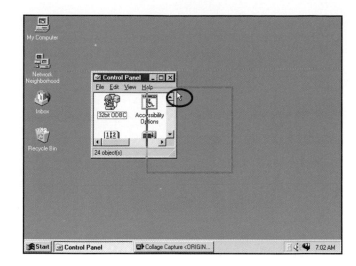

Task 4

Scrolling in a Window

Why would I do this?

Resizing a window may make it impossible for the window to display all of its contents. You can display window contents that are currently out of view by using the scroll bars.

In this task, you learn how to use the scroll bars.

1 Click once below the scroll box in the vertical scroll bar.

In Depth: When a window is too small to display all the information it contains, a *scroll bar* automatically appears on the side and/or bottom of the window. There are three ways to manipulate a scroll bar.

Clicking the *scroll arrow* at either end of the scroll bar will cause the contents of the window to move one line in that direction.

Clicking in the area outside the *scroll box* in the scroll bar will cause the contents of the window to move one page in that direction.

Dragging the scroll box will cause the contents to move in the direction of the dragging.

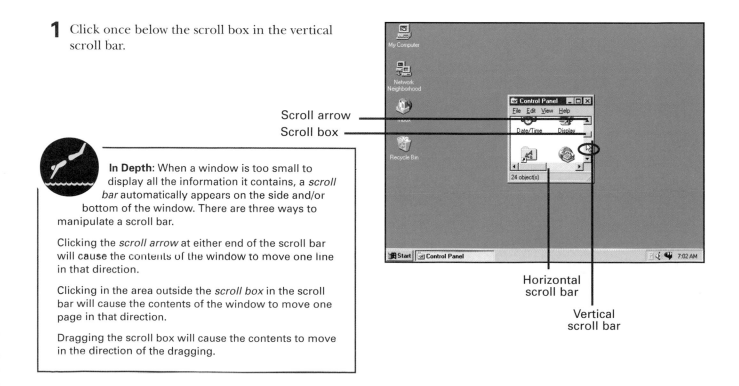

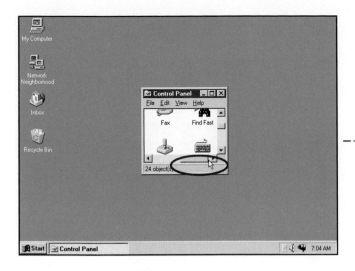

2 Click the horizontal scroll bar once to bring other icons into view.

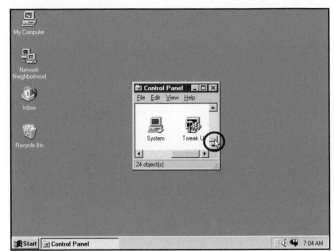

3 Drag the scroll box on the vertical scroll bar to the bottom of the scroll bar.

Task 5

Closing a Window

Why would I do this?

After you have finished working with a window, you should close it. Closing windows you are not using helps keep your desktop neat and conserves computer memory. You can close a window using a menu command such as Close, or you can click the window's Close button.

In this task, you learn how to close a window.

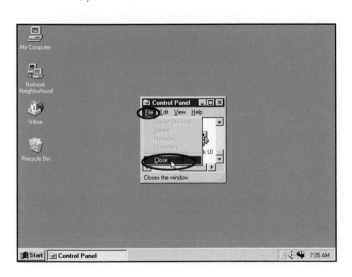

1 Click **File** on the menu bar and notice the Close command at the bottom of the menu. Do *not* click this command.

2 Position the pointer on the **Close** button in the Control Panel window.

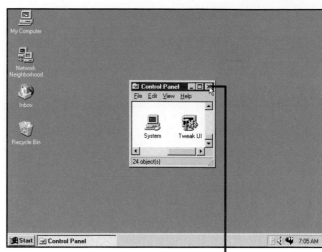

Close button

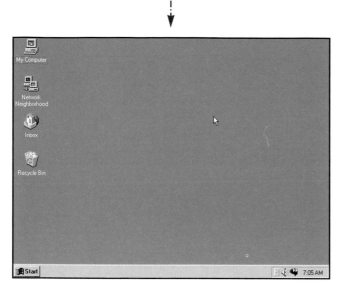

3 Click the **Close** button to close the Control Panel window.

Task 6

Working with Multiple Windows

Why would I do this?

One of the chief advantages of Windows 95 is its multitasking ability. *Multitasking* means running several applications at the same time. You can use the Cascade and Tile commands to control the display of all open windows on the desktop.

In this task, you learn how to work with more than one window on the desktop.

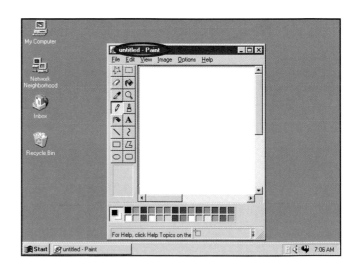

1 Click **Start, Programs, Accessories, Paint** to open the Paint application. Click the Restore button if necessary to display the application in a window.

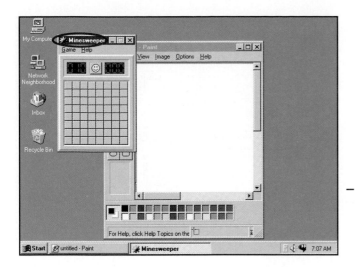

2 Click **Start, Programs, Accessories, Games, Minesweeper** to open the Minesweeper game.

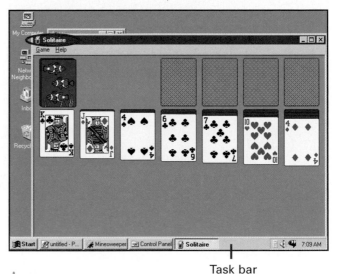

Task bar

3 Click **Start, Settings, Control Panel** to open the Control Panel window. Click **Start, Programs, Accessories, Games, Solitaire** to open the Solitaire game. At this point you have four applications open. Notice that the windows are stacked on top of each other so that you can only see the last window you opened clearly.

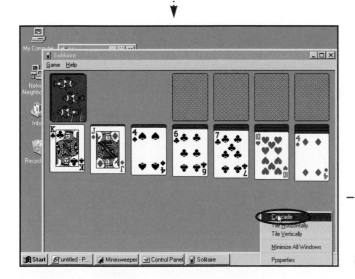

4 Right-click on an open space on the taskbar. A shortcut menu opens.

5 Click **Cascade** on the shortcut menu. The open applications display in a stack with their title bars showing.

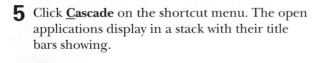

In Depth: When more than one window is open on the desktop, only one is active at a time. The *active window* is the window ready to accept your commands. You can tell which is the active window by its title bar. It will be in color or darker than the other title bars.

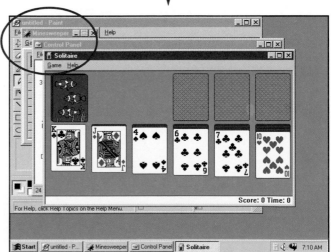

6 Right-click on an open space on the taskbar. Click **Tile Horizontally** on the shortcut menu.

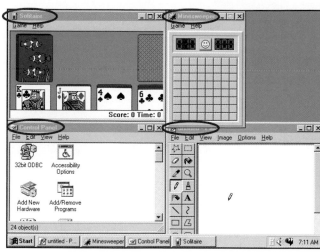

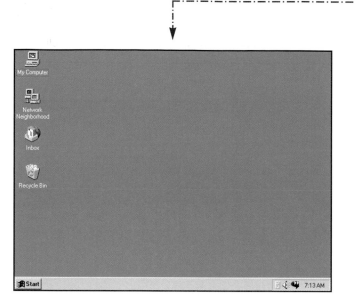

7 Close all open windows by clicking the **Close** button of each window.

Task 7

Using the Windows Help System

Why would I do this?

Because you may forget how to perform a task that you do not perform frequently, Windows 95 has a useful, friendly Help feature. This Help feature is organized by tabs (Contents, Index, and Find) to give you several different methods for obtaining help.

In this task, you learn how to use the Windows Help system.

1 Click **Start, Help**.

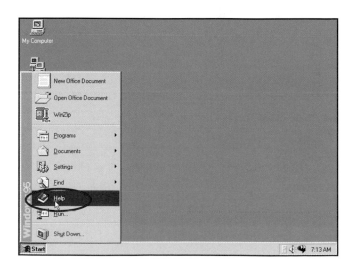

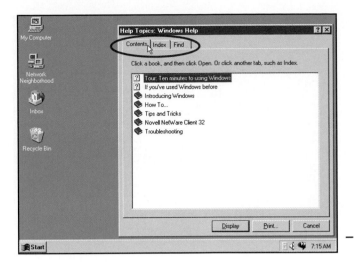

2 The Windows Help dialog box opens. Notice the tabs in the dialog box that give you three options for finding help: Contents, Index, and Find.

In Depth: The Windows Help window consists of three tabs that enable you to find Help in three different ways. The Contents tab acts as a table of contents. Double-click one of the "books" to see further Help topics in that area. The Index tab contains a listing of all the Help topics in the Help system. Scroll through the index list to find a topic or type part or all of the topic to see topics matching your request. The Find tab lets you locate any word or phrase in the Help system.

3 On the Contents tab, double-click the **Tips and Tricks** topic. A list of subtopics displays.

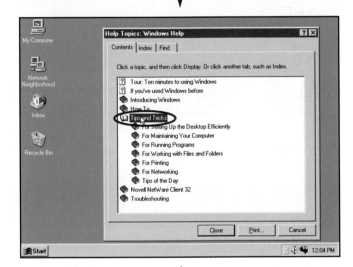

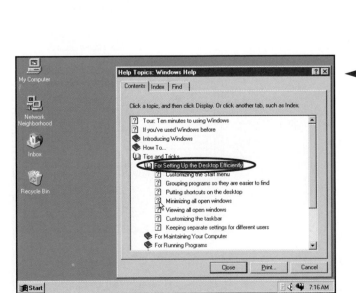

4 Double-click **For Setting Up the Desktop Efficiently**. A list of subordinate Help topics displays.

5 Double-click the Help topic **Minimizing all open windows**. The Help topic opens on the screen.

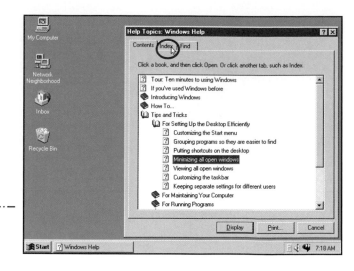

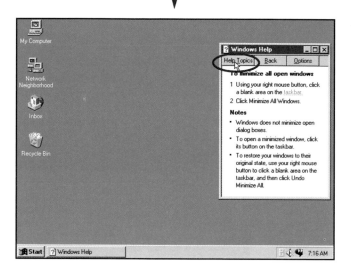

6 Click the **Help Topics** button to return to the main Help window.

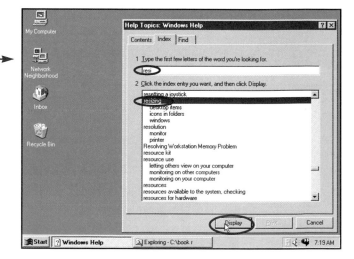

7 Click the **Index** tab. Locate Help information on the topic of resizing. In the text box at the top of the window, type the first few letters of the topic: **resi**. Windows scrolls through the index list to find the first topic with letters that match your typing.

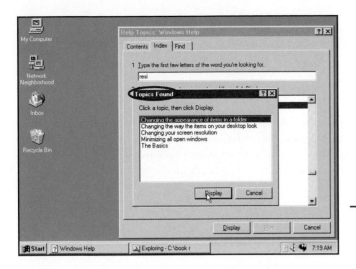

8 To narrow the search, click **Display**. Windows displays the **Topics Found** window, which gives a list of the Help topics about resizing.

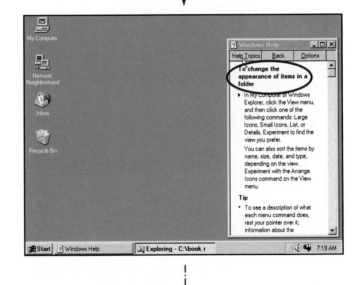

9 To see the Help topic that is first in the list, click **Display**. A Help topic displays describing how to change the appearance of items in a folder.

10 Close the Help topic by clicking its **Close** button.

Task 8

Shutting Down Windows

Why would I do this?

Shutting down Windows means to exit Windows. By shutting down your computer properly, Windows prepares your system to be turned off. Windows saves any system changes made since the last time you were on your system, and saves anything currently stored in memory to the hard disk. The Shut Down Windows dialog box also gives you other options, such as restarting your computer, restarting your computer in MS-DOS mode, or logging on to the computer as a different user.

In this task, you learn how to shut down Windows.

1 Click **Start, Shut Down**.

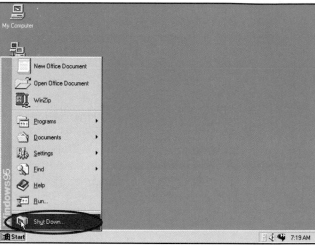

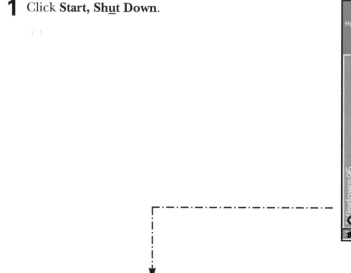

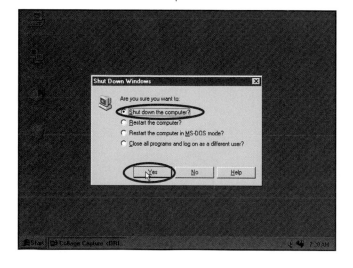

2 The **Shut Down Windows** dialog box opens. Make sure the **Shut down the computer?** option is selected.

3 Click the **Yes** button to exit Windows 95.

Student Exercises

True-False

For each of the following circle either T or F to indicate whether the statement is true or false.

T   F   **1.** When you click the Start button, you open a dialog box.

T   F   **2.** You can find help on a specific task from a list of topics by clicking the Index tab in the Help Topics dialog box.

T   F   **3.** You can change the size of a window.

T   F   **4.** After you have minimized a window, you can click the window's name on the taskbar to restore it.

T   F   **5.** After you have closed a window, you can click the window's name on the taskbar to restore it.

T   F   **6.** After a window is maximized, the Restore button replaces the Maximize button.

T   F   **7.** The first step to properly end a Windows 95 session is to click the Start button.

T   F   **8.** The Control Panel is listed on the Programs menu.

T   F   **9.** Dragging involves pointing, holding the left mouse button, and moving the mouse.

T   F   **10.** Double-clicking involves pressing the left mouse button, waiting a few seconds, and pressing the left mouse button a second time.

Identifying Parts of the Windows Desktop

Refer to the figure and identify the numbered parts of the screen. Write the letter of the correct label in the space next to the number.

1. E
2. D
3. B
4. F
5. C
6. J
7. A
8. I
9. G
10. H

  A. Start button
  B. Vertical scroll bar
  C. Horizontal scroll bar
  D. Taskbar
  E. Resizing arrow
  F. Desktop icons
  G. Scroll box
  H. Desktop
  I. Minimize button
  J. Maximize button

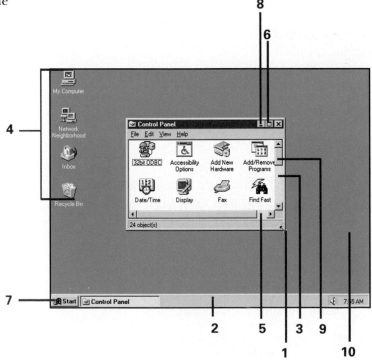

Matching

Match the following statements to the word or phrase that is the best match from the list. Write the letter of the matching word or phrase in the space provided next to the number.

1. _A_ A button that shuts an open window
2. _H_ A button that enlarges a window to fill the screen
3. _K_ A button that returns a window to its previous size
4. _E_ A button that reduces a window to a button on the taskbar
5. _I_ The bar at the bottom of the Windows 95 screen
6. _B_ The view that shows the title bars of all open windows
7. _F_ The view that shows all open windows arranged on the desktop
8. _C_ Pressing and holding the left mouse button while moving the mouse
9. _J_ The button that is the gateway to Windows 95 operations
10. _G_ The proper way to end a Windows 95 session

A. Close
B. Cascade
C. Dragging
D. Clicking
E. Minimize
F. Tile
G. Shut down
H. Maximize
I. Taskbar
J. Start
K. Restore

Application Exercises

Exercise 1

1. Open the Microsoft Word window.
2. Open the Control Panel window.
3. Cascade the windows.
4. Open the Microsoft Excel window.
5. Cascade the windows.
6. Resize the Control Panel window, making the window approximately one-third bigger.
7. Tile the windows vertically.
8. Close the Word window.
9. Close the Excel window.
10. Use the Windows 95 Help feature to learn how to close, minimize, and maximize.

Lesson 2
Windows 95 Disk and File Management

Task 1 Formatting a Disk

Task 2 Creating a File

Task 3 Creating a New Folder

Task 4 Copying a File

Task 5 Renaming a File or Folder

Task 6 Deleting a File or Folder

Introduction

In this lesson you use one of Windows 95's file management applications: Windows Explorer. Explorer is a tool that enables you to work easily and efficiently with files, folders, and disks.

Windows Explorer shows you the files and folders contained on the disk you are currently working with. Your Explorer window may not match exactly the illustrations shown in this lesson, but Explorer's features work the same way on every computer.

Visual Summary

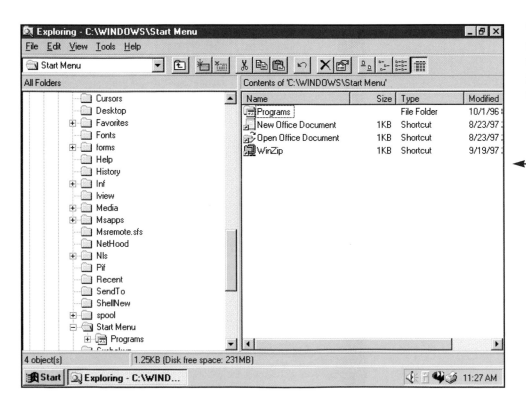

When you have completed this lesson, you will be able to use Windows Explorer for a number of file management tasks.

Task 1

Formatting a Disk

Why would I do this?

Although most new disks are already *formatted* when you buy them, you might want to format a disk to remove existing files or to check for disk integrity.

In this task, you learn how to format a disk.

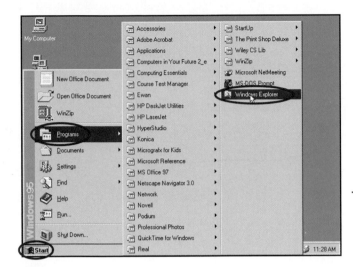

1 To open Windows Explorer, click **Start, Programs, Windows Explorer**.

In Depth: Disks are available in two capacities: double density (DD) and high density (HD). Double-density disks, which are rarely used, have a storage capacity of 720 kilobytes (KB); high-density disks have a capacity of 1.44 megabytes (MB).

Details button

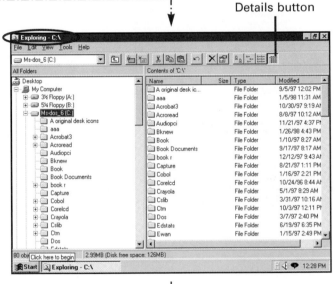

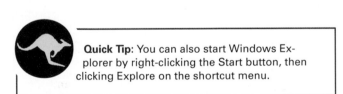

Quick Tip: You can also start Windows Explorer by right-clicking the Start button, then clicking Explore on the shortcut menu.

2 Windows Explorer opens on the desktop. If necessary, click the **Details** button on the toolbar to make your window view the same as the figures.

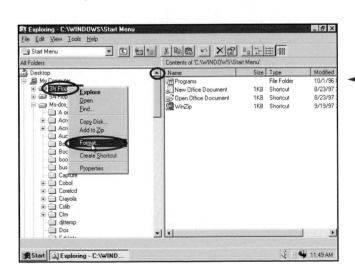

3 Place a disk you want to format in the A: disk drive. Scroll to the top of All Folders. Right-click on **3½ Floppy (A:)** to open a shortcut menu.

4 Click **Format** on the shortcut menu. The Format dialog box opens. Click the **Capacity** drop-down arrow to see the available capacities.

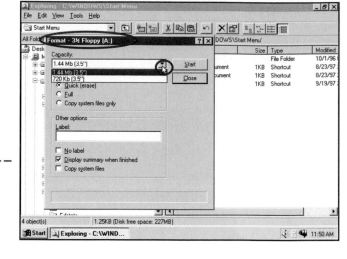

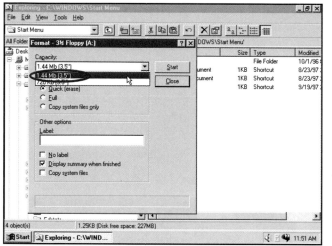

5 Select either **1.44MB (3.5")** or **720KB (3.5")** and click.

6 Select **Full** under Format type.

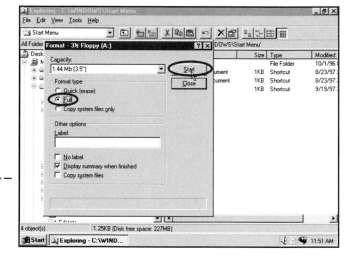

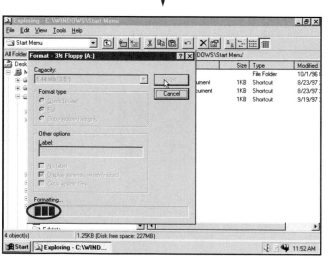

7 Click **Start** to begin the format. The blue bar at the bottom of the dialog box shows the progress of the format.

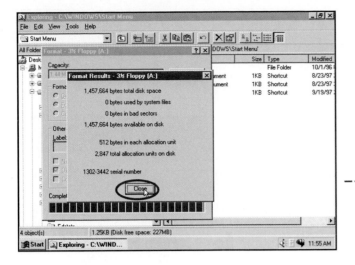

8 When the format is complete, a message box displays to show the results of the format.

9 Click **Close** in the message box.

10 Click **Close** in the Format dialog box.

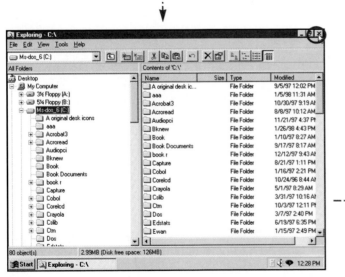

11 Click the **Close** button to close the Explorer window.

Task 2

Creating a File

Why would I do this?

In most instances, you create files in a specific application. For example, Word is used to create a word processing document, while Excel is used to create a spreadsheet document. There may be times, however, when you want to create a simple document. WordPad can do this for you.

In this task, you learn how to create a WordPad file that you can use to practice other Windows Explorer features.

1 Click **Start, Programs, Accessories, WordPad**.

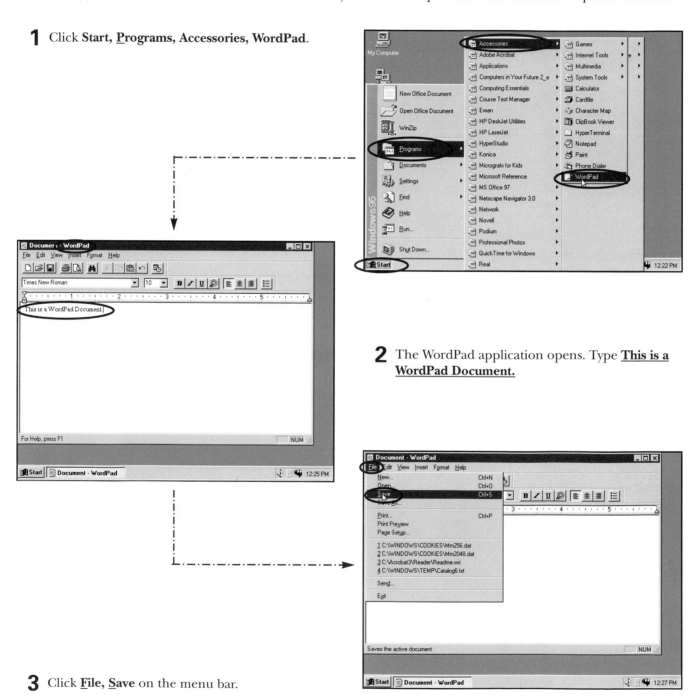

2 The WordPad application opens. Type **This is a WordPad Document.**

3 Click **File, Save** on the menu bar.

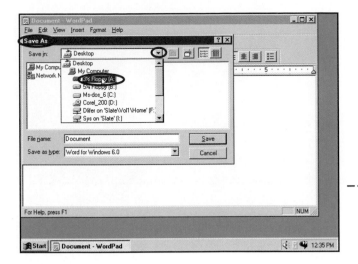

4 The **Save As** dialog box opens. Click the **Save in** drop-down arrow to display available places to save a document. **Click 3½ Floppy (A:).**

5 Double-click inside the **File name** box to highlight **Document**.

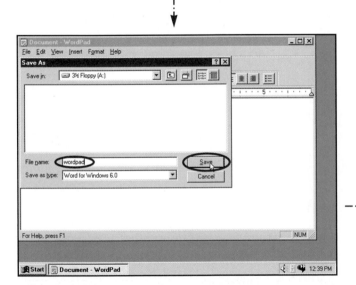

6 Type **wordpad** in the **File name** box.

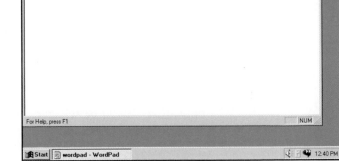

7 Click **Save** in the **Save As** dialog box. The WordPad document displays the new name in the title bar.

8 Click the **Close** button in the WordPad window to close WordPad.

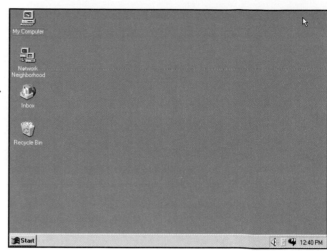

9 Start Windows Explorer. Click the scroll up arrow in All Folders and click **3¹/₂ Floppy (A:)**. Note that the file *wordpad* is now stored on the floppy disk.

Task 3

Creating a New Folder

Why would I do this?

Using *folders* is a way to keep files organized. One folder can be created to store all homework, while another folder can be created to store personal information.

In this task, you learn how to create a folder for saving homework.

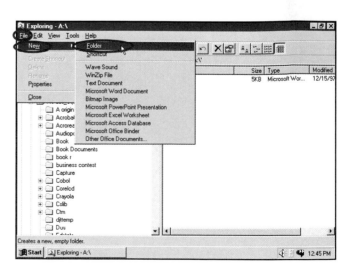

1 Windows Explorer should be open on your screen. The 3¹/₂ floppy drive should be selected in the All Folders pane. Click **File, New, Folder** from the menu bar.

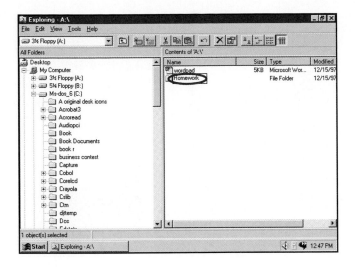

2 A new folder displays in the Contents pane of Explorer. Change the name of the folder by typing **Homework**.

In Depth: New folders are automatically named New Folder and the name is highlighted. To change the name of the new folder while the name is highlighted, simply type the name.

Task 4

Copying a File

Why would I do this?

Copying a file allows you to place a duplicate version of a file on another disk or in another folder. The Copy feature can help you keep archives of your work or share your work with others.

In this task, you learn how to copy the file you created in this lesson from the A: drive to the C: drive.

1 Click the **wordpad** file to select it.

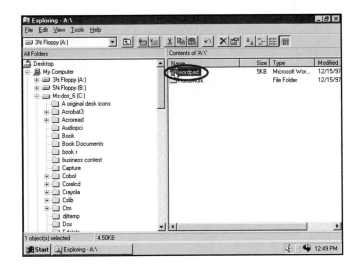

In Depth: To select a single file or folder in Explorer, click once on the file or folder. To select more than one file or folder, click the first file or folder, hold Ctrl down, and click additional files or folders. To select a block of adjacent files or folders, click the first file or folder, hold Shift down, and click the last file or folder of the block.

Pothole: Do not double-click a file you are selecting. Double-clicking will open the file and the application used to create it.

2 Drag the highlighted file to the **C:** drive. The file name and its icon attach to the pointer, along with a small white box containing a + sign. The + sign indicates that you are copying the file to the C: drive.

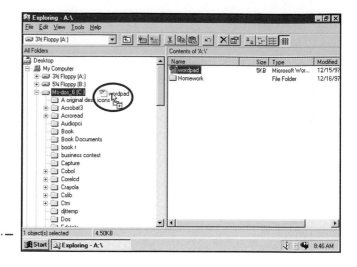

3 Release the mouse button when the **C:** drive name becomes highlighted.

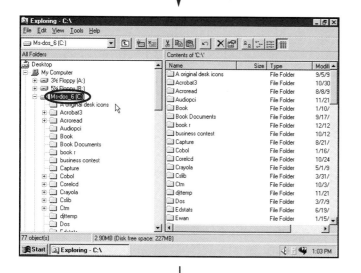

4 In the All Folders pane, click the **C:** drive. In the Contents pane, scroll down until you see the file you copied.

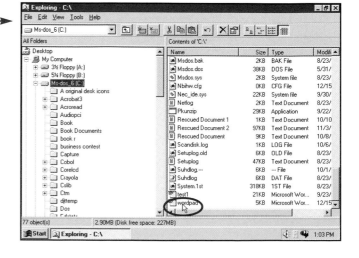

Task 5

Renaming a File or Folder

Why would I do this?

There may be times when you have created a folder or saved a file and then realized that you want to change the folder or file name to provide for better documentation. Because a file name in Windows 95 can be up to 255 characters long, you have a tremendous amount of freedom in naming your file.

In this task, you learn how to rename a file or folder.

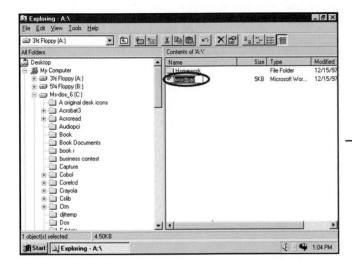

1 In the All Folders pane, click **3¹/₂ Floppy (A:)**. Click the **wordpad** file once to select it. After waiting several seconds (remember, double-clicking opens the file and its application), click the **wordpad** file again.

2 Type the new name **memo**. Click twice outside the selected box to remove the highlight.

3 Click the **Homework** folder once. After waiting several seconds, click **Homework** again.

4 Type the new name **Homework Fall Semester**.
Click twice outside the selected box.

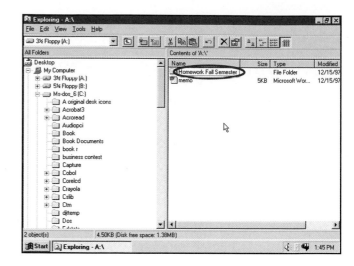

Task 6

Deleting a File or Folder

Why would I do this?

It is important to periodically delete old folders and files from your hard disk to keep it from filling up with out-of-date or unneeded files. Deleting a file or folder removes the file or folder from the hard disk and places the file or folder in the Recycle Bin. Until you delete the file or folder from the Recycle Bin you can retrieve a file or folder deleted by mistake. *Note that the Recycle Bin does not store files deleted from a floppy disk.*

In this task, you learn how to delete files and folders.

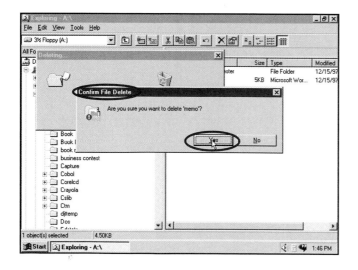

1 Click **memo** to select it. Press Del. A message box displays asking if you are sure you want to delete the file.

2 Confirm the deletion by clicking **Yes**. The file is removed from the disk. Select the **Homework Fall Semester** folder.

3 Press Del. A message box displays asking if you are sure you want to delete the folder.

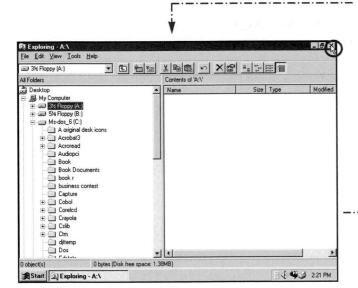

4 Confirm the deletion by clicking **Yes**. The floppy disk in the A: disk drive is now empty of files and folders.

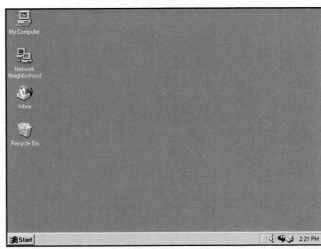

5 Close Windows Explorer by clicking its **Close** button.

Student Exercises

True-False

For each of the following, circle either T or F to indicate whether the statement is true or false.

T F **1.** There are two types of disks: high density and low density.

T F **2.** To start Explorer, right-click anywhere on the desktop.

T F **3.** You delete a folder by clicking the name of the folder in Explorer and pressing Del.

T F **4.** You can create a new folder on a disk by clicking New on the Edit menu.

T F **5.** The capacity of a high-density disk is 1.44MB.

T F **6.** Right-clicking the disk drive name in Explorer enables you to format a disk.

T F **7.** To copy a file, select it and then drag it from its current location to the location where you want the copy.

T F **8.** To rename a file, click the old file name once, wait, click again, and then type the new file name.

T F **9.** To rename a folder, double-click the folder name.

T F **10.** When you create a new folder, the folder is automatically named New Folder.

Identifying Parts of the Explorer Screen

going to collect

Refer to the figure and identify the numbered parts of the screen. Write the letter of the correct label in the space next to the number.

1. _____
2. _____
3. _____
4. _____
5. _____
6. _____
7. _____
8. _____
9. _____
10. _____

A. File menu
B. Paint file
C. Computers folder
D. Contents of the 3½ Floppy (A:) disk drive
E. All Folders pane
F. Contents pane
G. Close button
H. A folder on the C: drive.
I. Date file was last modified
J. C: drive

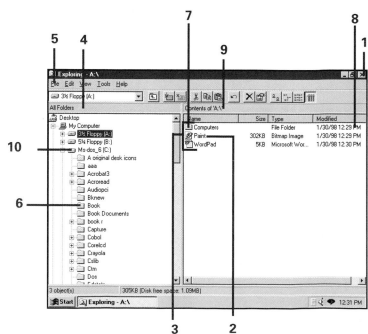

Matching *Going to collect*

Match the following statements to the word or phrase that is the best match from the list. Write the letter of the matching word or phrase in the space provided next to the number.

1. ___ Disk with the capacity of 1.44MB
2. ___ The name of the disk drive that uses a $3^1/_2$" disk
3. ___ The actual document saved on a disk
4. ___ Key used to remove a file or folder from a disk
5. ___ Place where related files can be stored
6. ___ Dragging files from one disk to another
7. ___ Disk with the capacity of 720KB
8. ___ Change the file name
9. ___ Process of making a new disk ready to use
10. ___ Name of the program that is used for file management

A. File
B. Copying
C. High density
D. Double density
E. Delete
F. Rename
G. Floppy or A:
H. Explorer
I. Dialog box
J. Folder
K. Format

Application Exercises

Exercise 1

1. Format a new disk.
2. Create a folder on your disk named **Spring**.
3. Create a folder on your disk named **Fall**.
4. Copy two files of your choice from the C: drive to the A: drive. Copy one to the **Fall** folder and one to the **Spring** folder.
5. Rename the **Fall** folder **Autumn**.
6. Delete all the files from the A: drive.
7. Delete all the folders from the A: drive.
8. Delete the **wordpad** document from the C: drive.

Lesson 3
Office 97 Basics

Task 1 Starting Office Applications

Task 2 Using the Office Shortcut Bar

Task 3 Opening an Existing Document

Task 4 Using the Office Assistant

Task 5 Exiting Office Applications

Introduction

Software suites such as Microsoft Office 97 combine individual applications into powerful, full-function software systems. The applications in the suite have similar designs and systems so that learning one application makes it easy to master other applications in the suite. Using a software suite is more cost-effective because bundled software is cheaper to purchase than individual application software programs. Because the applications in a software suite are designed to work together, you can easily integrate an object from one application into a document created in another application.

The Professional Edition of Microsoft Office 97 consists of five applications: Word (word processing), Excel (worksheet), Access (database), PowerPoint (presentation graphics), and Outlook (e-mail and information management).

Visual Summary

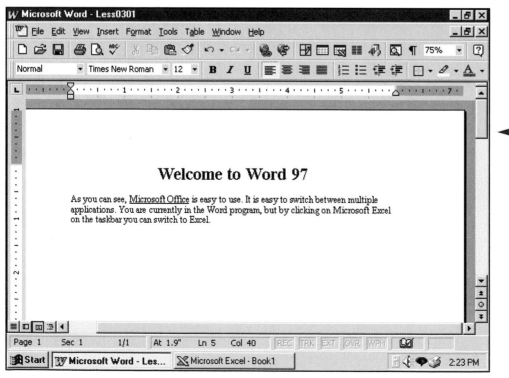

When you have completed Task 3, you will have an Office document on your screen that looks like this:

Task 1

Starting Office Applications

Why would I do this?

You can use Office 97 applications to perform a variety of tasks on your computer. You may, for example, want to create a letter using Word or create a database using Access. Office 97 gives you several ways to open an application. The two most common methods are using the Programs menu and using the Office Shortcut Bar.

In this task, you learn how to start an Office 97 application using the Programs menu.

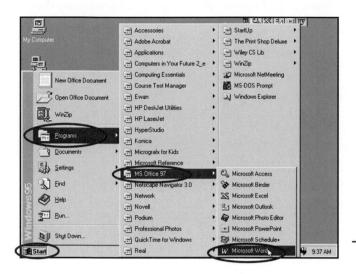

1 To open Word 97, click **Start, Programs, MS Office 97, Microsoft Word**.

Pothole: Depending on your installation, your Programs menu may look different from the one shown. If Microsoft Word is displayed on the Programs menu, click it to start Word.

2 The Microsoft Word application opens. Word displays a blank document named Document1. Notice the blinking *insertion point* at the top left of the document. This is where text displays when you begin typing the document. Notice also that the pointer takes the shape of an *I-beam* within the document area.

In Depth: All documents that you create with Office 97 applications share some common features. All of them have a *title bar* that gives the name of the application and sometimes the name of the document. A *menu bar* gives you access to the application's menu commands. The *Office Shortcut Bar* lets you quickly switch among Office applications. The *status bar* gives you information about the current document. Notice the Minimize, Maximize/Restore, and Close buttons for both the application (in the title bar) and the document.

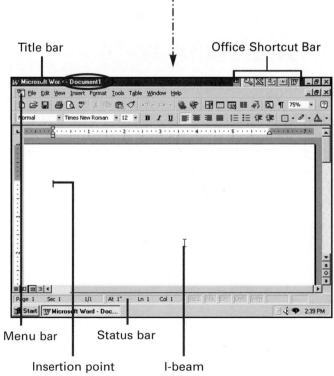

Title bar   Office Shortcut Bar

Menu bar   Status bar

Insertion point   I-beam

Task 2 don't do

Using the Office Shortcut Bar

Why would I do this?

The Office Shortcut Bar is a quick way to launch additional Office applications or access other Office programs, such as Outlook.

In this task, you learn how to start an Office application using the Office Shortcut Bar.

1 Click the **Excel** button in the Office Shortcut Bar to launch the Excel program.

> **In Depth:** Office 97 gives you many ways to customize the Office Shortcut Bar. Your Office Shortcut Bar may look different from the one shown, or it may not display at all. If you do not see the Office Shortcut Bar on your screen, start Excel in the same way you started Word.

Microsoft Excel

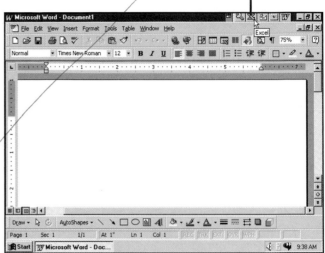

2 Microsoft Excel opens on your screen. The new blank workbook is entitled Book1. Notice the similarities between the Excel window and the Word window. Notice also that both Excel and Word have buttons on the taskbar, indicating that they are open applications.

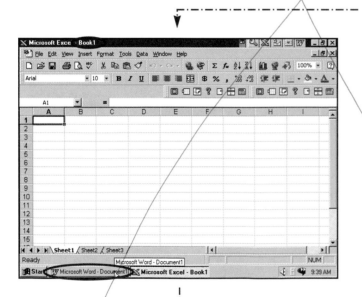

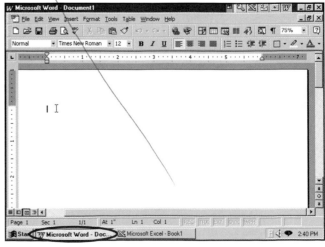

3 Click the **Microsoft Word** button on the taskbar to switch back to the Word application.

Task 3

Opening an Existing Document

Why would I do this?

Although in many cases you create new documents when you start an application, sometimes you will want to work on an existing document. You use the Open command to locate an existing document and open it on the application screen.

In this task, you learn how to open an existing document.

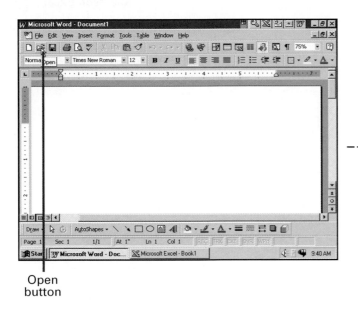

Open button

1 Click the **Open** button on the toolbar.

2 The **Open** dialog box appears. Place the student disk in the A: drive. Click the drop-down arrow in the Look in box. Click $3^1/2$ **Floppy (A:)**.

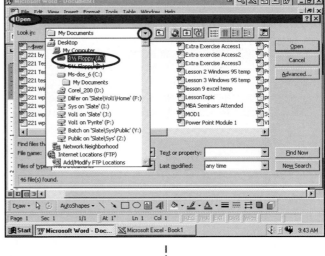

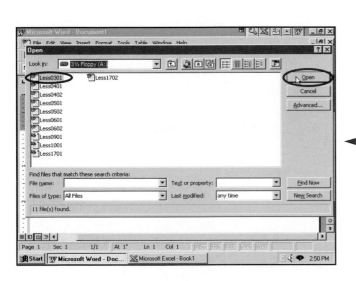

3 You should see a list of Word data files to be used with this course. Click **Less0301**.

4 Click the **Open** button. The file opens on your screen.

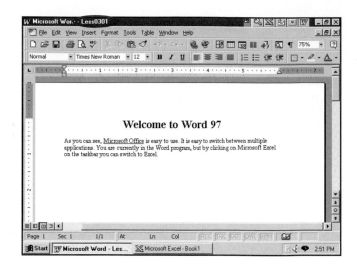

Task 4

Using the Office Assistant

Why would I do this?

Office 97 has an interactive Help feature called *Office Assistant*. Office Assistant provides context-sensitive help when you need it for particular tasks. Also, you can query Office Assistant to find information in the help system about particular features.

In this task, you learn how to use Office Assistant.

Office Assistant button

2 Click the **Office Assistant** button. The Office Assistant displays a balloon on the screen to ask what you would like to do. (The contents of the balloon may vary, depending on what task you have recently completed.)

1 Notice in the document that the words *Microsoft Office* are underlined. You can use the Office Assistant to give you information on how to underline text. Locate the **Office Assistant** button on the toolbar.

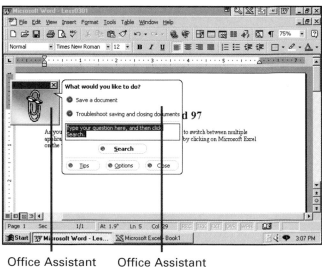

Office Assistant   Office Assistant balloon

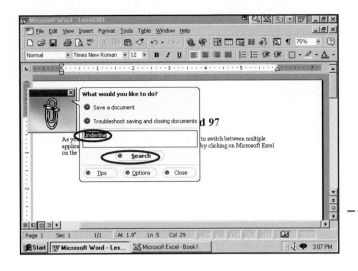

3 To ask the Office Assistant a question, type the question in the box that currently reads *Type your question here, and then click Search.* Type **<u>underline</u>** as shown.

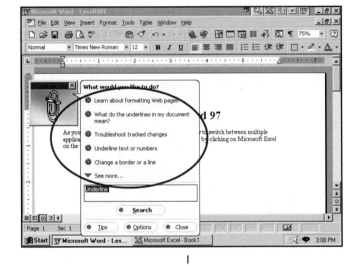

4 Click the **Search** button. The Office Assistant displays a list of Help topics relating to underlines.

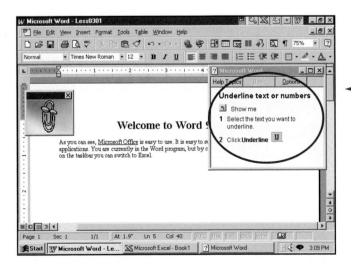

5 Click the **Underline text or numbers** Help topic. (You may need to click **See More** to see this topic.) The Office Assistant displays a Help topic that shows you how to underline text or numbers in your document.

6 Read the Help topic. Click the **Close** button in the Help topic. The Office Assistant remains on the screen after you close the Help topic.

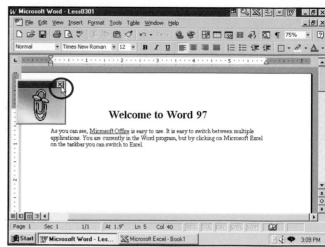

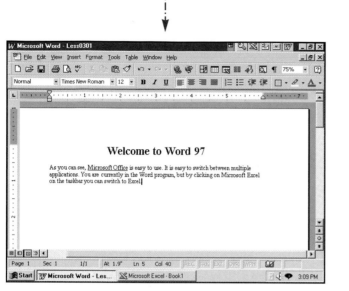

7 Click the Office Assistant **Close** button to remove it from the screen.

Task 5

Exiting Office Applications

Why would I do this?

Applications not in current use should be closed to conserve computer memory. There are two methods of closing an application: using the application's Close button or using the application's Exit command.

In this task, you learn how to exit Office applications.

Application Close button ——

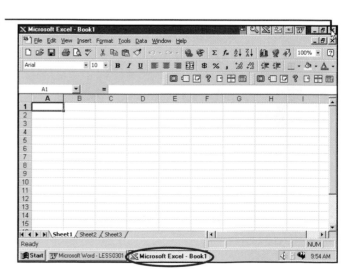

1 Click the **Microsoft Excel** button on the taskbar. The Microsoft Excel workbook displays.

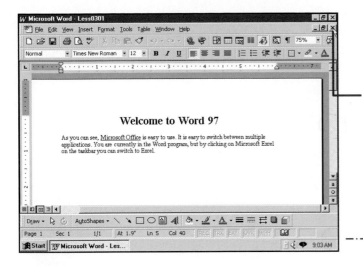

2 Click the application **Close** button to close both the workbook and the Excel application.

Document Close button

In Depth: The application Close button located in the title bar closes *both* the current document and the application. Choose this Close button if you want to completely leave the application when finished. The document Close button in the document's title bar (or directly below the application Close button if the document is maximized) closes *only* the document. Choose this Close button if you want to leave the document but wish to stay in the application. After you have closed a document, the title bar and menu bar of the application stay open so that you can start another new document if desired. Note that if you have made changes to the document since the last save, a dialog box prompts to save before closing either the document or the application.

3 Click the document **Close** button. Notice that the application remains open. To close it, click **File, Exit** on the menu bar.

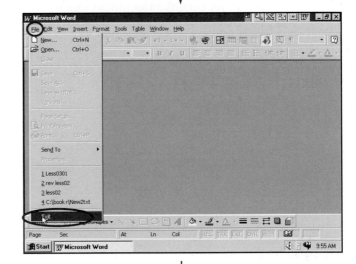

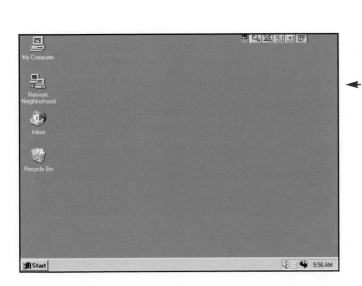

4 The application closes and you are returned to the Windows desktop.

Student Exercises

True-False

For each of the following, circle either T or F to indicate whether the statement is true or false.

(T) F **1.** Microsoft Word is a program used to create and modify documents.

(T) F **2.** A software suite combines individual applications into a full-function software system.

(T) F **3.** To start an application using the Office Shortcut Bar, just click on the icon of the application you want to use.

T (F) **4.** Each application in Office 97 has a very different look.

(T) F **5.** To open an existing document in any application, click the Document Open button on the toolbar.

(T) F **6.** The Office Assistant can give you context-sensitive help on your current task.

T (F) **7.** The menu bar tells you the name of the current application and sometimes the current document.

(T) F **8.** The insertion point indicates where text will appear when you type it.

(T) F **9.** The application Close button closes both the current document and the application.

T (F) **10.** After you click the document Close button, you are returned to the desktop.

Identifying Parts of the Word Screen

Refer to the figure and identify the numbered parts of the screen. Write the letter of the correct label in the space next to the number.

1. G
2. E
3. D
4. J
5. C
6. A
7. B
8. F
9. H
10. I

A. Open button
B. Title bar
C. I-beam pointer
D. Close document button
E. Status bar
F. Menu bar
G. Insertion point
H. Close application button
I. Office Shortcut Bar
J. Office Assistant button

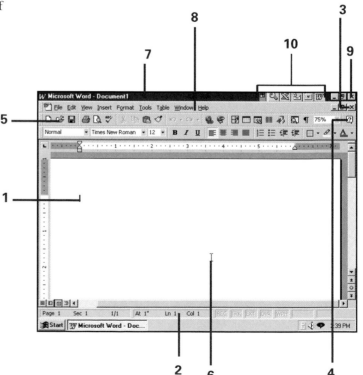

Matching

Match the following statements to the word or phrase that is the best match from the list. Write the letter of the matching word or phrase in the space provided next to the number.

1. **D** Group of icons you can use to access Office applications

2. **F** Marker that shows where text will appear when you type

3. **B** Office application for creating text documents

4. **C** Button that closes only the current document

5. **J** Office application for creating presentation graphics

6. **A** Button that enables you to bring an existing document to the screen

7. **G** Office application for creating databases

8. **I** Office application for creating worksheets

9. **E** Help tool that can give you context-sensitive help

10. **H** Bar that displays application and document names

A. Open

B. Word

C. Close document

D. Office Shortcut Bar

E. Office Assistant

F. Insertion point

G. Access

H. Title bar

I. Excel

J. PowerPoint

K. Close application

Application Exercises

Exercise 1

1. Use the Office Shortcut Bar to open Word and a new blank document.

2. Click the Office Assistant button on the toolbar. Ask the Office Assistant the question **How do I write a business letter** and click the Search button.

3. In the resulting balloon, click the blue button next to the entry *Quick ways to create letters, memos, and other documents.* Read the information in the Help window about the different kinds of wizards and templates available for use in Word.

4. Click the **Close** button in the Help window.

5. Close the Office Assistant.

6. Close the document and the application.

Exercise 2

1. Open Excel and a new blank workbook.

2. Click the Office Assistant button on the toolbar. Ask the Office Assistant the question **How do I enter data in a cell** and click the Search button.

3. Click the **Enter data in worksheet cells** topic to see a Help window asking you for more information about what you want to do. Click **Enter numbers, text, a date, or a time.**

4. Read the information. Close the Help topic window.

5. Close the Office Assistant.

6. Close the workbook and the application.

Lesson 4
Word 97: The Basics

Introduction

This lesson is the first of three lessons that cover features of Microsoft Word 97. Today, word processing programs are perhaps the most widely used of all applications. Working with Word enables you to create, modify, check, and print many professional-looking documents.

Word 97 has many new features not found in previous versions or in other word processing programs. You can save time with Word's automatic text features, which automatically correct misspellings, complete common text words and phrases, and replace abbreviations with full words. The grammar-checking feature helps you to locate grammar problems in your text. New wizards and templates guide you through the process of creating specific types of documents.

This lesson is designed to provide you with the basic skills you need to create, save, edit, and print a document.

Visual Summary

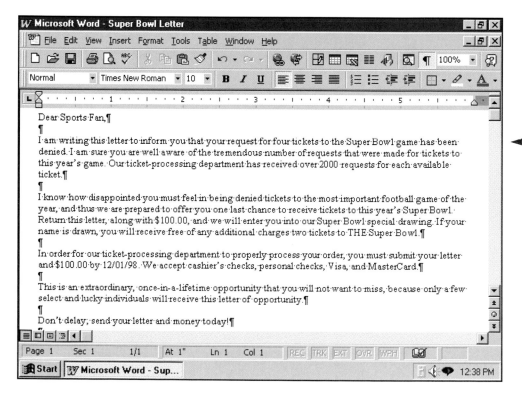

When you have completed Task 6, you will have created a document that looks like this:

Task 1

Launching Word 97

Why would I do this?

Launching Word starts the Word application so that you can begin creating a document.

In this task, you learn how to launch Word.

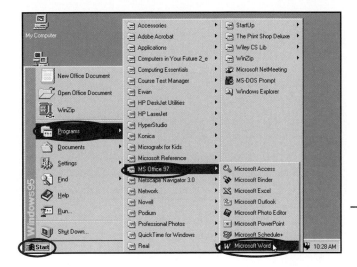

1 To start Word, click the **Start** button, click **Programs, MS Office 97,** and **Microsoft Word.**

Show/Hide ¶ button

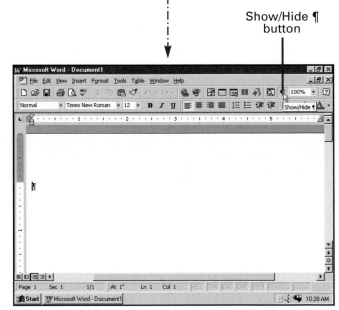

2 Microsoft Word opens and displays a new blank document. Click the **Show/Hide ¶** button to display nonprinting characters.

In Depth: You may find it helpful to display nonprinting characters on your screen. They will not appear on your printed document. Examples of nonprinting characters include paragraph marks (¶), created when you press ⏎Enter, and raised dots, created when you press the spacebar.

Task 2

Creating a Document

Why would I do this?

Look around at your school, office, or home and notice that you no longer see typewriters. Today, you can create a professional-looking document without the need for correction fluid, erasers, scissors, paste, and lost patience! With Word you can create, modify, save, and print a document which would have been impossible to accomplish just a few years ago.

In this task, you learn how to type text in a new document.

1 Type the document exactly as shown. As you type, do not press ⏎Enter at the end of a line. Allow the software to move any word that does not fit on the line you are typing to the next line. This is called *word wrap*. After you have completed typing the document, verify that your document is correctly typed.

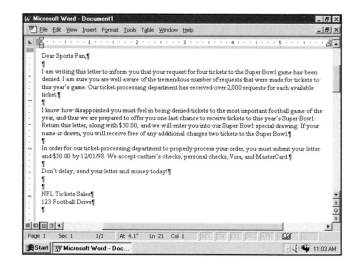

Dear Sports Fan,

I am writing this letter to inform you that your request for four tickets to the Super Bowl game has been denied. I am sure you are well aware of the tremendous number of requests that were made for tickets to this year's game. Our ticket-processing department has received more than 2,000 requests for each available ticket.

I know how disappointed you must feel in being denied tickets to the most important football game of the year, and thus we are prepared to offer you one last chance to receive tickets to this year's Super Bowl. Return this letter, along with $50.00, and we will enter you into our Super Bowl special drawing. If your name is drawn, you will receive free of any additional charges two tickets to the Super Bowl.

In order for our ticket-processing department to properly process your order, you must submit your letter and $50.00 by 12/01/98. We accept cashier's checks, personal checks, Visa, and MasterCard.

Don't delay; send your letter and money today!

NFL Tickets Sales
123 Football Drive

Pothole: If the Office Assistant appears after you type the first line of the document, click its Close button to remove it from the screen.

In Depth: As you type, you might notice wavy red or green lines appearing below some words in your document. Red wavy lines indicate a possible misspelling. Check any word underlined with a red wavy line to make sure you have spelled it correctly. A green wavy line indicates a possible grammar error. Do not worry about the green wavy lines. You will learn more about checking spelling and grammar in a later lesson.

Task 3
Saving and Closing a Document

Why would I do this?

Until you save your document, it is stored only in computer memory. Because computer memory is volatile (if the computer loses power, everything stored in the computer's memory is lost), you must store your document on a disk, which is not volatile. By saving your document to a disk, you can always retrieve it whenever you need to see, print, or modify it.

In this task, you learn how to save and close a document.

Save button

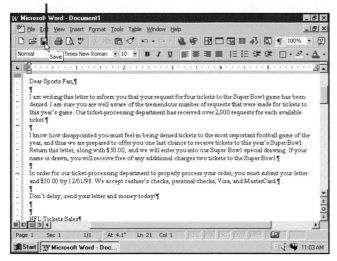

1 Click the **Save** button on the toolbar.

In Depth: On most computers, saving to the C: drive stores a file on the internal hard disk, while saving to the A: drive stores a file on the internal 31/2 floppy disk drive. Saving to the 31/2 floppy disk enables you to remove the disk and transport it elsewhere.

2 The **Save As** dialog box opens. Position your pointer inside the **Save in:** box and click to open a drop-down list of locations where you can save the file. Click **3¹/₂ Floppy (A:)**.

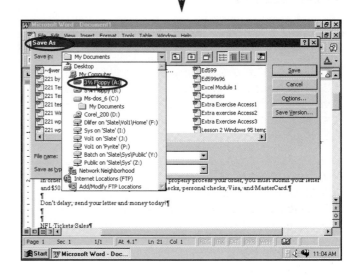

In Depth: Clicking the Save toolbar button is the fastest way to save a document. You can also use the Save or Save As command on the File menu. Use either the Save or Save As command the first time you save a document to open the Save As dialog box. After you have already saved a document, use Save to store subsequent changes to the document. You can use Save As to save a named document with a new name or to a new location.

Quick Tip: If you intend to save to the A: drive, make sure you have a disk in the drive before you click the Save button.

3 Highlight the suggested file name and type the new file name **Super Bowl Letter**.

 In Depth: A file name can be up to 255 characters in length and may contain spaces and commas.

4 Click the **Save** button. Notice that Word's title bar shows the new file name.

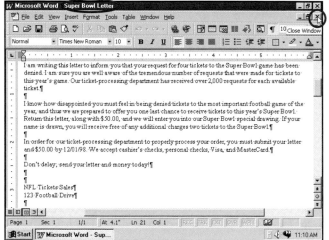

5 Close the document by clicking the document **Close** button.

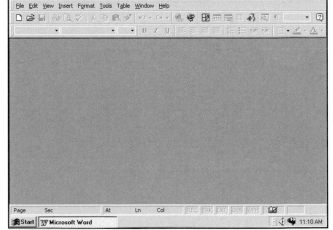

Task 4

Inserting New Text

Why would I do this?

There will be times when you want to add a word, a line, or a paragraph to an existing document. The capability to add text is a very important feature that typewriters lacked.

In this task, you learn how to insert text into an existing document.

Open
button

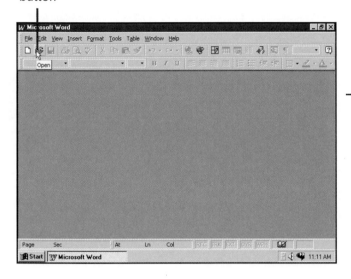

1 Click the **Open** button on the toolbar.

2 The **Open** dialog box opens. In the **Look in:** box, select **3½ Floppy (A:)**. Click the **Super Bowl Letter** document.

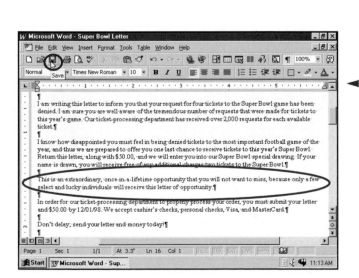

3 Click the **Open** button to open the document. Click the paragraph symbol following the second full paragraph of the letter body to position the insertion point. Press ⏎Enter once and type the following paragraph: **This is an extraordinary, once-in-a-lifetime opportunity that you will not want to miss, because only a few select and lucky individuals will receive this letter of opportunity**. Press ⏎Enter again. Save your changes.

Task 5

Moving Text

Why would I do this?

If you have information in your document that you want to move to a different location, such as changing the order of paragraphs in your document, you can cut (remove) the text and paste (relocate) it to a different area in your document.

In this task, you learn how to move text.

Cut button

1 Select the paragraph you inserted in the last task by clicking in the left margin and dragging down to the blank line below the paragraph.

> **In Depth:** Text that is cut or copied is placed on the *Clipboard*, a temporary Windows storage area. The Paste command places the text stored on the Clipboard at the insertion point. When you paste text into a document, the contents of the Clipboard are not erased. A new cut or copy replaces the Clipboard contents. After you turn your computer off, the contents of the Clipboard are erased.

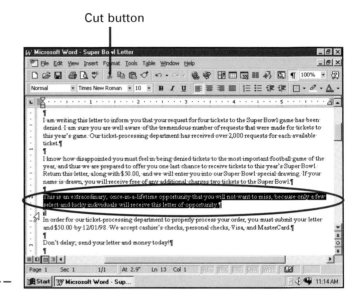

2 Click the **Cut** button. The selected paragraph is removed from your document and is now stored on the Clipboard.

Paste button

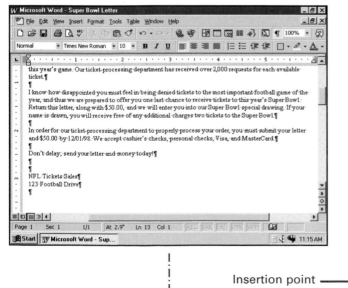

Insertion point

3 Position the pointer at the beginning of the paragraph *Don't delay; send your letter and money today!* and click to position the insertion point.

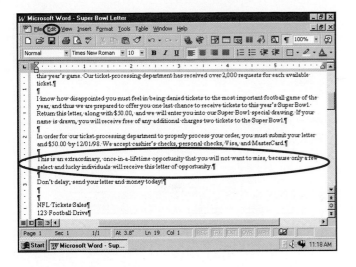

4 Cick the **Paste** button. The paragraph stored on the Clipboard is pasted at the insertion point. Save your changes.

Task 6

Using the Replace Command

Why would I do this?

Word's Replace command enables you to search for a particular word or phrase and replace it with something else. For example, if you typed a letter to send to the ABC Company but also wanted to send the same letter to the XYZ Company, you could search for all occurrences of ABC and replace them with XYZ without having to retype the entire letter.

In this task, you learn how to use the Replace command.

1 Click **Edit, Replace** on the menu bar.

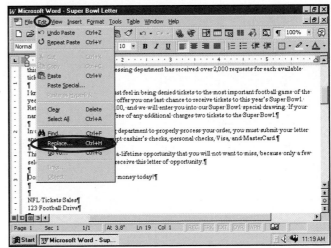

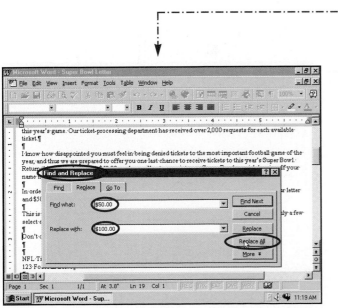

2 The **Find and Replace** dialog box opens. Type **$50.00** in the **Find what** field. Type **$100.00** in the **Replace with** field.

3 Click the **Replace All** button. Word displays a message informing you of the number of times the value $50.00 was found and replaced with the value $100.00.

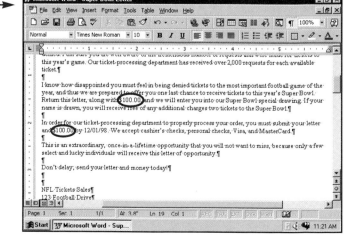

Pothole: Be careful when using the Replace All button because you may unknowingly replace something you do not want replaced. If unsure, use the Replace button, which prompts you at each occurrence. This gives you the option to replace or not replace that occurrence.

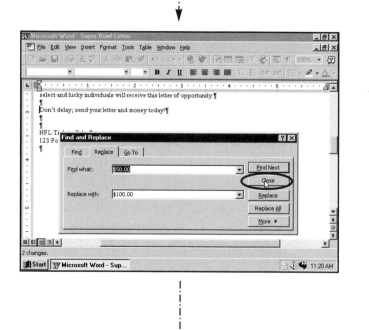

4 Click **OK** in the message box to close it.

5 Click **Close** in the Find and Replace dialog box. Save your changes.

Task 7

Previewing and Printing a Document

Why would I do this?

Using today's inexpensive color inkjet and laser printers, you can create professional-looking, print-shop quality documents. Word enables you to print a single page, page ranges, the entire document, and one or more copies of the document. Before printing, however, you should preview your work to make sure it looks just the way you want it to look.

In this task, you learn how to preview and print a document.

Print Preview button

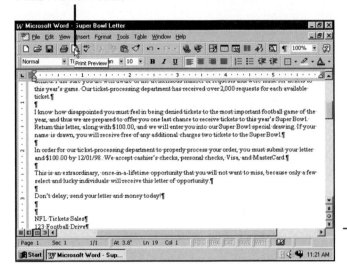

1 Locate the **Print Preview** button on the toolbar.

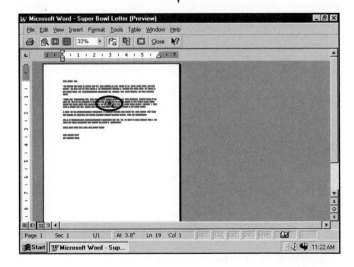

2 Click the **Print Preview** button. Your screen changes to show how your document will look when printed. Notice that the pointer has changed to a magnifying glass with a plus (+) sign.

3 To magnify a portion of your document, position the pointer on the first paragraph of the letter and click. Your document zooms in to a 100 percent magnification. Notice that the magnifying glass now contains a minus (-) sign.

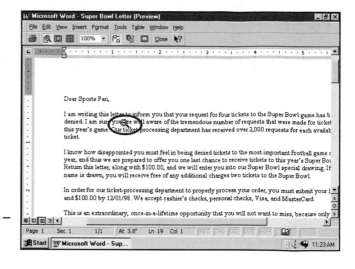

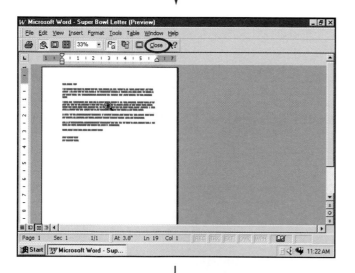

4 Click the mouse again to zoom back out to the original magnification.

5 To exit Print Preview, click **Close**. Click **File, Print** on the menu bar to open the Print dialog box.

Quick Tip: You can also print a document quickly by clicking the Print button on the toolbar. When you click this button, you bypass the Print dialog box and send the document directly to your printer.

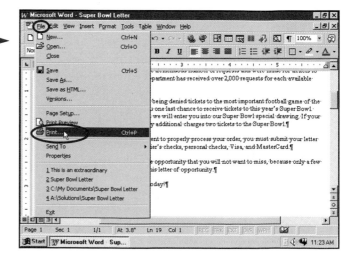

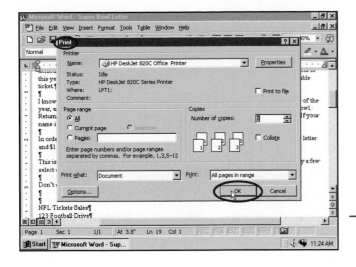

6 The **Print** dialog box opens. Review the options available in this dialog box.

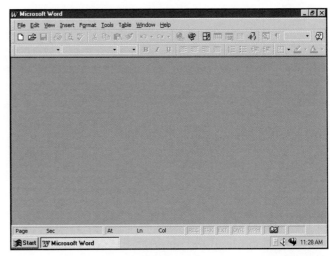

In Depth: The Print dialog box enables you to select from a number of options to print your document. You can select a new printer from a list of available printers. You can also select the page range of All, the Current page, or specific pages (2-5 would only print pages 2 through 5). You can even use the Number of copies scroll arrows to select the number of copies to print.

7 Click **OK** to print the document. Save your changes. Close the document.

Student Exercises

True-False

For each of the following, circle either T or F to indicate whether the statement is true or false.

T (F) **1.** To place text on the Clipboard, simply highlight it.

T (F) **2.** The fastest way to launch Word is to right-click the Start button.

T (F) **3.** When entering text, you should always press ⏎Enter at the end of each line.

T (F) **4.** When adding text to a document, the new text must be inserted at the end of the document and then moved to the desired location.

T (F) **5.** Both Cut and Paste place text on the Clipboard.

(T) F **6.** You cannot use the Replace command without first using the Find command.

T (F) **7.** Print Preview displays a smaller version of the printout on the printer.

T (F) **8.** When saving a file to a disk, you must use a filename that does not exceed eight characters.

T (F) **9.** Closing a document automatically saves the document.

T (F) **10.** Opening a document while you are working on another document erases the original document.

Identifying Parts of the Word Screen

Refer to the figure and identify the numbered parts of the screen. Write the letter of the correct label in the space next to the number.

1. C
2. B
3.
4. G
5.
6. A
7. D
8. E
9. I
10. F

A. Open button
B. Document name
C. Scroll arrow
D. Cut button
E. Scroll bar
F. Paste button
G. Scroll box
H. Show/Hide ¶ button
I. Print Preview button
J. Save button

Matching

Match the following statements to the word or phrase that is the best match from the list. Write the letter of the matching word or phrase in the space provided next to the number.

1. A A button that shows hidden symbols and spaces
2. I The button to launch the Word program
3. E The menu to select if you want to use the Replace command
4. K A button that looks like a disk
5. C A command that places the contents of the Clipboard in the document
6. D A command that removes text from the document and places it on the Clipboard
7. F The button used to load a document from the disk
8. G The menu to select if you want to use the Save or Save As command
9. J A button that looks like a blank sheet of paper with a magnifying glass
10. H A word automatically moving to the next line when it does not fit on the current line

A. Show/Hide
B. Print
C. Paste
D. Cut
E. Edit
F. Open
G. File
H. Word wrap
I. Start
J. Print Preview
K. Save

Application Exercises

Exercise 1

1. Type the following document.

September 12, 199X

Mr. George Huff
B & L Computer Supplies
126 West Center Street
Columbus, OH 43210

Dear Mr. Huff,

I appreciated your recent telephone call to Ajax Computer requesting information on our new products. It is with much pleasure that I provide to you, free of charge, a catalog listing all of our inventory components.

During the past several months, we have been very busy in reviewing and evaluating all of our products to see if they meet the highest standards of quality that you expect from Ajax Computer components. After all, if you are not completely satisfied with our products, we have not accomplished our job!

I trust that you will call me if you have any questions that may arise which are not answered in our catalog. On behalf of Ajax Computer, I thank you for your inquiry concerning our computer products.

William L. Fellow
V.P., Marketing Division
Ajax Computer Inc.
1957 Maple Canyon Dr.
Columbus, OH 43221

2. Save the document as **Computer Supplies**.

3. Modify the document to include the following text as the third paragraph:

I would like to mention that we will be having a fall clearance sale during the month of October. All items ordered during this month that we have in our current stock of inventory will be reduced by 35% over our already low prices.

4. Move the third paragraph to the end of the letter.

5. Use Replace to replace all references to *Ajax Computer* with the newly formed company called **Creative Computer Resources**.

6. Save the document using the same name.

7. Print the document. Close the document.

Exercise 2

You are a travel agent for the Sunshine Booking Company. You have been asked by the local college to distribute a letter to all college students suggesting ways to make the upcoming spring break more enjoyable and safer.

1. Type the following letter.

To all people planning a spring trip.
Explore Options
Inquire about Travel Companions
Shop for the Best Package Prices
Make Reservations
Schedule the Itinerary
Pack Sensibly
Spring break is the time of year when college people look forward to rest and relaxation. Many times this rest and relaxation includes a trip. Planning is an important part of a successful trip. The following tips should be used for a successful trip.

2. Save the letter as **Travel Letter**.

3. Use Replace to change the word *people* to **students**.

4. Use Cut and Paste to move the last paragraph to follow the first sentence.

5. Save the document again using the same name.

6. Print the document. Close the document.

Exercise 3

As the owner of a large retail nursery, you send out letters in the fall to all customers who have placed an order for spring planting.

1. Type the following letter:

September 12, 199X

Ms. Emily Jones
234 Elm Street
Ashland, OH 44805

Dear Ms. Jones,

According to our experts, the best time to plant these trees in your area is April 1st. We will ship the trees to arrive at your home on or around April 1st of next year. The total amount due must be paid before we ship your order.

Thank you for your recent order.

Jimmy Smith
The Tree Farm
231 East Orchard Park Road
Butler, OH 44822

2. Save the letter as **Tree**.

3. Add the following paragraph to the beginning of the document:

This letter is to confirm that your order was received on August 20. Our records show that you ordered 5 maple trees at $9.00 each, 10 white pine trees at $4.00 each, and 2 apple trees at $18.00 each. The total for your order is $211.00.

4. Change the total amount of the order from *$211.00* to **$121.00**.

5. Save the document again using the same name.

6. Print the document. Close the document.

Exercise 4

You are the president of the student senate and must write a letter to the president of the university thanking her for speaking to your group last week.

1. Type the following letter.

<Type the name of the president of your university>
<Your university address>
<Your city, state zip code>

Dear Dr. <your president>,

We students feel that the fee should not be increased by more than 3.5%. We realize that it is very expensive to run an institution of this size, but a fee increase of 6%, as you mentioned to us last week, will make it impossible for some of the current students to return to campus next year.

Sincerely,

<your name>
Student Senate President

2. Save the document as **President**.

3. Add the following paragraph to the end of the document.

Thank you very much for speaking to the student senate last week. The feedback from the students has been very positive. We were especially happy to hear that the administration is planning an informal session next week to discuss the proposed fee increase.

4. Use Replace to replace the word *fee* with the word **tuition**. (Be careful not to use Replace All. You do not want to change the *fee* in *feedback*.)

5. Use Cut and Paste to switch the paragraphs so that the paragraph you just added is the first paragraph.

6. Save using the same name.

7. Print the document. Close the document.

Exercise 5

The Eagle Corporation

As the administrative assistant to the president of Eagle Corporation, you are responsible for informing all employees of the annual company picnic. Create a document using Microsoft Word 97 that will provide pertinent information concerning this annual picnic. Be sure to include in your document the time, place, schedule of events, and any other necessary information an employee would need to be well informed.

Lesson 5
Formatting Text in Word 97

Introduction

As you have learned, you can create a document in Word 97 quickly and easily. Most documents can be improved by using formatting options to emphasize portions of text or adjust the placement of text on the page. Formatted documents can be easier to read and understand.

This lesson is designed to provide you with the ability to improve the appearance and quality of your document.

Visual Summary

When you have completed Task 8, you will have created a document that looks like this:

NFL TICKETS

Dear Sports Fan,

I am writing this letter to inform you that your request for four tickets to the Super Bowl game has been denied. I am sure you are well aware of the tremendous number of requests that were made for tickets to this year's game. Our ticket-processing department has received more than 2,000 requests for each available ticket.

I know how disappointed you must feel in being denied tickets to the most important football game of the year, and thus we are prepared to offer you one last chance to receive tickets to this year's Super Bowl. Return this letter, along with $100.00, and we will enter you into our Super Bowl special drawing. If your name is drawn, you will receive free of any additional charges two tickets to the **Super Bowl**.

In order for our ticket-processing department to properly process your order, you must submit your letter and $100.00 by 12/01/98. We accept cashier's checks, personal checks, Visa, and MasterCard.

This is an exceptional, _once-in-a-lifetime opportunity_ that you will not want to miss, because only a few select and lucky individuals will receive this letter of opportunity.

Don't delay; send your letter and money today!

NFL Tickets Sales
123 Football Drive
Buffalo, NY

Task 1

Checking Spelling and Grammar

Why would I do this?

It is important to make sure that your documents contain no spelling or grammar errors. Word helps you with these tasks using several automated checking features. As you may already have noticed, Word underlines possible misspellings with a red wavy line and possible grammar errors with a green wavy line. You can correct these errors "on the fly" using the right mouse button, or you can review errors in the Spelling and Grammar dialog box.

In this task, you learn how to check spelling and grammar in a document.

Spelling and Grammar button

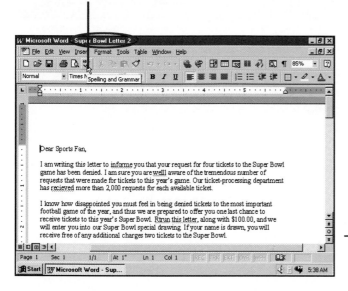

1 Open **Less0501** and save it on your disk as **Super Bowl Letter 2**. Make sure the insertion point is at the beginning of the document. Locate the **Spelling and Grammar** button on the toolbar.

2 Click the **Spelling and Grammar** button on the toolbar. Word begins checking spelling and grammar and locates the misspelled word *informe*. Word displays the **Spelling and Grammar** dialog box so that you can correct the error. Word automatically suggests the proper spelling, *inform*.

In Depth: If Word finds a spelling or grammar error, it highlights the word or phrase and opens the Spelling and Grammar dialog box. This dialog box lets you select the proper spelling from the Suggestions list or correct the spelling in the Not in Dictionary pane of the dialog box. If the word is correct as is, click Ignore or Ignore All to tell Word to skip the word. The Add button lets you add words that are not in Word's spelling dictionary to a custom dictionary so that they will not be flagged in the future as misspellings. If the insertion point is not at the beginning of the document when you start the spelling and grammar check, Word checks the document from the insertion point to the end of the document and then asks if you want to check the rest of the document as well.

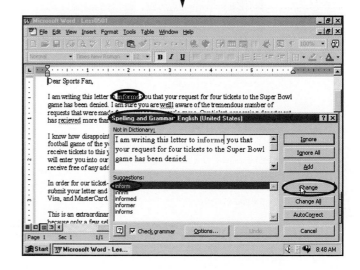

3 To accept the suggested change and find the next spelling error, click **Change**. Word highlights the misspelled word *welll* and suggests the correct spelling.

Quick Tip: You can check spelling and grammar quickly by right-clicking on a word or phrase underlined with a red or green wavy line. Word opens a shortcut menu that shows a list of possible spellings or grammar corrections. Click one of the choices to correct the word or phrase. You can also access the Spelling and Grammar dialog box from this shortcut menu.

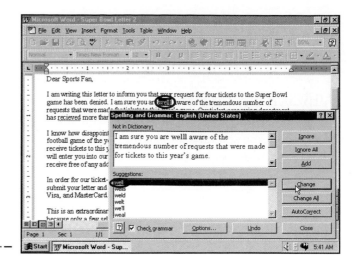

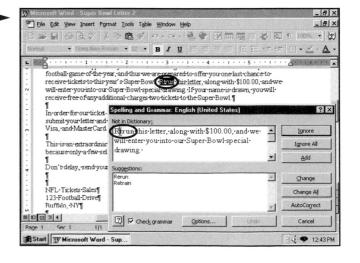

4 To accept the suggested change and find the next error, click **Change**. Word suggests the correct replacement for the misspelled word *recieved*.

5 To accept the change and find the next mistake, click **Change**. Word highlights the next error. The word *Return* has been spelled as *Rtrun*. Word does not have a correct suggested replacement.

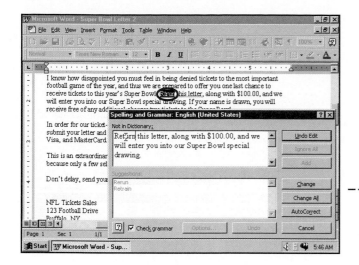

6 In the top pane of the dialog box, highlight the red word *Rtrun*. Type the correct word, **Return**.

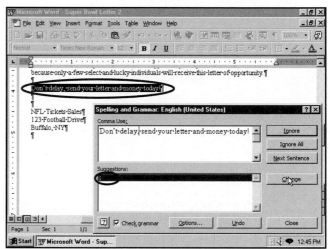

7 Click **Change** to make the change in the document and find the next error. The grammar checker alerts you to a grammar problem in the last sentence of the document. It suggests you use a semicolon instead of a comma.

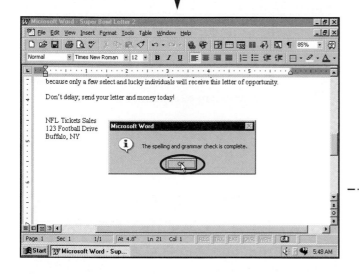

8 Click **Change** to continue with the check. When the entire document has been checked for spelling and grammar, Word displays a message telling you the check is complete.

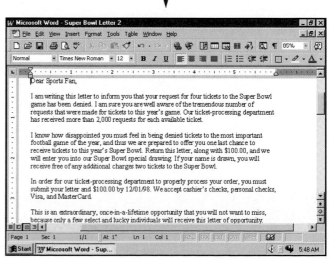

9 Click **OK**. Save your changes.

Task 2

Using the Thesaurus

Why would I do this?

The thesaurus gives you a quick and easy way to find *synonyms* and *antonyms*. Use the thesaurus to improve the content of your document by finding the words that make your point most effectively.

In this task, you learn how to use the thesaurus.

1 Position the pointer on the word *extraordinary* in the fourth paragraph and click. Click **Tools, Language, Thesaurus** on the menu bar.

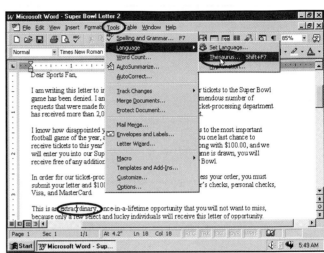

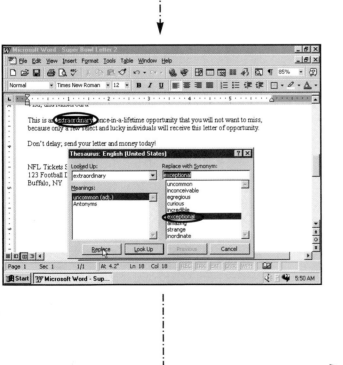

2 Click the synonym **exceptional**.

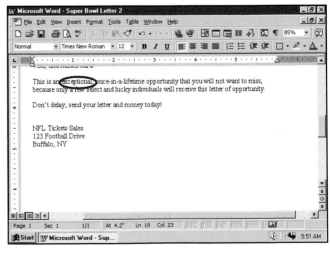

3 Click **Replace**. Word replaces *extraordinary* with *exceptional* and adjusts the word spacing. Save your changes.

Task 3

Changing Font, Font Size, and Color

Why would I do this?

Changing the font, font size, and color can help draw attention to important headings, words, and phrases in your document. If you are using a color printer to output your document, you can greatly improve the overall appearance and quality of your document by using color for specific items of text.

In this task, you learn how to change the font, font size, and color of the text.

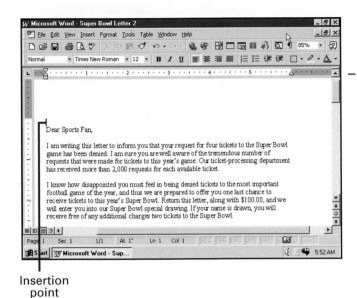

Insertion point

1 Position the insertion point to the left of the first word in the document. Press ⏎Enter once to insert a blank line. Move the insertion point up one line.

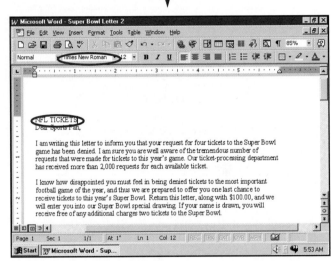

2 Type in all capital letters **NFL TICKETS**.

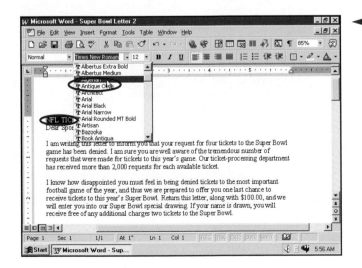

3 To change the font of the *NFL TICKETS* heading, select the heading, click the **Font** list box on the toolbar, and locate the **Algerian** font. (If you do not have the Algerian font, choose any other font except Times New Roman.)

> **In Depth:** A *font* consists of all characters and numbers from a particular typeface in a specific size. A *typeface* is a specific design of type. Typefaces have unique names, such as Times New Roman, Ariel, or Algerian. Typefaces can be divided into two main groups: *serif* and *sans serif*. Serif faces have small lines at the ends of the strokes that make up the characters. Sans serif typefaces do not have these lines. This note is set in a sans serif typeface, and the text of the steps in this book is set in a serif typeface. Word has a default font that it uses whenever you start typing a new document.
>
> You can also change the font of your text by clicking Font on the Format menu. The Font dialog box lets you select a number of options for changing the appearance of text.

4 Click the **Algerian** font choice.

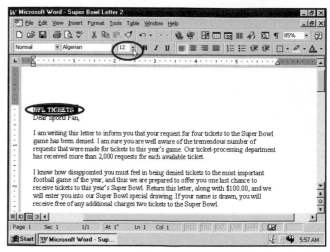

5 To change the size of the heading, make sure the heading is still selected and click the **Font Size** list box to display a list of selectable font sizes. Using the scroll down arrow, locate and highlight **48**.

In Depth: If you know the font size you want, you can type the number in the Font Size box. When selecting a font size, keep in mind that 1 point = 1/72 of an inch. Word has a default font size that it uses whenever you start typing a new document.

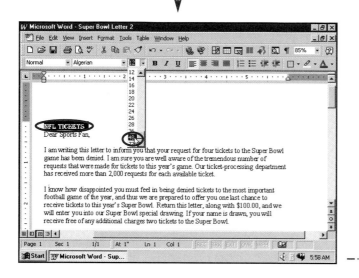

6 Click **48** on the Font Size drop-down list. The heading characters are now 48 point. To change the color of the heading, make sure the heading is still highlighted. Position the pointer on the Font Color drop-down arrow and click to display the Font Color palette.

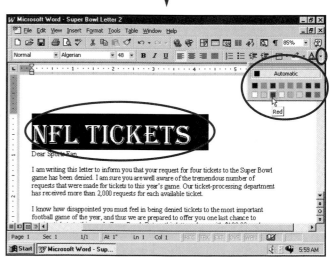

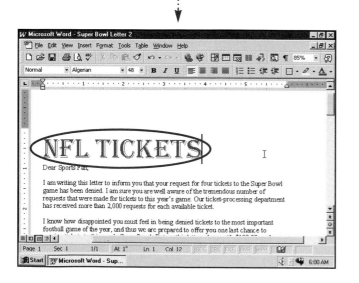

7 Click the **Red** palette color. Click anywhere in the document to remove the highlight on the heading and see the new color. Save your changes.

Task 4

Changing Font Styles

Why would I do this?

To make specific text in your document stand out, you can change its font style. *Font styles* are changes made in the appearance of text, such as **bold**, <u>underline</u>, or *italics*. Font styles often have specific uses. For example, titles of books and films are usually in italics, and terms or important phrases are frequently in bold.

In this task, you learn how to apply font styles to text.

Bold button

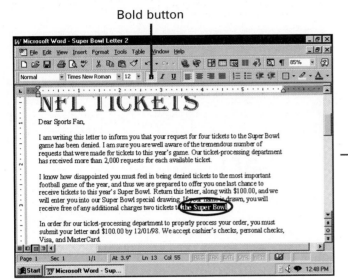

1 To make the phrase *the Super Bowl* stand out at the end of the second paragraph, select all three words and click the **Bold** button on the toolbar.

Underline button

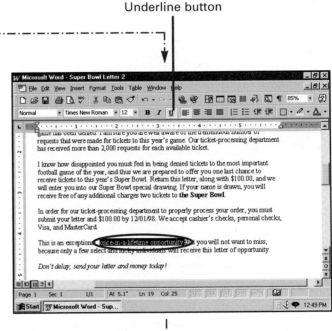

2 To emphasize the phrase *once-in-a-lifetime opportunity*, select the phrase and click the **Underline** button on the toolbar.

Italic button

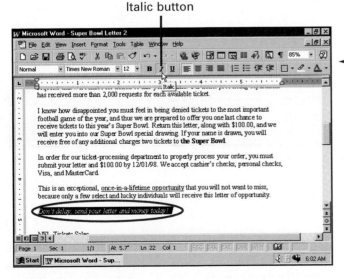

3 To emphasize the sentence *Don't delay; send your letter and money today!*, select the sentence and click the **Italic** button on the toolbar. Save your changes.

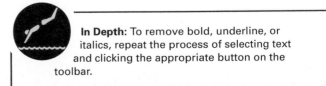

In Depth: To remove bold, underline, or italics, repeat the process of selecting text and clicking the appropriate button on the toolbar.

Task 5

Adjusting Text Alignment

Why would I do this?

By default, Word aligns your text flush with the left margin. There will be times, however, when you will want to align some portions of your text differently. In Word, you can align left, align right, center, or justify (flush with both margins). Using the alignment options can make your text easier to read or emphasize parts of it for the reader.

In this task, you learn how to change text alignment.

1 Position the insertion point on the heading *NFL TICKETS*. Center the heading by clicking the **Center** button on the toolbar.

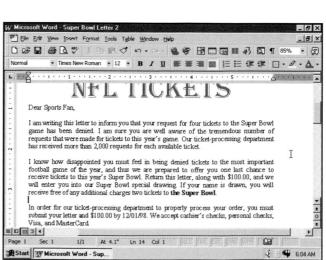

Center button

Justify button

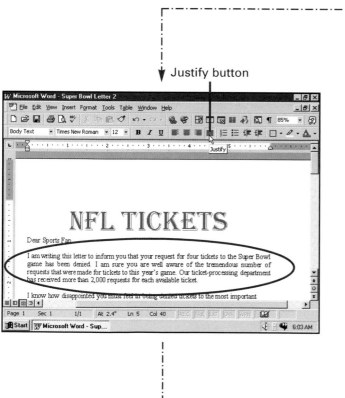

2 To justify the text in the first paragraph, click in the paragraph and then click the **Justify** button on the toolbar.

3 Justify the remaining paragraphs in the document. Save your changes.

Task 6

Setting Indents

Why would I do this?

An *indent* is space inserted to move a paragraph away from the edge of the text. Indents can help you set off text from either the left or right margin or, both. Indented paragraphs help the reader follow your text and can emphasize particularly important paragraphs.

In this task, you learn how to use indents to set off paragraphs.

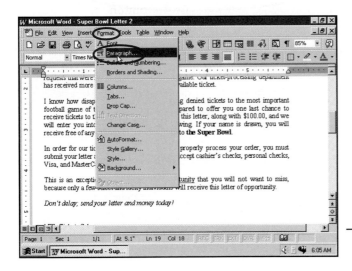

1 To emphasize the paragraph that begins *This is an exceptional*, indent it from both the left and right margins. Position the insertion point anywhere in the paragraph. Click **Fo̲rmat, P̲aragraph** on the menu bar.

2 The **Paragraph** dialog box opens. In the Indention area, click the Left scroll up arrow until the box shows a value of **0.5"**. Click the right scroll up arrow until this box shows a value of **0.5"**.

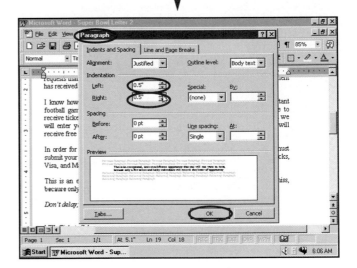

In Depth: The Paragraph dialog box gives you a number of indent options. You can set a specific value for a left or right indent. Click the Special drop-down list arrow to see two additional types of indents. The First line option moves the first line of a paragraph a specified distance from the left margin. The Hanging option moves all lines in a paragraph *except* the first line a specified distance from the left margin.

You can also set indents using the Left Indent, Hanging Indent, First Line Indent, and Right Indent markers on the ruler. Just drag a marker on the ruler to create the indent for the current paragraph or selected paragraphs.

3 Click **OK** to apply the left and right indents. The paragraph is indented from both the left and right margins by .5 inches.

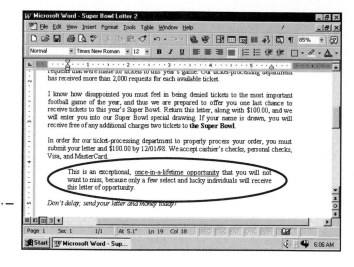

4 To set a first-line indent for the last three lines of the document, select them. Click **Format, Paragraph** on the menu bar. In the Paragraph dialog box, click the **Special** drop-down list arrow. Click **First line**.

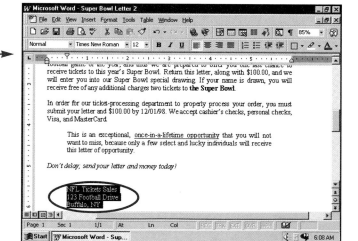

5 Click **OK** to apply the indent. The address is indented. Save your changes.

Task 7

Setting Line Spacing

Why would I do this?

By default, Word uses single spacing for new documents. This means that there is no extra space between lines of text. You might want to change this default line spacing to make the document easier to read. Word's 1.5 line spacing inserts half a line between lines of text. Double spacing inserts an entire blank line between lines of text. Some types of documents have specific line spacing requirements. For example, manuscripts and term papers usually require double spacing. Business letters are usually single spaced. You can also use line spacing to control the number of document pages. If you want your text to take up more pages, use 1.5 lines or double spacing. If you need to squeeze your document into fewer pages, use single spacing.

In this task, you learn how to set line spacing.

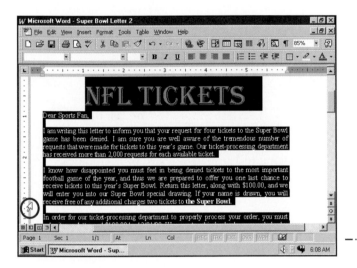

1 Select the entire document by positioning the pointer in the left margin and triple-clicking.

In Depth: You do not have to use the same line spacing throughout a document. To make some paragraphs a different line spacing, select them and then change the spacing option.

2 Click **Format, Paragraph** on the menu bar.

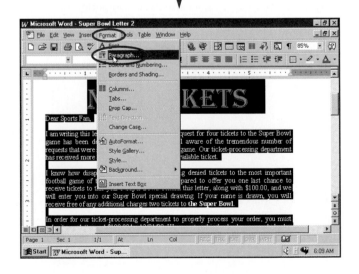

3 The **Paragraph** dialog box opens. Position the pointer on the Line spacing drop-down arrow and click. Highlight **1.5 lines**.

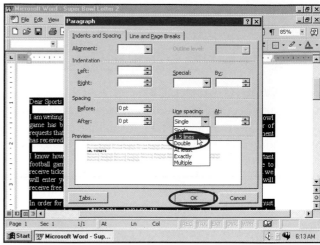

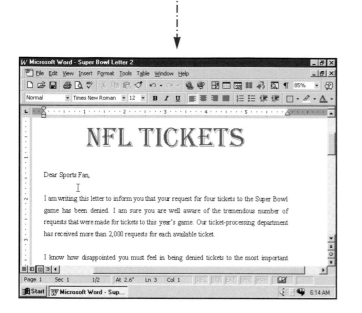

4 Click **OK** to apply the new line spacing. Your document's line spacing changes from single spacing to 1.5 spacing. Save your changes.

Task 8

Setting Margins

Why would I do this?

Margins are the white spaces between the edge of the paper and your text. Changing the margins of a document enables you to fit more text on a page or provide more white space around the text to improve the look of a page.

In this task, you learn how to set new margins for your document.

1 Click **File, Page Setup** on the menu bar.

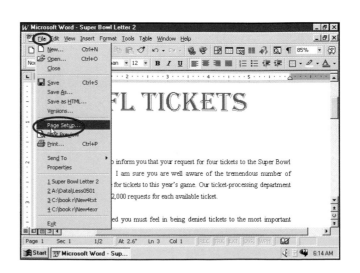

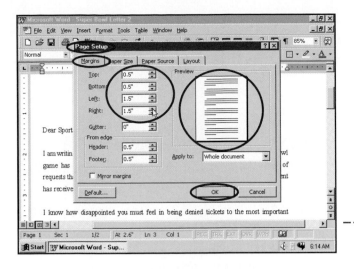

2 The **Page Setup** dialog box opens. On the **Margins** tab in the dialog box, click the Top scroll down arrow until the box shows a value of **0.5"**. Click the Bottom scroll down arrow until this box shows a value of **0.5"**. Click the Left scroll up arrow until the box shows a value of **1.5**. Click the Right scroll up arrow until this box shows a value of **1.5**. The Preview changes to reflect your new left, right, top, and bottom margin settings.

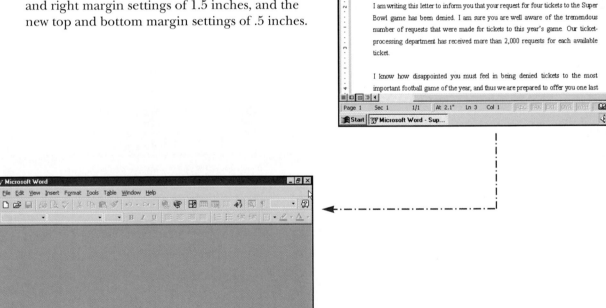

3 Click **OK**. Your document displays the new left and right margin settings of 1.5 inches, and the new top and bottom margin settings of .5 inches.

4 Save your changes. Print the document. Close the document. 5

Student Exercises

True-False

For each of the following, circle either T or F to indicate whether the statement is true or false.

T   F   **1.** If you choose Ignore in the Spelling and Grammar dialog box, Word ignores all spelling errors in the document.

T   F   **2.** To start the Thesaurus feature, you must first click the Language menu on the menu bar.

T   F   **3.** The margins in a document must be changed before you begin to type.

T   F   **4.** Word underlines possible misspellings with a red wavy line.

T   F   **5.** Line spacing must be consistent throughout the entire document.

T   F   **6.** There are only two types of text alignment, left and center.

T   F   **7.** A font size of 12 is bigger than a font size of 10.

T   F   **8.** A font size of 72 creates characters that are about 1 inch tall.

T   F   **9.** Centering text using the Center button places the text equally between the left and right margins.

T   F   **10.** Font colors may be changed anywhere in the document.

Identifying Parts of the Word Screen

Refer to the figure and identify the numbered parts of the screen. Write the letter of the correct label in the space next to the number.

1. _____
2. _____
3. _____
4. _____
5. _____
6. _____
7. _____
8. _____
9. _____
10. _____

A. Spelling and Grammar button
B. Font Size button
C. Font button
D. Bold button
E. Italic button
F. Underline button
G. Center button
H. Font Color button
I. Left indent
J. Right indent

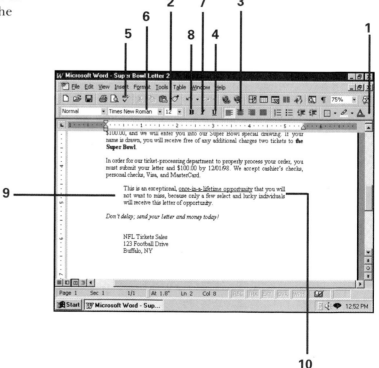

Matching

Match the following statements to the word or phrase that is the best match from the list. Write the letter of the matching word or phrase in the space provided next to the number.

1. ___ A tool to find synonyms
2. ___ Justifying text at the left margin
3. ___ Measurement of font size
4. ___ A tool to check for misspellings
5. ___ Formatting text so that characters appear darker
6. ___ The menu to select if you want to change line spacing
7. ___ Set of characters with the same typeface
8. ___ Aligning text with both the left and right margins
9. ___ The space between the edge of the paper and a document's text
10. ___ The menu to select to change page margins

A. Point

B. Font

C. Margin

D. File

E. Align left

F. Bold

G. Green wavy line

H. Spelling and grammar

I. Thesaurus

J. Format

K. Justify

Application Exercises

Exercise 1

1. To complete this exercise, you must have completed Application Exercise 1 in Lesson 4. Open the document you created and saved in Lesson 4 Application Exercise 1 named **Computer Supplies**. Save the document as **Computer Supplies 2**.

2. Check the spelling of the document.

3. Use the Thesaurus to change the word *pleasure* in the first paragraph to another word with a similar meaning.

4. In the last paragraph, bold the words *fall clearance sale*.

5. In the last paragraph, underline *35%*.

6. At the top of the document, insert the heading **Creative Computer Resources**.

7. Change the font of the heading to **Ariel**. Change the font size of the heading to **22** point. Apply the **Bold** font style.

8. Right-align the heading.

9. Move the last three lines of the document, the company's address, above the date. Change the alignment of these three lines to right. Change the size of the text in these three lines to **14** point.

10. Indent the last paragraph half an inch from the left and right margins.

11. Save your changes. Print the document. Close the document.

Exercise 2

1. To complete this exercise, you must have completed Application Exercise 2 in Lesson 4. Open the document you created and saved in Lesson 4 Application Exercise 2 named **Travel Letter**. Save the document as **Travel Letter 2**.

2. Open **Less0502**. Select all the text in this document. Click the **Copy** button to copy the text to the Clipboard. Close this document.

3. Paste the copied text at the end of **Travel Letter 2**. Insert one blank line above the pasted material to separate it from the original text of **Travel Letter 2**.

4. Check the spelling and the grammar of the entire document.

5. Change the font size for all the text in the document to **12** point if necessary.

6. The pasted text consists of headings followed by paragraphs of text. To make the headings more visible, apply a bold font style to them. (The first is *Explore Options*, just below the blank line.)

7. Apply a font color to the headings to make them even more visible.

8. Indent the first lines of the paragraphs under each of these headings by **0.25** inch.

9. Italicize the last line in the document, *Don't forget the sunscreen!*

10. Change the line spacing of the entire document to **1.5** lines.

11. Save your changes. Print the document. Close the document.

Exercise 3

1. To complete this exercise, you must have completed Application Exercise 3 in Lesson 4. Open the document you created and saved in Lesson 4 Application Exercise 3 named **Tree**. Save the document as **Tree 2**.

2. Right-align the date on the first line of the document.

3. In the second paragraph, underline *The total amount due must be paid before we ship your order.*

4. In the last paragraph, italicize *Thank you for your recent order.*

5. Justify the paragraphs that form the body of the letter.

6. At the top of the document, insert the heading **THE TREE FARM**.

7. Change the font of the heading to **Algerian** (or a font of your choice). Change the font size of the heading to **36** point. Change the font color of the heading to **Bright Green**.

8. Center the heading.

9. Change the left and right margins of the entire document to **1.75** inches.

10. Save your changes. Print the document. Close the document.

Exercise 4

1. To complete this exercise, you must have completed Application Exercise 4 in Lesson 4. Open the document you created and saved in Lesson 4 Application Exercise 4 named **President**. Save the document as **President 2**.

2. Add and right-align the date on the first line of the document

3. In the last paragraph, underline **3.5%**.

4. In the last paragraph, bold **6%**.

5. At the top of the document, insert the heading **From the desk of <your name>**

6. Change the font of the heading to **Architect** (or a font of your choice). Change the font size of the heading to **24** point. Change the font color of the heading to **Teal**.

7. Right-align the heading.

8. Change all margins to **2** inches.

9. Save your changes. Print the document. Close the document.

Exercise 5

The Eagle Corporation

As the assistant to the manager of human resources, it is your responsibility to generate and post a monthly document that shows the availability of job opportunities within Eagle Corporation. Create a monthly job opportunities document for August for the positions of accounts payable clerk, janitor, and secretary for the sales department. Include in your document a brief job description and the minimum requirements to be considered for the job.

Lesson 6
Special Features in Word 97

Introduction

Now that you are able to create and format documents, you are ready to use some of the special features available in Word to enhance the overall appearance of your documents. This lesson will show you how to create more professional-looking documents.

Visual Summary

When you have completed Task 8, you will have created a document that looks like this:

Spring Break Announcement

To all students planning a spring trip.

Spring break is the time of year when college students look forward to rest and relaxation. Many times this rest and relaxation includes a trip. Planning is an important part of a successful trip. The following tips should be used for a successful trip.

- Explore Options
- Inquire about Travel Companions
- Shop for the Best Package Prices
- Make Reservations
- Schedule the Itinerary
- Pack Sensibly
- Chart Your Stops
- List Important Events

Explore Options

Planning for a vacation is a very big job. Your best bet is to start thinking about spring break in the fall. Make a list of vacation spots that you might like to explore and gather information on these various places.

Task 1

Inserting Clip Art

Why would I do this?

You can add existing Word clip art graphics to add emphasis to your document. By adding graphics, you can make your document "come alive."

In this task, you learn how to insert a clip art picture.

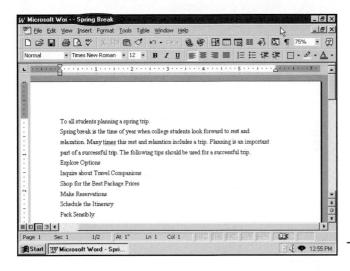

1 Open **Less0601** and save it on your disk as **Spring Break**.

In Depth: The amount of clip art you have available depends on your installation of Word. If you are using a computer on which previous versions of Word have been installed, you probably have a good selection of clip art. If you are using a computer on which only Office 97 has been installed, you may have few clip art choices on your hard disk. However, you have the option of accessing clip art pictures stored on the Office 97 installation CD or on the Microsoft Clip Gallery Web page.

2 Position the insertion point to the left of the first word in the body of the document. Click **Insert, Picture,** and **Clip Art** on the menu bar.

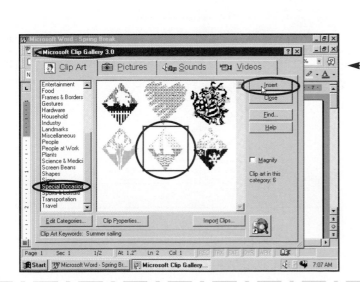

3 The **Microsoft Clip Gallery 3.0** dialog box opens. Click the **Special Occasion** category. Click the sailboat graphic (labeled Summer sailing).

Pothole: Depending on your installation, the sailboat graphic shown may appear in the Seasons category, the Special Occasions category, or the Sports & Leisure category. You may need to have your Office 97 installation disk in the CD drive in order to insert the graphic.

4 Click **Insert** to insert the picture. The clip art picture displays at the location of the insertion point.

In Depth: When a picture is first inserted, it is surrounded by small squares called *handles*. Handles indicate that the picture is selected. If you want to move or resize the picture, click it once to select it and display the handles. While the picture is selected, you can easily move it by placing the pointer inside the picture, clicking, and dragging the picture to a new location.

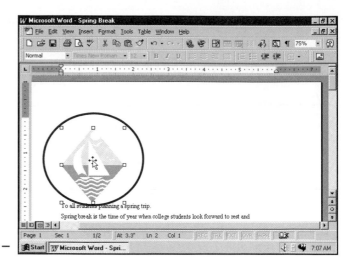

5 If the selection handles are not visible around the picture, click once inside the picture to select it. Drag the picture to the right and center it between the left and right margins.

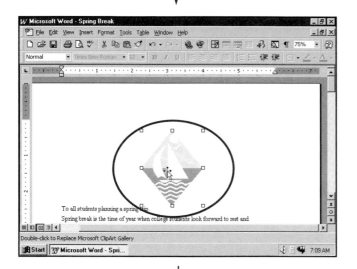

In Depth: To resize a graphic, use the selection handles. Drag a handle inward to reduce size and outward to increase size. Side handles control width. Top and bottom handles control height. Corner handles change both width and height at the same time.

6 To reduce the size of the picture, click the bottom corner handle and drag inward at a 45-degree angle about a quarter of an inch.

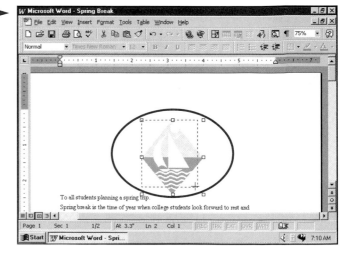

7 Place the pointer on the first line of text and click the **Center** button on the toolbar. Save your changes.

In Depth: Clip art pictures automatically move text out of the way as they are inserted in a document. By default, pictures move text above and below the picture. You can change the way text wraps around a picture using the Text Wrapping button on the Picture toolbar that displays whenever a picture is selected.

Task 2

Adding a Border

Why would I do this?

Adding a border to paragraphs in your document makes the information stand out. It is a nice way to draw attention to a particular phrase, paragraph, or section of your document that you want to emphasize.

In this task, you learn how to insert a border to emphasize text.

1 Drag the pointer in the left margin to select the six tips starting with *Explore Options* and ending with *Pack Sensibly*.

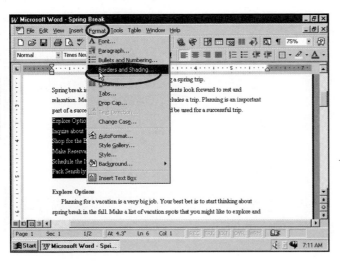

2 Click **Format, Borders and Shading** on the menu bar.

3 The **Borders and Shading** dialog box opens. Scroll down in the Style box until you see the double line. Click to highlight the double line.

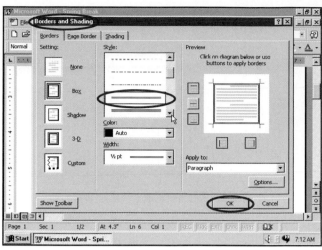

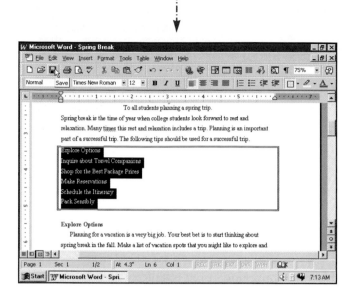

4 Click **OK**. A double line border will be placed around the highlighted text. Save your changes.

Task 3

Creating Bulleted and Numbered Lists

Why would I do this?

Bulleted and numbered lists help you present information and ideas in a clear step-by-step approach. By placing numbers or bullets in front of information in your document, you are enabling the reader of your document to follow important points or issues in your document.

In this task, you learn how to create bulleted and numbered lists.

1 Highlight the six tips again. Click **Format, Bullets and Numbering** on the menu bar.

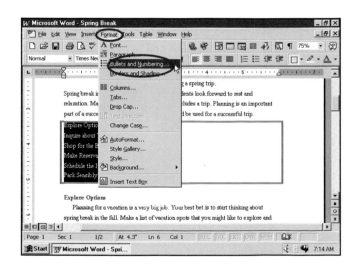

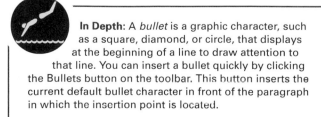

In Depth: A *bullet* is a graphic character, such as a square, diamond, or circle, that displays at the beginning of a line to draw attention to that line. You can insert a bullet quickly by clicking the Bullets button on the toolbar. This button inserts the current default bullet character in front of the paragraph in which the insertion point is located.

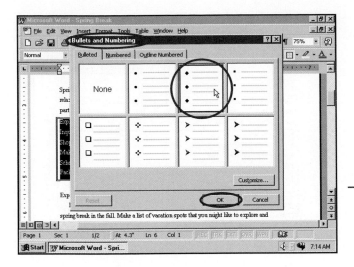

2 The **Bullets and Numbering** dialog box opens. Position the pointer inside the diamond bullet box and click.

3 Click **OK**. Each of the highlighted six tips is now preceded by a diamond bullet. Click outside the highlighted list to deselect the highlighted area.

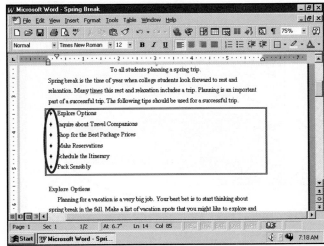

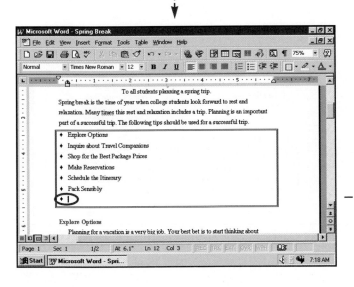

4 Position the insertion point after the last word of the last bulleted tip (*Pack Sensibly*). Press ⏎Enter to create a new bullet item.

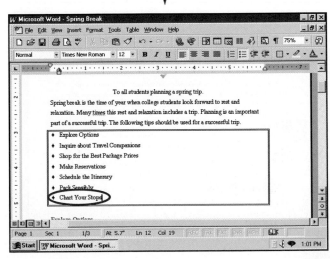

5 Type **Chart Your Stops**.

6 Press ⏎Enter to insert another new bullet item. Type **List Important Events**.

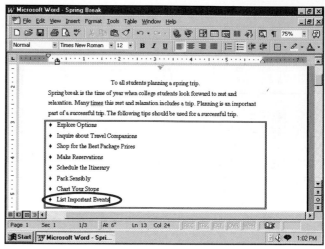

Numbering button

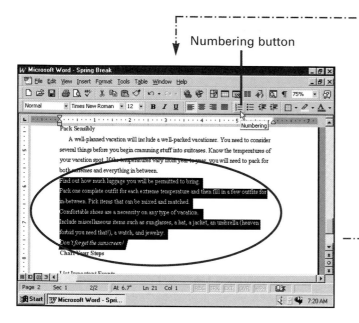

7 Scroll to the bottom of page 2. Under the *Pack Sensibly* heading, highlight the text beginning with *Find out how much luggage you will be permitted to bring* and ending with *Don't forget the sunscreen!*

8 Click the **Numbering** button on the toolbar. The highlighted text is automatically numbered for you. Click outside the highlighted list to deselect the highlighted area.

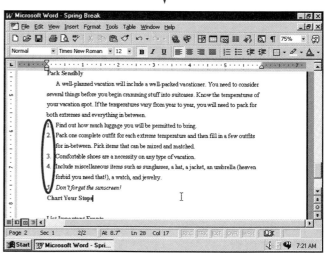

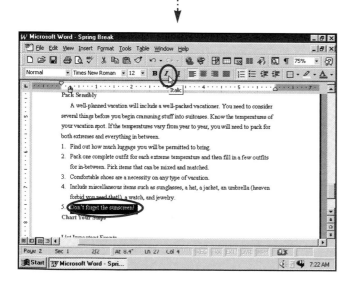

9 Notice that the italic style on the last item also italicizes the number 5. To remove the italic style, highlight the last numbered item and click the **Italic** button on the toolbar. Save your changes.

Task 4

Inserting Page Breaks

Why would I do this?

As you create a document, Word inserts an automatic *page break* to mark the end of each full page. You may not like where an automatic page break falls, however. A page may break in the middle of a table, for example. Or a heading may appear on one page and the paragraph following the heading appear on the next page. You can adjust page endings yourself by inserting a manual page break. All text after a manual page break moves to the next page.

In this task, you learn how to insert a page break.

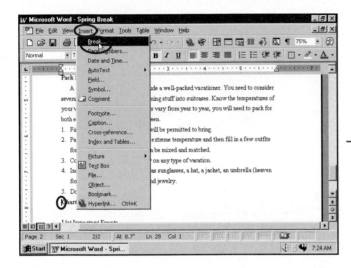

1 The heading *Chart Your Stops* displays toward the bottom of page 2 of your document. To move this and the next heading (*List Important Events*) to the next page, position the insertion point to the left of the word Chart in the heading. Click **Insert, Break** on the menu bar.

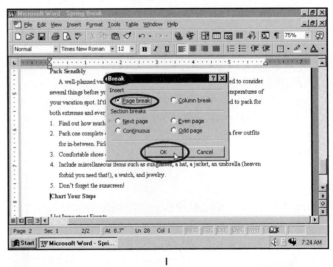

2 The **Break** dialog box opens. The default choice in the dialog box is **Page break**.

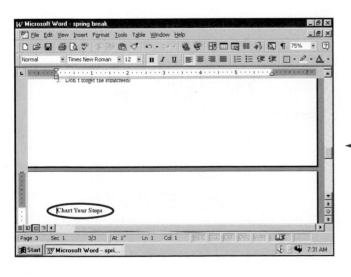

3 Click **OK** to insert the page break. The heading moves to the next page. Save your changes.

Task 5

Working with Tabs

Why would I do this?

Instead of using the Spacebar to position your insertion point at a specific point in your document, you can use Word's tab feature to set a tab stop. By default, Word sets a tab stop every half inch. You can set tab stops anywhere on the ruler. When you press ⓣab↹, your insertion point automatically moves to the tab stop.

In this task, you learn how to set and use tabs to organize text.

1 Position the cursor on the line after the *Chart Your Stops* heading. Click **Format, Tabs** on the menu bar.

> **In Depth:** You can set four different types of tabs using Word's tab feature. A left tab aligns text at the left of the tab stop. A right tab aligns text at the right. A center tab centers text on the tab stop. A decimal tab aligns numbers by their decimal points at the decimal tab stop. You can set all four types of tabs in the Tabs dialog box or you can set tabs directly on the ruler by clicking the tab button at the far left of the ruler (it usually shows a left tab symbol) until it shows the type of tab you want to set. Then click the ruler where you want the tab stop.

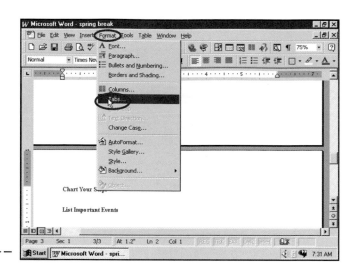

2 The **Tabs** dialog box opens. First, specify a left tab at the 0.5-inch position. Type **.5** in the Tab stop position box. Click the **Left** option button in the Alignment area if it is not already selected.

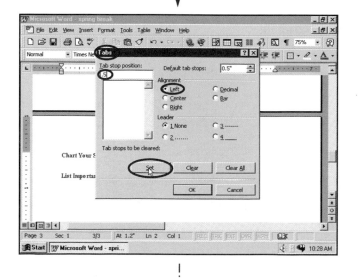

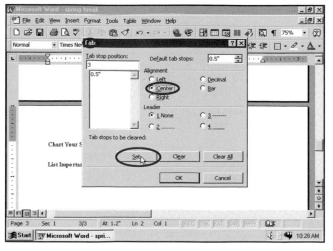

3 Click **Set** to set the tab. Notice that the 0.5" tab stop displays in the Tab stop list. Insert the next tab. Type **3** in the Tab stop position box. Click the **Center** option button in the Alignment area.

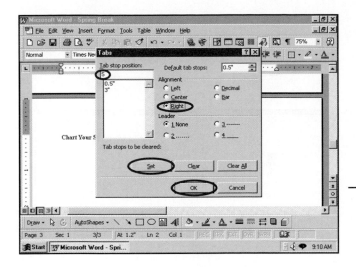

4 Click **Set** to set the tab. The new tab stop displays in the Tab stop list. Type **5** in the Tab stop position. Click the **Right** option button in the Alignment area.

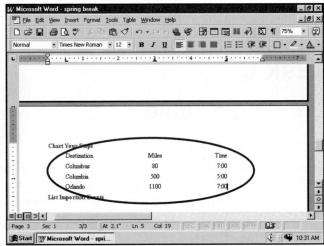

5 Click **Set** to set the tab. Click **OK** to close the Tabs dialog box. Type the text as shown. Press the Tab↹ before each word or number.

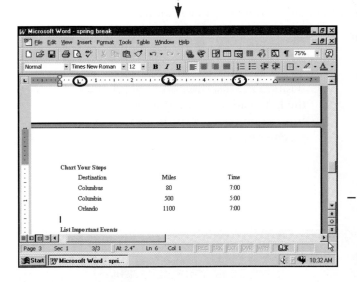

6 With your insertion point at the end of the last entry, press ↵Enter to insert a blank line above the last heading. Look at the ruler to see whether the tab stops you set display for this new blank line.

7 Click **Format, Tabs** on the menu bar to open the **Tabs** dialog box. Click the **Clear All** button to remove the tabs you set and return to the default setting of tabs every half inch.

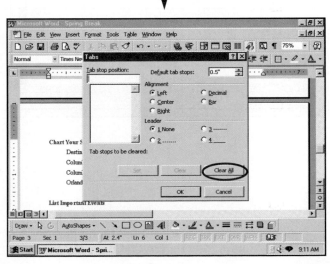

8 Click **OK** to close the Tabs dialog box. Notice that the ruler now shows no tab symbols. Save your changes.

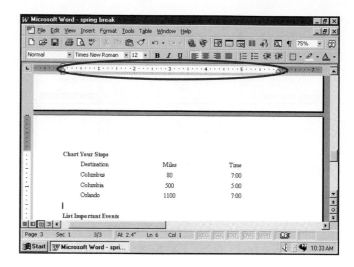

Task 6

Creating a Table

Why would I do this?

As you have seen, you can use tabs to organize information in your document into rows and columns. Tabs work fine if you have only a few rows and columns. For more complex material that may have many rows and columns, you should use Word's table feature. A table improves the readability of complex tabular information.

In this task, you learn how to create a table in a document.

Insert Table button

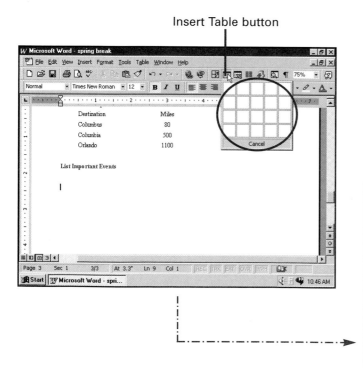

1 Position the insertion point on the line after the last heading, *List Important Events*. Click the **Insert Table button** on the toolbar. The table palette displays.

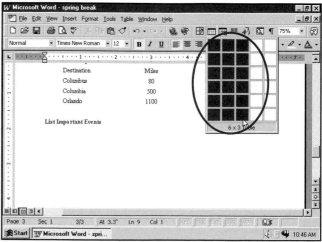

2 Hold down the mouse button and highlight three columns and six rows in the table palette.

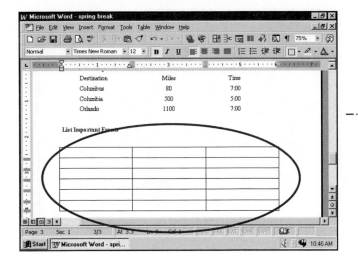

3 Release the mouse button. The table grid displays in your document.

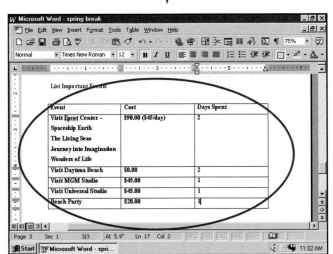

4 Type the text into the table cell locations as shown. Press (Tab⇆) to move from column to column and to new rows. Press (↵Enter) to create new lines within a table cell. Save your changes.

Task 7

Formatting a Table

Why would I do this?

Word lets you format a table in a number of ways to improve its appearance and readability. Changing font size and style enables you to fit more text into table cells or make text easier to read. Word's AutoFormat feature offers predesigned formats to control the appearance of a table.

In this task, you learn how to format a table.

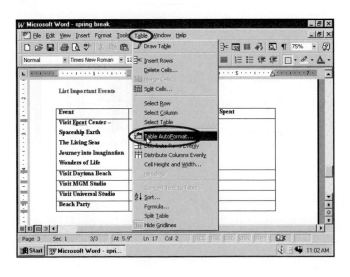

1 With the insertion point anywhere in the table, click **Table, Table AutoFormat** on the menu bar.

2 The **Table AutoFormat** dialog box opens. Highlight the **Colorful 2** format.

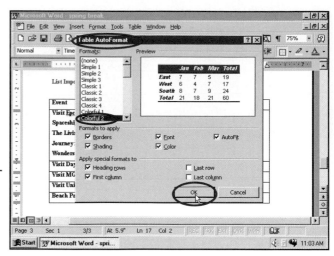

3 Click **OK** to close the dialog box. The Auto-Format you chose is applied to the table.

Insert Columns button

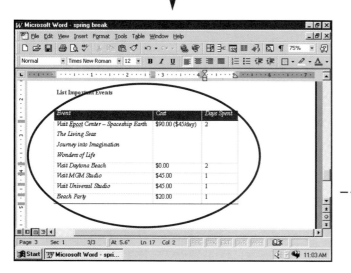

4 To insert a column in the table, position the insertion point at the top border of the *Cost* column, until the pointer becomes a heavy downward-pointing arrow. Click once to highlight the entire column.

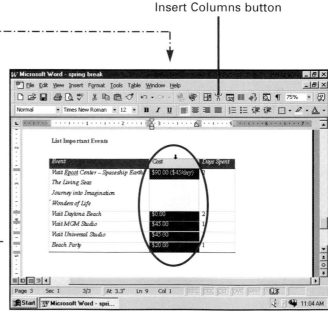

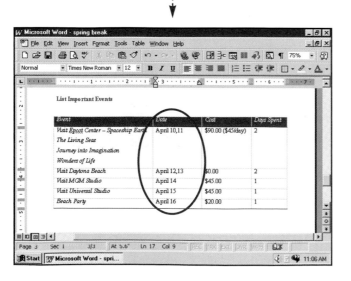

5 Click the **Insert Columns** button on the toolbar to insert a new column to the left of the Cost column. Insert text in this column as shown.

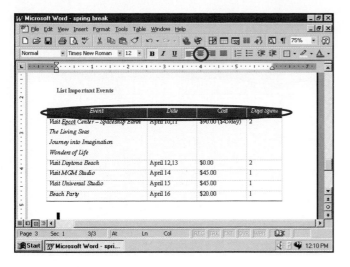

6 To center the column heads, click the pointer in the left margin next to the first row of the table (the row that contains the headings). Click the **Center** button on the toolbar. Save your changes.

Task 8

Inserting Headers, Footers, and Page Numbers

Why would I do this?

A *header* is text that displays at the top of every page in a document. A *footer* is text that displays at the bottom of every page in a document. Headers and footers can deliver helpful information about the document, such as the date, time, total number of pages in the document, filename, and so on. You can also include page numbers in either a header or footer. Word keeps track of page numbers and adjusts them if you add or delete pages in your document.

In this task, you learn how to insert a header and page number in a document.

1 Press Ctrl+Home to move the insertion point to the beginning of the document. Click **View, Header and Footer** on the menu bar.

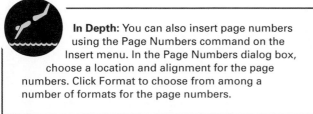

In Depth: You can also insert page numbers using the Page Numbers command on the Insert menu. In the Page Numbers dialog box, choose a location and alignment for the page numbers. Click Format to choose from among a number of formats for the page numbers.

2 The Header and Footer toolbar displays on the screen, along with a text area where you can type a header.

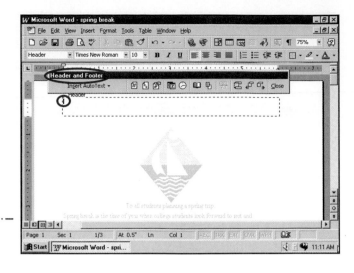

Quick Tip: By default, Word displays the header area on the screen. To insert a footer, click the Switch Between Header and Footer button on the Header and Footer toolbar. Word then displays the footer area.

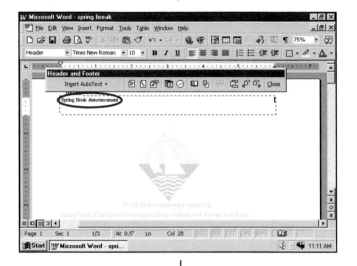

3 In the header text area, type the header **Spring Break Announcement**. Press Tab↹ twice.

Insert Page
Number button

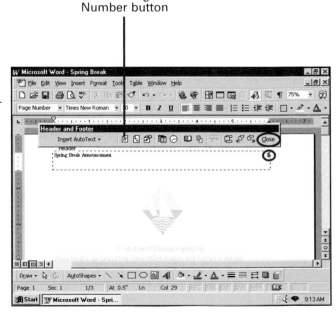

4 Click the **Insert Page Number** button on the toolbar to insert page numbers on all pages.

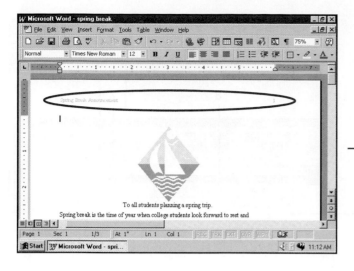

5 Click the **Close** button on the Header and Footer toolbar to close the header text area. Notice the header and page number at the top of the first page of the document.

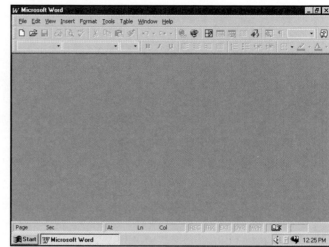

6 Save your changes. Print the document. Close the document.

10.

Student Exercises

True-False

For each of the following, circle either T or F to indicate whether the statement is true or false.

T (F) **1.** The default tab stop setting is every 1 inch.

(T) F **2.** The Header and Footer command is located on the View menu.

T (F) **3.** Clip art is special art that you must draw before you can use it.

T (F) **4.** When creating a table, you must have the same number of rows and columns.

T (F) **5.** Page numbers are always printed at the bottom of the page.

(T) F **6.** Pressing Ctrl + Home places the insertion point at the beginning of the document.

(T) F **7.** The Borders and Shading command is located on the Format menu.

(T) F **8.** To resize a graphic, use the selection handles.

T (F) **9.** Bullets and numbers are applied using the same toolbar button.

T (F) **10.** There are three types of tabs: Left, Center, and Decimal.

Identifying Parts of the
Word Screen

Refer to the figure and identify the numbered parts of the screen. Write the letter of the correct label in the space next to the number.

1. C
2. F
3. A
4. E
5. H
6. B
7. G
8. D

A. Insert Table button
B. Clip art picture
C. Header text area
D. Insert Page Number button
E. Close Header/Footer button
F. Close document button
G. Numbering button
H. Bullets button

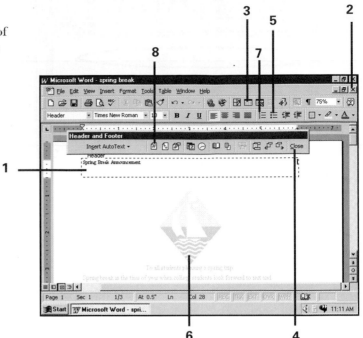

Matching

Match the following statements to the word or phrase that is the best match from the list. Write the letter of the matching word or phrase in the space provided next to the number. Some letters may be used more than once.

1. A The menu that gives you choices to format a table

2. D Area at the bottom of each page that can be used for text

3. F The menu used to insert clip art

4. B A box placed around text

5. E Area at the top of each page that can be used for text

6. C Special symbol placed at the beginning of a list of important points

7. G The menu to select to create a bulleted list

8. H The menu to select to place a header in a document

9. G The menu to select to place a border in a document

10. G The menu to select to set tabs

A. Table
B. Border
C. Bullet
D. Footer
E. Header
F. Insert
G. Format
H. View

Application Exercises

Exercise 1

1. To complete this exercise, you must have completed Application Exercise 1 in Lesson 5. Open the document you created and saved in Lesson 5 Application Exercise 1 named **Computer Supplies 2**. Save the document as **Computer Supplies 3**.

2. Place a border around the last paragraph.

3. Save your changes. Print the document. Close the document.

Exercise 2

1. Open **Less0602** and save it on your disk as **Weather**.

2. Create a heading called **Weather** for the document, using a font, style, and size of your choice. Align the heading at the left and change its color if you wish.

3. Click in the heading and insert a border beneath it: In the Borders and Shading dialog box, choose a line width of 3 points and a color to match your heading. Click at the bottom of the sample paragraph to set the border line. Then click **OK**.

4. Insert a clip art picture that relates to weather below the heading. Position the picture so that no text appears between the picture and the heading's border. Text should wrap at the right side of the picture.

5. Change the format of the first paragraph of the text to remove the first line indent.

6. Number the six points in the fifth paragraph. Place a border around the numbered list.

7. Create a header with the date centered in the header area. (**Hint:** Use the Date button on the Header and Footer toolbar to insert the date.) Create a footer with the page number centered. (**Hint:** With the Header and Footer toolbar still open, click the Switch Between Header and Footer button to move to the Footer area.)

8. Save your changes. Print the document. Close the document.

Exercise 3

1. To complete this exercise, you must have completed Application Exercise 3 in Lesson 5. Open the document you created and saved in Lesson 5 Application Exercise 3 named **Tree 2**. Save the document as **Tree 3**.

2. Change the alignment of the date and the heading to left alignment.

3. Position the insertion point to the left of the heading and insert a clip art picture that relates to trees. Using the Picture toolbar, change the text wrap option to Square so that the heading and date appear to the right of the clip art picture. Resize the picture or change the size of the heading text so that the heading fits on one line. Change the heading color if desired to complement the color of the picture.

4. In the second sentence of the first paragraph, type a colon after the word *ordered* and delete the rest of the text in the paragraph. Press ⏎Enter twice to insert a blank line.

5. Insert the following material and organize it using tabs. Use a center tab for the Quantity numbers and decimal tabs for the Price Each and Total Cost numbers.

Item	Quantity	Price Each	Total Cost
Maple trees	5	$9.00	$45.00
White pine trees	10	$4.00	$40.00
Apple trees	2	$18.00	$36.00
			$121.00

6. Save your changes. Print the document. Close the document.

Exercise 4

The Eagle Corporation

As the public relations manager of Eagle Corporation you have been given the task to create a newsletter to send to potential customers. This letter should explain to customers why Eagle Corporation is the best store for purchasing their office supplies. The newsletter should contain the following features:

1. Clip art

2. Borders

3. Table

4. Numbered list

5. Bulleted list

6. Headers/footers and page numbers

Lesson 7
Excel 97: The Basics

Introduction

Microsoft Excel 97 is a spreadsheet program designed to help you organize and analyze financial and statistical data. In today's businesses, schools, and homes, spreadsheets have become a standard tool to capture and evaluate both textual and numerical information.

This lesson is designed to help you become comfortable with the basic features of Excel 97.

Visual Summary

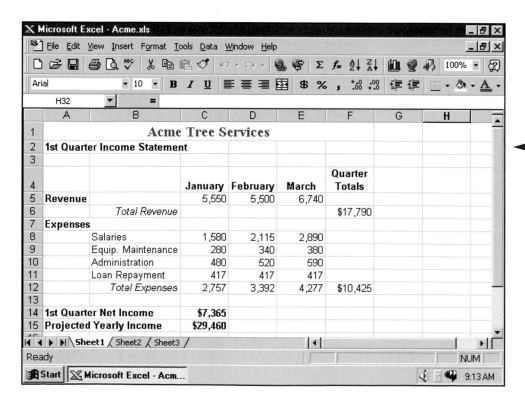

When you have completed Task 9, you will have created a worksheet that looks like this:

Task 1

Launching Excel 97

Why would I do this?

Launching Excel starts the Excel application so that you can begin creating a worksheet.

In this task, you learn how to launch Excel.

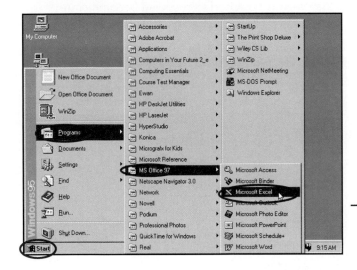

1 To start Excel, click the **Start** button and then click **Programs, MS Office 97, Microsoft Excel**.

2 Microsoft Excel opens and displays a new workbook entitled Book1.

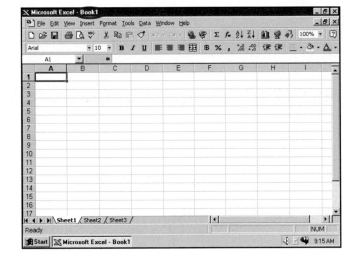

In Depth: When Excel opens on your screen, the document you see is called a *workbook*. A workbook consists of a number of *worksheets*. Each worksheet is identified by a tab at the bottom of the window labeled Sheet1, Sheet2, and so on. Usually, you work with only one worksheet at a time. But you may use several worksheets in a workbook to keep track of related data. For example, you might have a workbook devoted to invoices, which contains a worksheet for May invoices, a worksheet for June invoices, and so on.

Task 2

Navigating the Worksheet

Why would I do this?

An Excel worksheet is organized in numbered *rows* and lettered *columns*. You enter data into specific *cells*. A cell is the intersection of a row and a column. An Excel worksheet can be extremely large, handling as many as 256 columns and 65,536 rows, for a total of 16,777,216 unique cell locations. In addition, each individual cell can contain as many as 32,000 characters. To use any worksheet efficiently, you must know how to navigate among the rows, columns, and cells.

In this task, you learn how to move within a worksheet.

1 To see another worksheet in the workbook, click the tab at the bottom of the window labeled **Sheet2**.

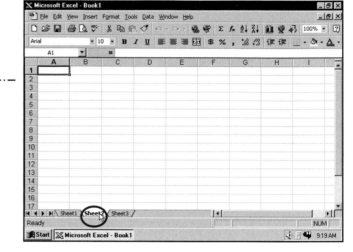

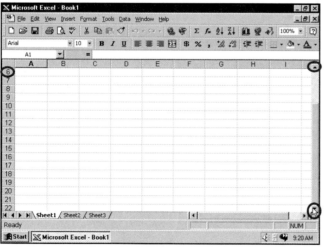

2 Return to Sheet1 by clicking the **Sheet1** tab at the bottom of the window. Position your pointer on the scroll down arrow on the vertical scroll bar and click five times. Row 6 is now the first row on your screen.

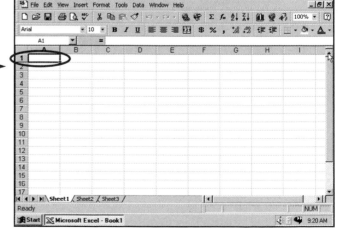

3 Click the scroll up arrow on the vertical scroll bar until row 1 displays.

Quick Tip: Using ⟨PgUp⟩ and ⟨PgDn⟩ moves up or down the worksheet by as many rows as can fit in the document window.

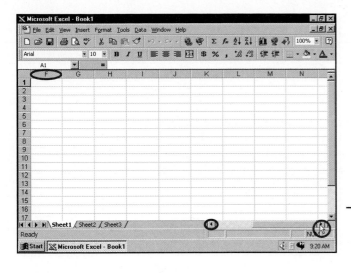

4 Position your pointer on the scroll right arrow on the horizontal scroll bar and click five times. Column F is now the first column on your screen.

5 Click the left arrow on the horizontal scroll bar until column A displays.

 Quick Tip: You can also drag the vertical or horizontal scroll box to move within your worksheet.

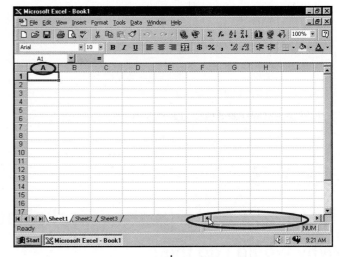

Name box

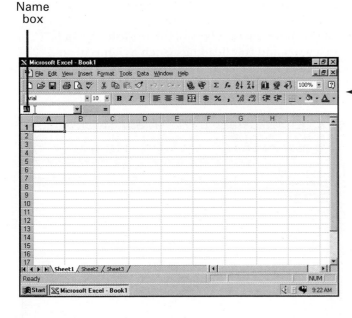

6 Position the pointer in the **Name** box and click to highlight the current cell address.

In Depth: You identify a specific cell in a worksheet by the column letter and the row number that intersect in that cell. This is called the *cell address*. For example, the cell where column C and row 3 intersect is called cell C3. When a cell is selected, it is surrounded by a heavy outline that is sometimes called the *cell pointer* or highlight. The currently selected cell is called the *active cell*.

7 Type **X55** in the Name box and press ↵Enter to go directly to cell location X55.

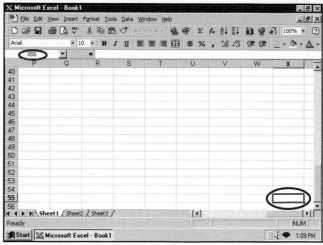

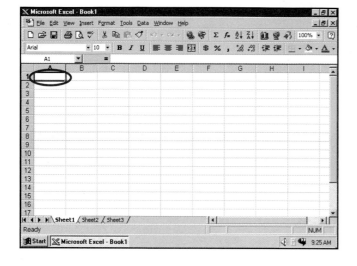

8 Hold down Ctrl and press Home to return to row 1, column A (called the home position) of your worksheet.

Task 3

Entering Data in the Worksheet

Why would I do this?

You can enter text or numbers in a cell. Text provides information about the numbers in the worksheet. For example, you use text for column headings (such as months in a year) and row headings (such as items in an invoice). Numbers are the chief form of data that you organize and analyze in a worksheet.

In this task, you learn how to enter text and numbers in a worksheet.

1 Click inside cell **A1** if that cell is not currently highlighted. Type **Acme Tree Service** and press ↵Enter to confirm the entry.

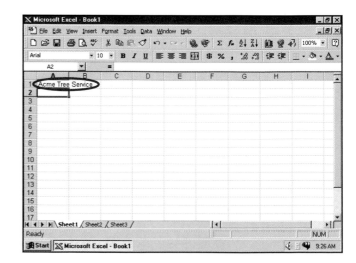

Pothole: After you position your pointer in a cell location, be sure to click to select that cell, otherwise you may enter data in another cell that is currently active.

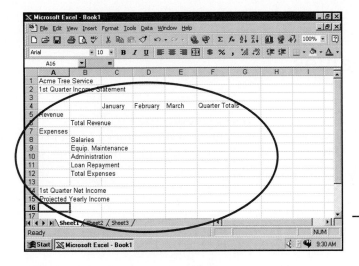

2 In cell **A2** type **1st Quarter Income Statement** and press ⏎Enter to confirm the entry. Refer to the figure and type the remaining text entries. Press ⏎Enter or Tab⇄ to confirm each entry. Notice that when your entry is longer than the cell is wide, the text flows into the next cell.

 In Depth: In a worksheet, text entries are often called *labels* and number entries are often called *values*.

3 You enter numbers the same way you enter text. Refer to the figure and type the numbers in the worksheet.

Pothole: Notice that the numbers you entered for January expenses cover part of the text you entered in column B. Don't worry! All the text is still stored in the cells. You learn how to adjust column widths to display all data later in this lesson.

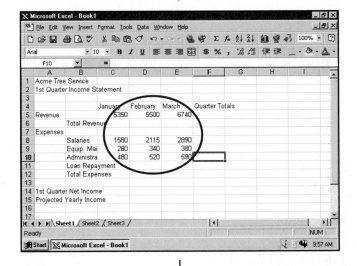

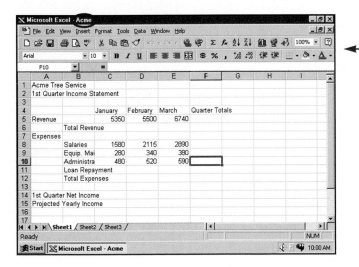

4 Save the workbook on your disk with the name **Acme**.

In Depth: You save a workbook just as you save a word processing document: Click the Save button, specify the location where you want to save the file in the Save As dialog box, and type a name for the file.

Task 4

Using Formulas to Calculate Values

Why would I do this?

After you have entered values in a worksheet, you can analyze them in many ways to provide you with further information. You can use *formulas* to instruct Excel how to analyze values. For example, you can enter a formula in a cell that instructs Excel to add the value in one cell to the value in another cell and then display the sum.

In this task, you learn how to create formulas to calculate values in the worksheet.

1 To calculate total revenue for the first quarter, click in cell **F6**. Type the formula **=C5+D5+E5**.

In Depth: The equal sign (=) informs Excel that you want to enter a formula at this location. The cell addresses (C5, D5, and E5) tell Excel where to find the values for the calculation. The plus sign (+) is a *mathematical operator* that tells Excel that you want to add the values in the specified cell references. Any future changes to these cells automatically change the value of cell F6. Other common mathematical operators are - (for subtraction), * (for multiplication), and / (for division).

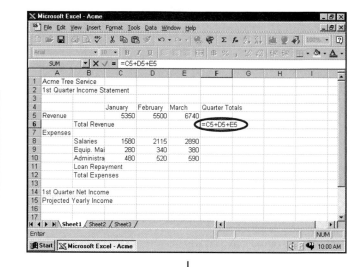

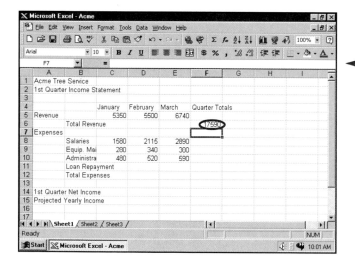

2 Press ⏎Enter to confirm the entry.

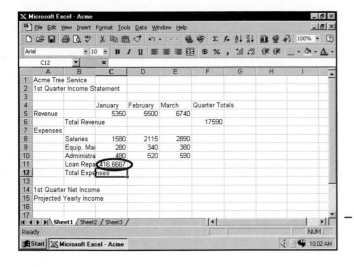

3 Cell B11 refers to a loan repayment expense. The tree service borrowed $5,000 for a year. To calculate the monthly repayment, click cell **C11** and type the formula **=5000/12**. Press (↵Enter) to confirm the entry.

4 The loan repayment amount should be the same for the months of February and March. You can use Copy to insert the same formula in cells D11 and E11. Click in cell **C11** to make it active. Click the **Copy** button on the toolbar. A moving marquee surrounds cell C11. Click in cell D11 and drag to the right to highlight cell E11 as well.

> **In Depth:** When you select a group of cells, Excel does not highlight the first cell in the selected area. A group of adjacent cells that have been selected is called a *cell range*. Cell ranges are identified by the first cell at the top left of the range, a colon, and the last cell at the bottom right of the range. Excel gives you several additional ways to select groups of cells. Click the column header letter to select an entire column. Click the row header number to select an entire row. Click the Select All button (the light gray rectangle at the top left of the worksheet where the columns and rows meet) to select all cells in the worksheet.

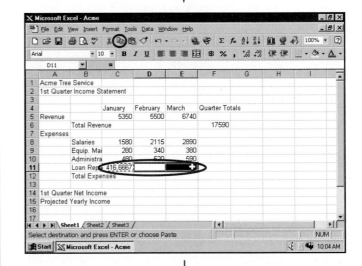

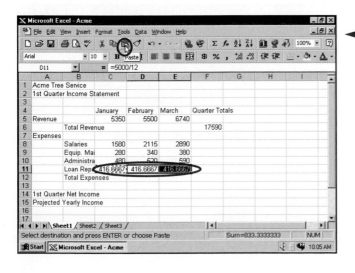

5 Click the **Paste** button on the toolbar. The copied formula displays in cells **D11** and **E11**.

> **Quick Tip:** To save time when entering formulas, you can simply click in the cell you want to include in the formula. For example, to create a formula that adds the values in cells B3 and B4, type the = sign, click in cell B3, type the + sign, and click in cell B4. Then press (↵Enter) or (Tab⇄) to confirm the entry.

6 Now you can total the expenses for each month and for the entire quarter. In cell **C12**, type the formula **=C8+C9+C10+C11**. Copy the formula in cell C12 to cells **D12** and **E12**. In cell **F12**, type the formula **=C12+D12+E12**. Press ⏎Enter to confirm the entry.

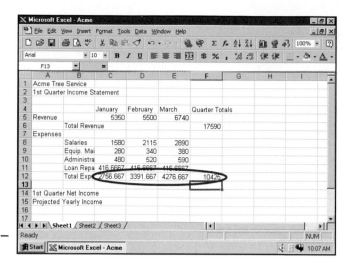

7 To determine the net income, you need to subtract total expenses from total revenue. Click in cell **C14** and type the formula **=F6-F12**. Press ⏎Enter.

In Depth: You can instruct Excel to perform more than one operation in a formula. For example, you can create a formula that adds two values and then multiplies the sum by another value. Excel performs these operations according to *rules of precedence*: any multiplication operation is performed first, followed by division, addition, and then subtraction. To control the order in which Excel performs calculations, you can enclose operations within parentheses. Excel always performs the calculation within parentheses first.

8 You can project the year's profits by subtracting expenses from revenues and multiplying the remainder by 4 (for the four quarters in the year). Click in cell **C15** and type the formula **=(F6-F12)*4**. This formula tells Excel to first subtract expenses from revenues and then to multiply the resulting value by 4. Press ⏎Enter. Save your changes.

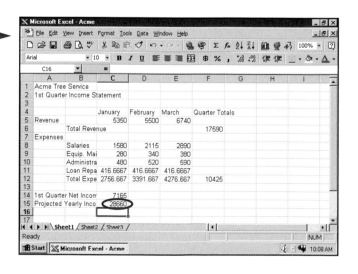

Task 5

Editing Cell Contents

Why would I do this?

Suppose you type text, numbers, or formulas into a cell and then decide to change the contents of the cell because you made a mistake or have received revised data. You can easily change the contents of a cell after you have entered data.

In this task, you learn how to edit cell contents.

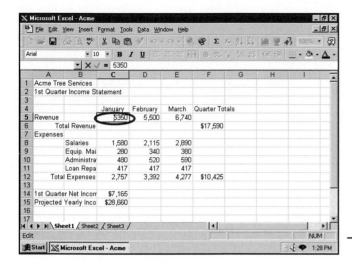

1 The Revenue number for January is incorrect. It should read 5550. To correct the data, double-click in cell **C5**. An insertion point displays within the cell.

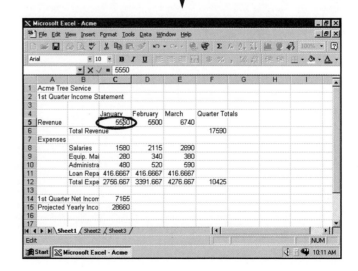

2 Position the insertion point to the left of the number 3 and press Del. Type **5**.

3 Press ⏎Enter to confirm the change. Notice that some of the formulas you entered in the last task have recalculated to account for the new value.

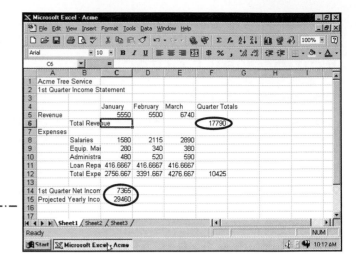

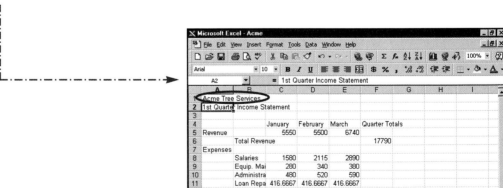

4 To change the worksheet's main heading, double-click in cell **A1**. Position the insertion point to the right of the last word in the heading.

5 Type **s** and press ⏎Enter. Save your changes.

Task 6

Adjusting Column Width

Why would I do this?

You have probably already noticed that when you type data into a cell, it can run over into adjacent cells if those cells have no data in them. If you type a long entry into a cell whose adjacent cells have data, however, the entry is truncated. The data is still in the cell—you just can't see all of it. You can display all of the data in the cells by widening the column.

In this task, you learn how to adjust column width.

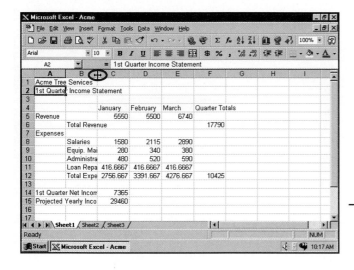

1 Column B is not wide enough to display the expense items. You can widen the column by dragging its border in the column header row. Move the pointer up to the vertical line that marks the boundary between column B and column C. The pointer becomes a double-pointed arrow.

2 Hold down the mouse button and drag the arrow pointer to the right to widen the column until all expense items show. Save your change.

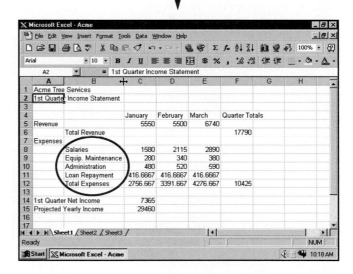

Quick Tip: Another method to widen a column is to double-click the right boundary of the column heading. Excel automatically widens the column to fit the widest entry in the column.

In Depth: You can increase or decrease row height using a similar process. Position the pointer on the boundary line between two rows and drag up or down to decrease or increase the size of the row.

Task 7

Changing Data Alignment

Why would I do this?

Excel can left, center, or right-align data within a cell or a group of cells. This feature is used to improve the appearance of the worksheet. By default, Excel left-aligns text entries and right-aligns number entries, but you can change the alignment of any type of data in a cell. You can also wrap text in a cell and center text across several cells.

In this task, you learn how to change data alignment.

1 To center the column headings, highlight the cell range **C4:F4**. Click the **Center** button on the toolbar to center the text within each cell.

> **In Depth:** To align data in cells, you can use both toolbar buttons and the Format Cells dialog box. Use the toolbar buttons for common alignments such as center, left, right, and merge and center. Use the Format Cells dialog box to wrap text and change vertical alignment.

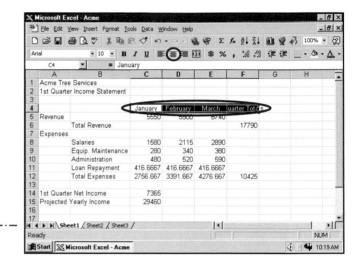

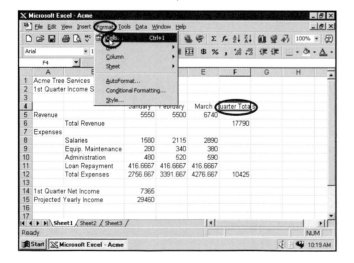

2 Notice that the centered heading *Quarter Totals* is now truncated. You can wrap the text in this cell to avoid having to widen the cell to display all the text. Click in cell **F4** to make it active. Click **Format, Cells** on the menu bar.

3 The **Format Cells** dialog box opens. Click the **Alignment** tab. Click the **Wrap text** check box.

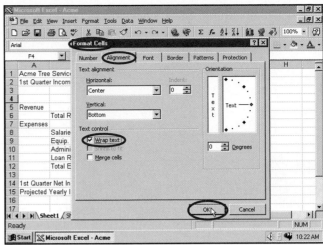

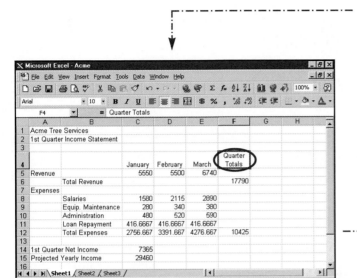

4 Click **OK** to close the dialog box. Notice that the long text entry now appears on two lines and the row height has adjusted automatically to accommodate the two lines.

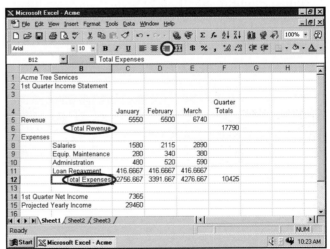

5 To make the *Total Revenue* entry stand out, click cell **B6** and then click the **Align Right** button on the toolbar. Perform the same operation to right align the *Total Expenses* entry in cell **B12**.

Merge and
Center button

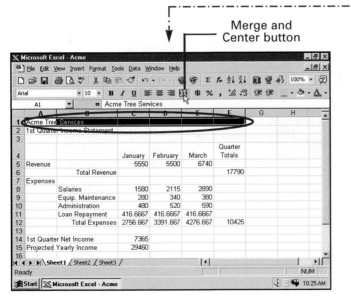

6 To center the title *Acme Tree Services* across all the columns containing data, first select the cell range **A1:F1**.

7 Click the **Merge and Center** button on the toolbar to center the title across the worksheet data. Click in another cell to remove the highlight. Save your changes.

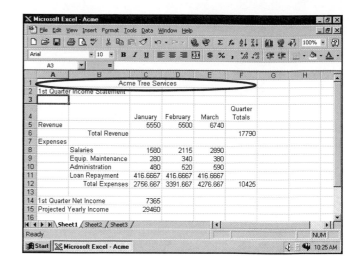

In Depth: When you merge and center data, the data is still stored in the original cell (in this case, A1) even though it looks as if it begins in another cell.

Task 8

Formatting Text

Why would I do this?

Formatting text in a worksheet can make it more useful for the reader. By making column headings bold, for example, you draw attention to them. Changing the font or font size can make text more readable or interesting. You can even use color to emphasize specific portions of the worksheet.

In this task, you learn how to format text in the worksheet.

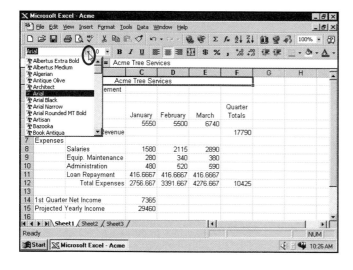

1 Click in cell **A1** to select the *Acme Tree Services* title. To change the font of the title, click the down arrow on the **Font** box on the toolbar. The font list displays.

In Depth: Text formatting in Excel is almost identical to text formatting in Word. You can use toolbar buttons to make many character formatting changes. You can also click Cells on the Format menu, then the Font tab, to access other text formatting options.

2 Scroll to find the **Times New Roman** font and click the font name to apply it to the title.

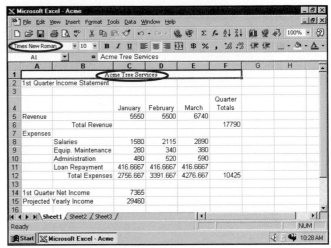

3 The heading would draw more attention if it were larger. Click the **Font Size** down arrow on the toolbar and choose **14** from the drop-down list.

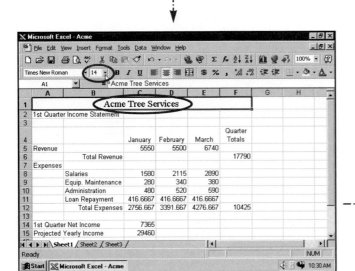

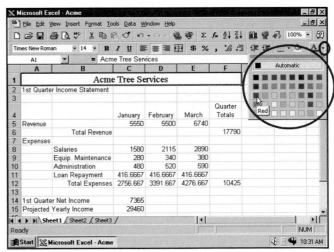

4 With the heading still selected, click the **Font Color** drop-down arrow on the toolbar to display the color palette.

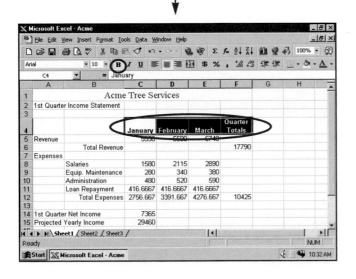

5 Click the **Red** palette choice. Select the cell range **C4:F4**. Click the **Bold** button on the toolbar.

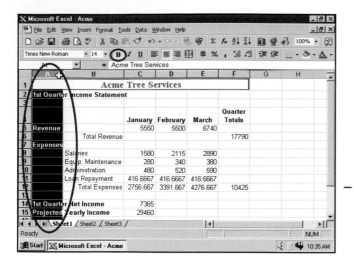

6 To boldface all the entries in column A, click the column heading (the letter A at the top of the worksheet) to select the entire column. Click the **Bold** button on the toolbar.

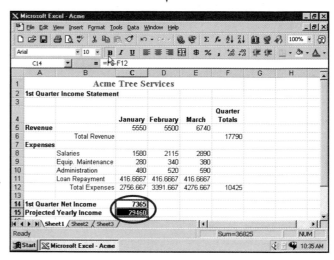

7 Select the cell range **C14:C15** and click the **Bold** button on the toolbar.

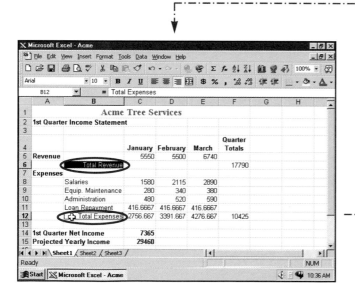

8 Select cell **B6**. Hold down Ctrl and select cell **B12**.

Quick Tip: Holding down Ctrl enables you to highlight multiple nonadjacent cells in your worksheet.

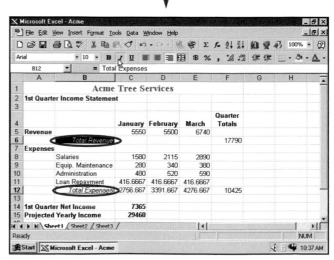

9 Click the **Italic** button on the toolbar. Save your changes.

Task 9

Formatting Numbers

Why would I do this?

Besides giving you a number of ways to format text, Excel offers a number of ways to format numbers. Using number formats saves you the effort of typing dollar signs, commas, or percent signs in cells. Number formats also let you choose how many decimal places to display, if any, and how to display negative numbers.

In this task, you learn how to apply number formats to values in the worksheet.

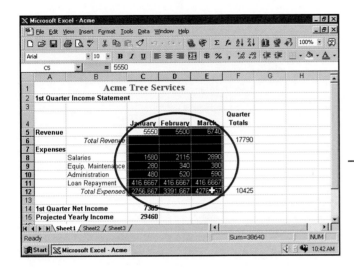

1 The revenue and expense numbers are currently in two different formats—some with decimal places and some without. Apply a format to make all the numbers look the same. Select the cell range **C5:E12**.

2 Click **Format, Cells** on the menu bar. The **Format Cells** dialog box opens. Click the **Number** tab if necessary.

> **Quick Tip:** You can apply some types of number formats using buttons on the toolbar.

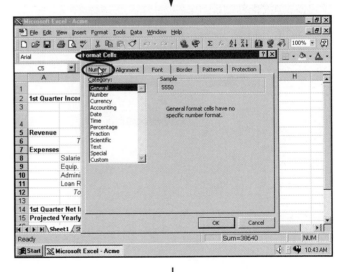

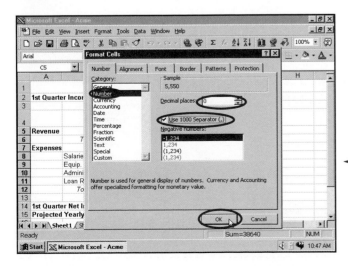

3 Click the **Number** format in the **Category** list. In the **Decimal places** box, click the down arrow until **0** displays. Click the **Use 1000 Separator** box until a check mark appears.

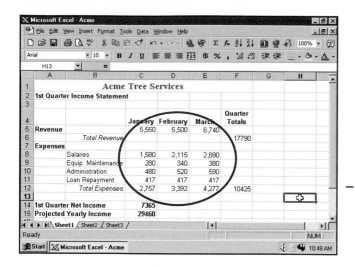

4 Click **OK** to apply the format to the cell range. Click outside the highlighted text to see the results.

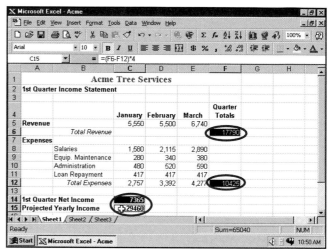

5 To indicate that the Quarter Totals, the Net Income, and the Projected Yearly Income numbers are currency, you can apply the Currency format. Select cell **F6**, hold down Ctrl, and select **F12**, **C14**, and **C15**.

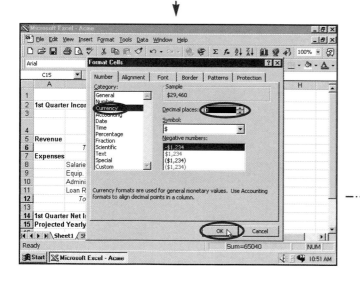

6 Click **Format, Cells** to open the Format Cells dialog box again. In the **Category** list, click **Currency**. In the **Decimal places** box, click the down arrow until **0** displays.

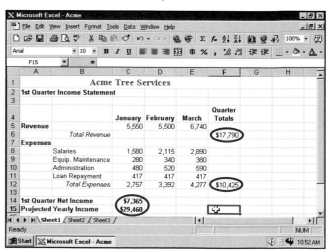

7 Click **OK** to apply the formatting. Click in any cell to remove the highlights. Save your changes.

Task 10

Previewing and Printing a Worksheet

Why would I do this?

The trend today with computer output is digital imaging. Information is stored in electronic format that is accessible to any user who logs onto the computer and views information on the monitor. There still exists, however, the need for hard copy. You can view a hard copy, write comments on it, forward it to someone else for review, or simply file it for future reference. Before you print your worksheet data, you should preview it. Worksheets can become very large, with many columns and rows of data. If you see in the preview window that your worksheet is too wide to fit a portrait page, you can change the print orientation to landscape to save paper.

In this task, you learn how to preview and print a worksheet.

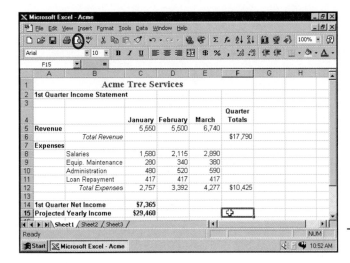

1 Click the **Print Preview** button on the toolbar to preview your worksheet.

2 The **Print Preview** window opens to show you what the worksheet will look like when printed.

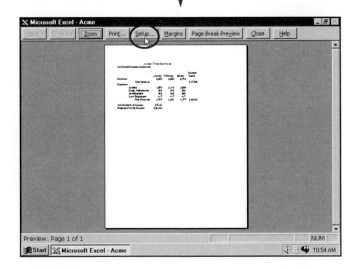

> **In Depth:** Excel's Page Setup dialog box gives you a number of options on four tabs for printing your worksheet. Besides changing the print orientation from portrait to landscape, you can insert a header or footer, change worksheet margins, or choose whether to print *gridlines* or row and column headers.

3 Click the **Setup** button on the Print Preview toolbar. The **Page Setup** dialog box opens. Click the **Sheet** tab.

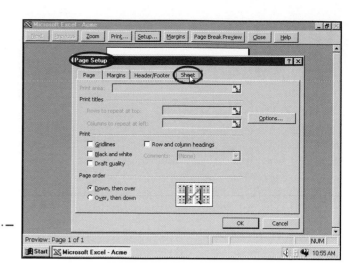

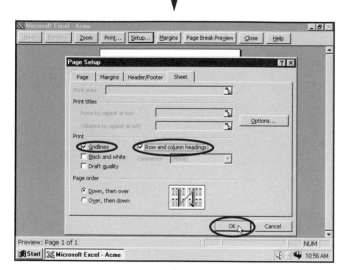

4 Click the **Gridlines** and **Row and column headings** check boxes so that Excel displays and prints these parts of the worksheet.

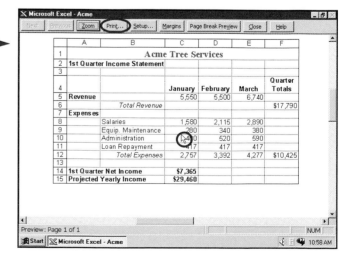

5 Click **OK** to close the dialog box and return to the Print Preview window. Click the magnifying pointer once on the worksheet preview to see the data in a magnified view.

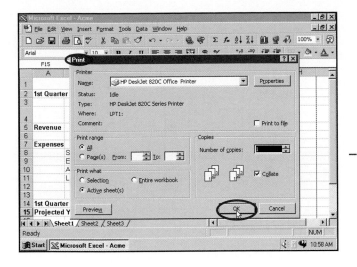

6 Click the **Print** button on the Print Preview toolbar. The **Print** dialog box opens.

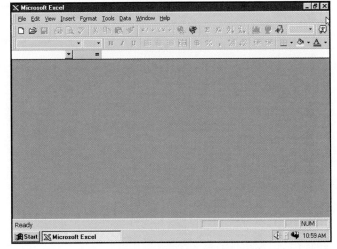

7 Click **OK** to print a hard copy of your worksheet. Save your changes. Close the worksheet by clicking its **Close** button.

Student Exercises

True-False

For each of the following, circle either T or F to indicate whether the statement is true or false.

T (F) **1.** You can type text and numbers in a cell, but you must use a toolbar button to enter a formula.

T (F) **2.** Double-clicking in a cell deletes the contents of the cell.

(T) F **3.** Pressing ⏎Enter while in cell B4 moves the highlight to and selects cell B5.

T F **4.** You bold and center text in Excel the same way as you do in Word.

T F **5.** You must select a cell before you can enter text or numbers.

T F **6.** Excel's Merge and Center feature centers the contents of data across multiple cells.

T F **7.** A worksheet and a workbook are exactly the same.

T F **8.** Pressing Tab⇆ twice while in cell F5 moves the highlight to and selects cell F7.

T F **9.** Cell addresses C20 and 20C mean the same thing in an Excel worksheet.

T F **10.** You can tell in Excel which cell is selected because that cell has a dark border around it.

Identifying Parts of the Excel Screen

Refer to the figure and identify the numbered parts of the screen. Write the letter of the correct label in the space next to the number.

1. h
2. E
3. g
4. a
5. A
6. D
7. i
8. D
9. C
10. J

A. Column header
B. Center button
C. Font button
D. Active cell
E. Row header
F. Wrapped text
G. Currency format
H. Font Size button
I. Merge and Center button
J. Align Right button

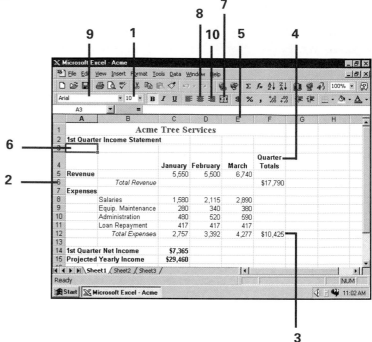

Matching

Match the following statements to the word or phrase that is the best match from the list. Write the letter of the matching word or phrase in the space provided next to the number.

1. C Button used to launch Excel
2. F The arithmetic sign used to begin typing a formula
3. J The intersection of a row and column
4. L Location to widen a column
5. G The proper reference for row 8, column F
6. K Keystrokes used to move from cell B14 to H14
7. I Button used to properly center text across multiple cells
8. b A group of selected adjacent cells
9. h Operation that Excel will perform first in a formula
10. E Cell currently selected

A. F8
B. Cell range
C. Start button
D. 3 1/2 floppy disk
E. Active cell
F. The = sign
G. 8F
H. Multiplication
I. Merge and Center button
J. Cell
K. Press Tab⇆ six times
L. Border line between columns

Application Exercises

Exercise 1

1. Create the worksheet shown in the figure.

2. Save the worksheet on your disk as **Fish Farm**.

3. Center the *Joe's Fish Farm* heading across columns A–G. Change the font size to **16** and the font color to **Teal**.

4. Bold the subtitle.

5. Format the fish name column headings as bold, centered, and teal.

6. Format the row headings (the locations) as bold italic.

7. Format the *Total Count* entry as bold and teal.

8. In cell B10, create a formula to add the values for salmon in all locations. Copy the formula to cells C10:F10 to add the numbers for the other fish.

9. Format all the numbers as Number with no decimal places and the 1000 separator.

10. Adjust column widths to display all data.

11. Save your changes.

12. Preview the worksheet. Use the Setup button to open the Page Setup dialog box. Specify that gridlines print.

13. Print the worksheet. Close the worksheet.

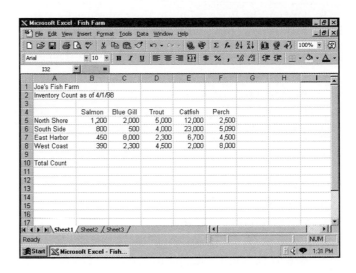

Exercise 2

1. Create the worksheet shown in the figure.

2. Save the worksheet on your disk as **Creative Computers**.

3. Click the **Select All** button to select all the cells in the worksheet. Change the font to **Times New Roman**.

4. Center the title *Creative Computer Resources* across columns A-E. Change the font size to **14** point and the color to **Blue**.

5. Center the subtitle *Fall Clearance* across columns A-E, italicize the text, and change the color to Blue.

6. Center and bold the four column headings (Item, Model, Quantity, and Price).

7. The entry in cell A6 should read **Laser Printer**. Make this change. The price for paper is incorrect. The price should be **17.75**. Make this change.

Select All button

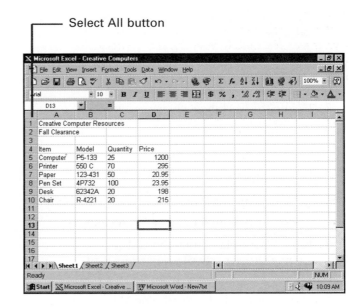

8. Center the entries in the Model and Quantity columns.

9. Format the Price values in the Currency format with two decimal places and dollar signs.

10. Adjust column widths as necessary to display all data.

11. Save your changes. Print the worksheet. Close the worksheet.

Exercise 3

1. Create the worksheet shown in the figure.

2. Save the worksheet on your disk as **Tree Farm**.

3. Wrap the text in cells B4:D4 if you did not do so when entering the data.

4. Change the font of the title to **Algerian** and its size to **16** point. Change the color to **Green**. Underline the text.

5. Bold and center the column headings.

6. Format the tree values with 1000 separators and no decimal places.

7. Bold the names of the trees.

8. Enter a formula to calculate the percent of loss. In cell E5, type the formula **=(C5+D5)/B5**. Copy the formula to cells E6:E9. Format the % Loss column in Percentage format with no decimal places.

9. Save your changes. Print the worksheet. Close the worksheet.

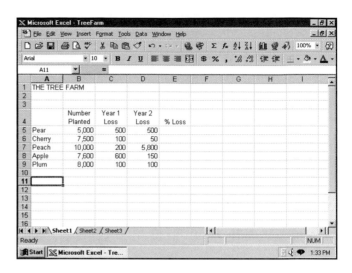

Exercise 4

1. Create the worksheet shown in the figure.

2. Save the worksheet on your disk as **Student Senate**.

3. Change the worksheet title (*Student Senate Office*) to 14 point Times New Roman bold. Change the subtitle to 12 point Times New Roman italic. Use colors of your choice for the title and subtitle.

4. Enter a formula to total the college expense for each of the five school years (rows 6-10).

5. Bold and center the column headings. Use a color of your choice for the headings. Adjust column widths to display all data.

6. Bold the row headings.

7. Format all the numbers as currency with no decimal places.

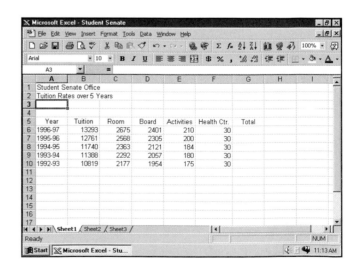

8. Save your changes. Print the worksheet with gridlines. Close the worksheet.

Exercise 5

The Eagle Corporation.

As the manager of the shipping department at Eagle Corporation, you are responsible for keeping track of all expenditures within your department. Those expenditures include, but are not limited to, paper supplies, equipment (such as a copy machine or a computer), and miscellaneous expenses (such as money for the coffee fund).

Design and create a worksheet using Excel that would enables you to effectively control and monitor your department's expenditures. Name the worksheet **Shipping**.

Lesson 8
Special Excel Features

Introduction

Now that you are able to create, format, save, and print a worksheet, you are ready to use additional capabilities available in Excel to enhance the overall effectiveness of your worksheet. This lesson shows you how to create a more professional worksheet.

This lesson is designed to introduce you to some of Excel's special features.

Visual Summary

When you have completed Task 9, you will have created a workbook that looks like this:

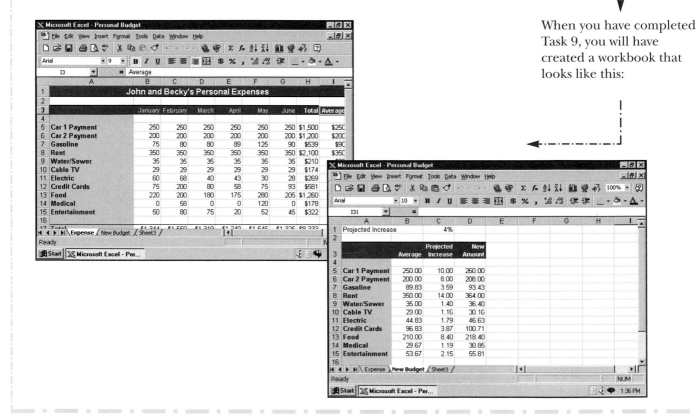

Task 1

Using the Fill Handle to Insert Data

Why would I do this?

In Lesson 7, you used Copy and Paste to duplicate the contents of one cell in other cells. To speed the data entry process, you can also use Excel's fill options. Excel's *fill handle* enables you to fill cells adjacent to a selected cell with the same value as is in that cell. The fill handle can also be used to continue items in a series. For example, you can enter the word *Monday* in a cell and use the fill handle to insert the other days of the week in adjacent cells. Using the fill handle saves time and reduces the chance of data entry errors.

In this task, you learn how to use the fill handle.

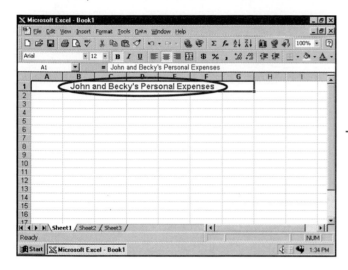

1 Open a new workbook in Excel. Type **John and Becky's Personal Expenses** in cell **A1**. Make the heading 12 point, bold, red, and merge and center the heading across cell range A1:G1.

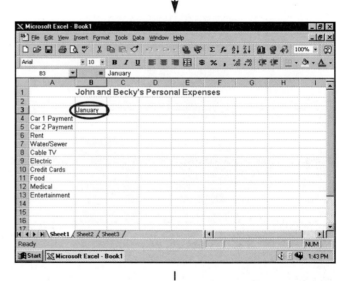

2 Type the expense items as shown in cells **A4** through **A13**. Adjust the width of column A to display all text. Type **January** in cell **B3**. After confirming the entry, click in cell **B3** again to select it.

3 Position the pointer on the fill handle, the small square at the lower right corner of cell B3. The pointer becomes a plus (+).

> **Quick Tip:** Excel has additional fill commands on the Edit menu to help you enter data quickly. To fill a group of adjacent cells below a cell with that cell's value, select the cell and the additional cells to fill. Then click Edit, Fill, Down. To fill a group of cells to the right, use Fill Right. You can also fill up or fill left.

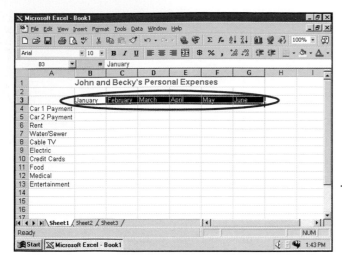

4 Drag the pointer to the right to cell G3 and release the mouse button. Excel understands that you want to continue a series starting with the month *January* and fills the cells with the months of February through June.

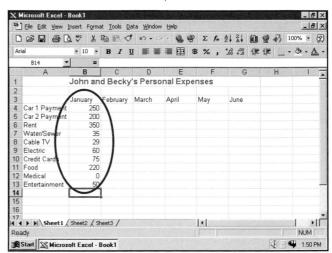

5 Type the expense numbers for January as shown in cells **B4** through **B13**.

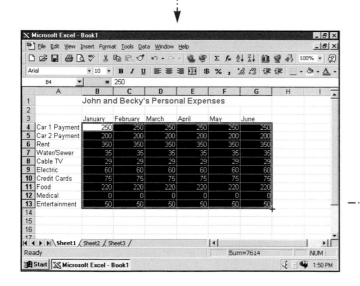

6 Select the numbers you just entered. Click the fill handle at the lower right corner of cell **B13** and drag the fill handle to the right to cell **G13**. Release the mouse button. Excel fills the cells across the worksheet with the values in the selected cells.

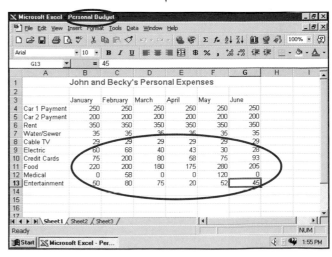

7 Change the expense items as shown in cells **B9** through **G13**. Save the worksheet as **Personal Budget**.

Task 2

Moving Data in the Worksheet

Why would I do this?

You can relocate data in a worksheet to a different area of the worksheet using the *drag and drop* feature. Moving data saves you the labor of having to re-enter it in another location.

In this task, you learn how to move data in a worksheet using the drag and drop feature.

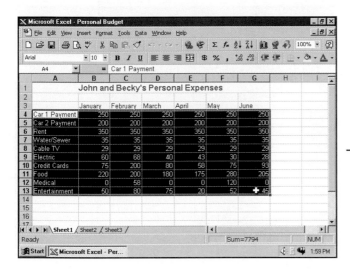

1 Select the cell range **A4:G13**.

2 Place the pointer on the lower border of the highlighted cells until it becomes an arrow.

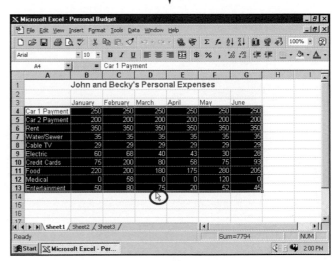

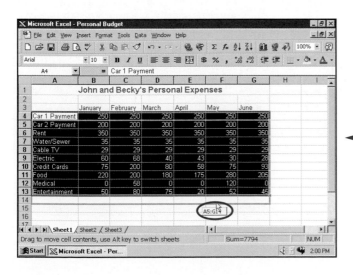

3 Drag the pointer down one row to row 14 and release the mouse button. The highlighted data moves down one row. Save your changes.

Task 3

Inserting Rows and Columns

Why would I do this?

You may need to make room in your worksheet for additional data that has been left out. Or you simply may want to add rows or columns to make the worksheet easier to read.

In this task, you learn how to insert a row in the worksheet.

1 Click in the row 7 header (the number 7) to select the entire row.

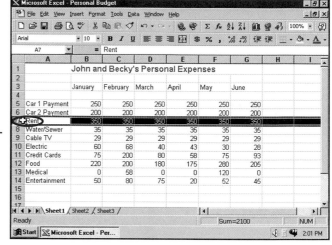

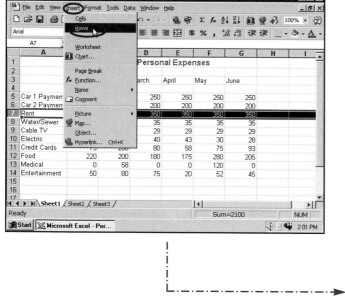

2 Click **Insert**, **Rows** on the menu bar.

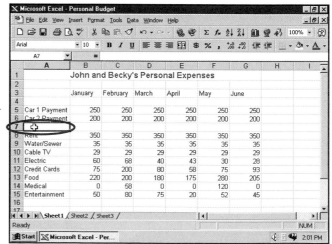

3 A new row 7 is added to your worksheet. The previous row 7 is now row 8. Click in cell **A7**.

In Depth: To insert a column, click the column header (the letter) of the column that will be to the right of the new column. Click Insert, Columns. The new column displays, and columns to the right automatically move up one letter. Note that you cannot insert a column within an area of the worksheet where you have merged and centered text.

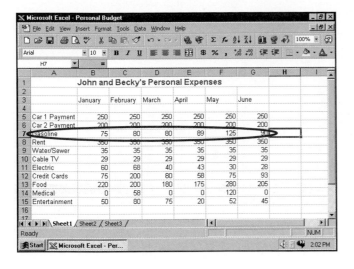

4 Type **Gasoline** in cell **A7**. Type the gasoline expenses for January through June as shown in cells **B7** through **G7**. Save your changes.

Task 4

Calculating Totals Using SUM

Why would I do this?

In the last lesson, you used a simple formula to add numbers for a total. If you have many numbers to add, using a formula can be time-consuming. You can also easily miss numbers or cell references that you should include in the total. Excel's AutoSum feature lets you automatically sum the numbers in a column or row. Using AutoSum saves time and ensures the accuracy in your totals. AutoSum uses Excel's SUM function to create the total. You can type the SUM function yourself to total columns or rows of numbers.

In this task, you learn how to use AutoSum and SUM to total numbers in a worksheet.

1 In cell **A17** type **Total** and press [Tab⇥] to move to cell B17. Locate the **AutoSum** button on the toolbar.

> **In Depth:** The AutoSum feature inserts a *function* in the active cell. A function is a formula that has already been created for you to perform a specific calculation. The AutoSum feature uses Excel's SUM function to total numbers automatically.

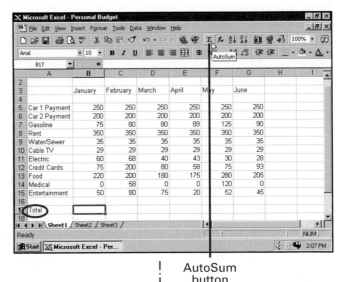

AutoSum button

2 Click the **AutoSum** button on the toolbar. Excel inserts the sum function in cell B17. Notice that Excel assumes you want to sum the numbers in the column directly above. Excel surrounds the cell range B5:B16 with a dashed marquee to indicate that these are the numbers it will sum.

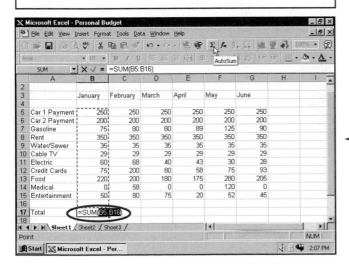

3 Press ↵Enter to accept the proposed sum range. The total automatically calculates. Future changes to any value in cells B5 through B16 will automatically change the total in cell B17.

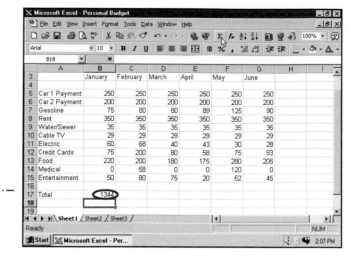

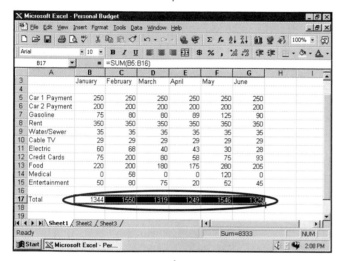

4 Use the fill handle to copy the function in cell B17 to the cell range **C17:G17**.

In Depth: When you copy a formula or a function, Excel automatically adjusts cell references to reflect the column that the formula or function has been copied to. For example, the function currently in cell B17 is =SUM(B5:B16). If you copy this function to cell G17, the function becomes =SUM(G5:G16). Excel anticipates that you will want to perform the same kind of calculation in this cell as you did in cell B17, only using the new cell range G5:G17. Excel's reference to the new cell range is called a *relative cell reference* because it changes relative to the location of the formula.

5 Format the total cells in cell range **B17:G17** for currency with no decimal places.

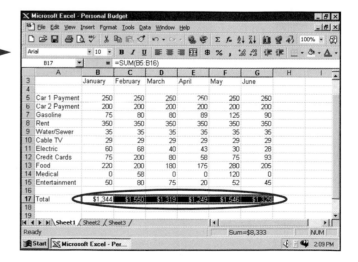

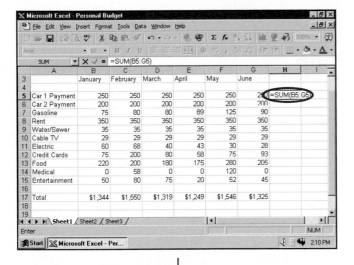

6 Now try creating a SUM function yourself to total each budget item for the six-month period. Click in cell **H5** and type the function **=SUM(B5:G5)**.

In Depth: Functions begin with equal signs in the same way formulas do, in order to let Excel know you want to create a calculation. The function name tells Excel what function to use. Function names usually reflect the type of calculation they perform. For example, SUM calculates a sum of cell values and MAX finds the maximum value in a cell range. The cell references in parentheses are called the *argument*. The argument contains cell references or other values that are used in the calculation.

7 Press ↵Enter to perform the calculation. Use the fill handle to copy the function to the cell range **H6:H15**. Format the totals for currency with no decimal places.

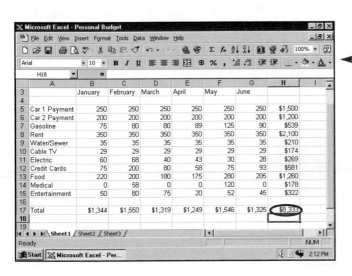

8 Click cell **H17** and use the **AutoSum** button to calculate the total of the cell range **B17:G17**. Save your changes.

Task 5

Working with Statistical Functions

Why would I do this?

As you have already learned, Excel offers functions to help you perform specific types of calculations. The SUM function you used in the last task is designed to total the numbers in a particular cell range. Excel includes many other functions designed for many categories of calculations, such as mathematical, financial, and statistical calculations. Using Excel's functions enables you to perform sophisticated calculations without having to create the formulas yourself.

In this task, you learn how to use some of Excel's statistical functions (AVERAGE, MIN, MAX, and COUNT) to analyze the budget figures.

1 In cell **A18** type **Count,** in cell **A21** type **Average Credit Cards ==>**, in cell **A22** type **Minimum Food ====== >**, and in cell **A23** type **Maximum Food ===== >**.

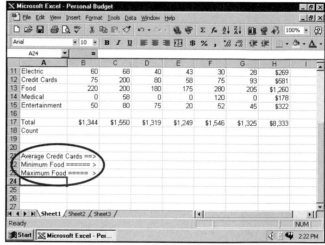

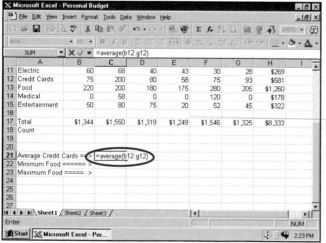

2 Click in cell **C21** and type the following function: **=average(b12:g12)**.

In Depth: You can type a function directly in a cell, like a formula, if you know the syntax of the function. To get help inserting functions or to see the functions available in various categories, click the Paste Function button on the toolbar. The Office Assistant displays to offer help with the process of selecting and entering a function.

3 Press (←Enter) to confirm the entry. In cell C21 Excel displays the average of the numbers in the cell range B12:G12.

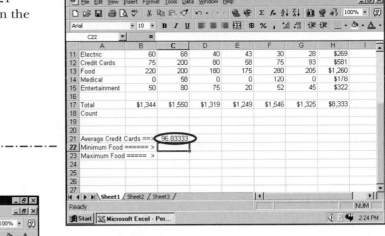

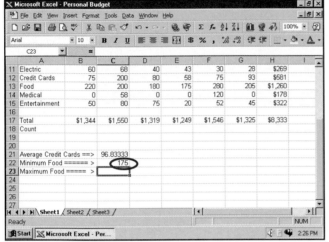

4 In cell **C22** type the function **=min(b13:g13)** and then press (←Enter) to confirm the entry. In cell C22 Excel displays the smallest number (the minimum) in the cell range B13:G13.

5 In cell **C23** type **=max(b13:g13)** and press (←Enter) to confirm the entry. In cell C23 Excel displays the largest (the maximum) number in the cell range B13:G13.

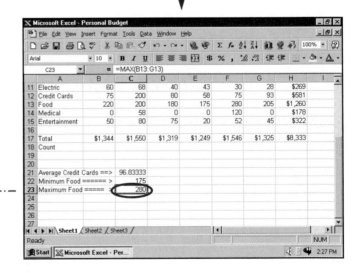

6 In cell **B18** type **=count(b5:b15)** and press (←Enter) to confirm the entry. Excel displays a number showing how many cells have data in the cell range B5:B15.

7 Format the cell range **C21:C23** for currency with no decimal places. Use the fill handle to copy the function in cell B18 to the cell range **C18:G18**.

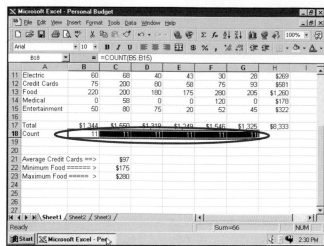

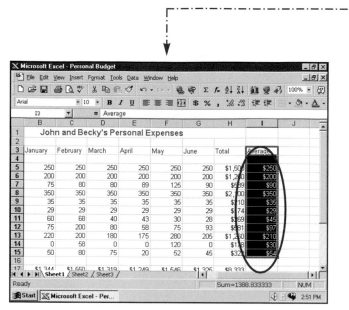

8 In cell **H3** type **Total**. In cell **I3** type **Average**. In cell **I5** type the function **=average(b5:g5)**. Use the fill handle to copy the function in cell I5 to the cell range **I6:I15**. Format the cells in cell range I5:I15 for currency with no decimal places. Save your changes.

Task 6

Using Borders and Shading

Why would I do this?

Borders are lines you can add to any side of a cell or to all sides to create an outline. Borders help emphasize areas of the worksheet. *Shading* is a color or pattern you add to cells. Shading not only makes your worksheet more attractive, but it can also draw attention to specific parts of the worksheet.

In this task, you learn how to use borders and shading to enhance the worksheet data.

Borders button

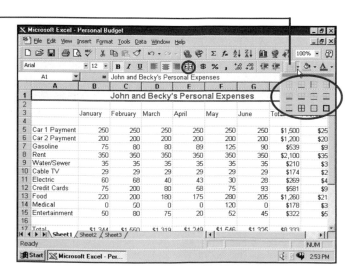

1 First, adjust the position of the worksheet title. Select cell range **A1:I1** and click the **Merge and Center** button. Then click the **Borders** drop-down arrow on the toolbar. The Borders palette displays.

2 Click the heavy solid outline border in the far right bottom corner of the palette. The outline border is applied to the heading's cell range. (You cannot see the heading because of the selection highlight on the cells.)

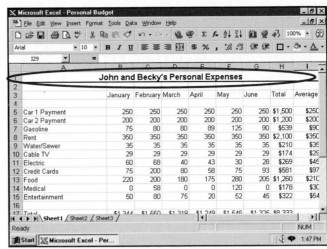

Fill Color
button

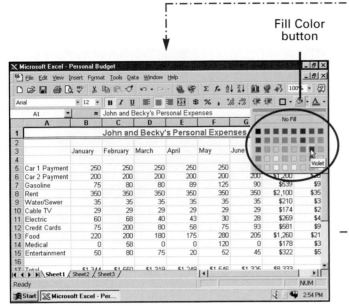

3 With the title still selected, click the **Fill Color** drop-down arrow. The Fill Color palette displays.

Font
Color
button

4 Click the **Violet** palette color. With the title still selected, click the **Font Color** drop-down arrow. The Font Color palette displays.

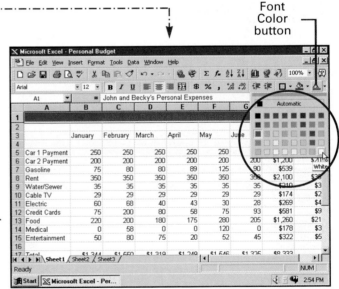

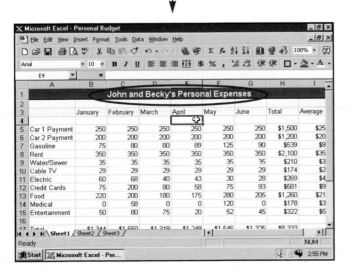

5 Click the **White** palette color. Click outside the selected cells to remove the highlight. Save your changes.

Task 7

Using the AutoFormat Feature

Why would I do this?

By using the AutoFormat command, you can apply predefined formats to your worksheet. AutoFormat saves time you might have spent trying out various border and shading options.

In this task, you learn how to format a worksheet using the AutoFormat command.

1 Select the cell range **A3:I23**. Click **Format, Auto-Format** on the menu bar.

> **In Depth:** Excel assumes your worksheet is in a standard form, with labels going down the left column and across the top row. If your worksheet is not set up this way, select the rows and columns you want to format.

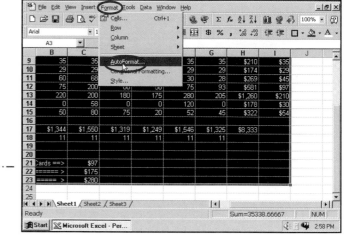

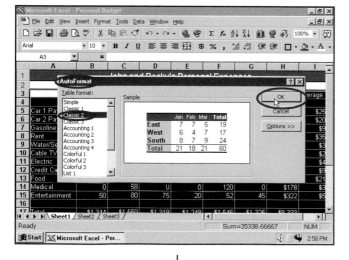

2 The **AutoFormat** dialog box opens. Highlight the **Classic 2** table format.

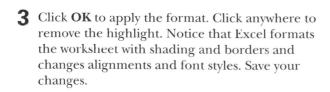

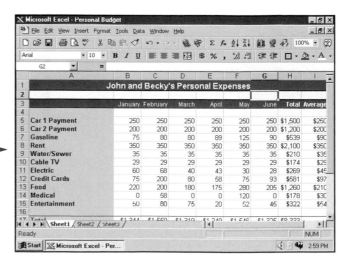

3 Click **OK** to apply the format. Click anywhere to remove the highlight. Notice that Excel formats the worksheet with shading and borders and changes alignments and font styles. Save your changes.

Task 8

Working with Multiple Sheets in a Workbook

Why would I do this?

Up to this time, you have created and modified only one worksheet in a workbook. As you saw in Lesson 7, however, workbooks can contain more than one worksheet. Using multiple worksheets in a workbook enables you to create separate but related information in each worksheet. By using an additional worksheet in the current workbook, you can create a new worksheet projecting a budget increase.

In this task, you learn how to work with multiple worksheets within a single workbook.

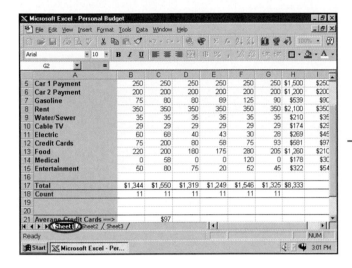

1 First, change the name of the current worksheet from the default name *Sheet1*. Double-click the **Sheet1** tab at the bottom of the window. The default sheet name is selected.

2 Type **Expense** as the new sheet name. The new name displays on the worksheet tab.

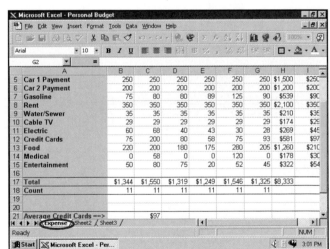

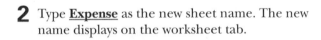

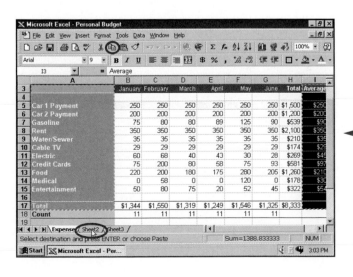

3 To transfer information from the Expense worksheet to a new worksheet, select the cell range **A3:A17**. Press and hold Ctrl to also select the cell range **I3:I17**. Click the **Copy** button on the toolbar.

4 Click the **Sheet2** tab to move to the next work-sheet in the workbook. Click in cell **A3**.

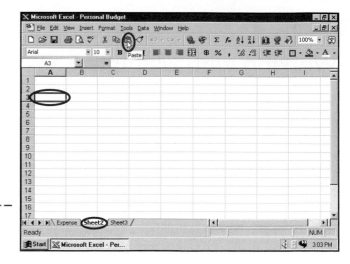

5 Click the **Paste** button on the toolbar. The contents of the clipboard are placed into the Sheet2 worksheet. Click outside the highlighted text. Adjust the width of column A to show all data.

6 Double-click the **Sheet2** tab and type **<u>New Budget</u>** as the new name for the sheet. Click anywhere in the worksheet to accept the new name. Save your changes.

Task 9

Working with Absolute Cell References

Why would I do this?

When copying formulas, Excel automatically assumes the cell references are relative, meaning that copied formulas change (are variable) based on the rows or columns where the data is located. An *absolute cell reference* does not change (is constant) and refers to a specific cell location. To let Excel know you want to use an absolute address, you must precede the row number or column letter with a dollar sign ($).

In this task, you learn how to use absolute cell references.

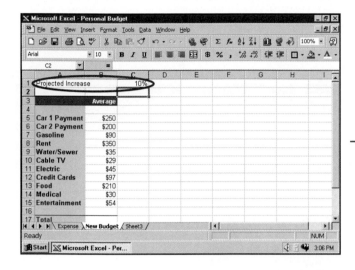

1 In cell **A1** type **Projected Increase**. In cell **C1** type **.10** (for 10%). Format cell C1 as a percent with no decimal places.

Format Painter button

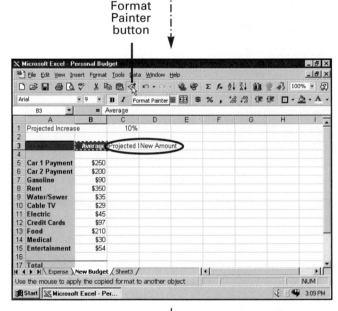

2 In cell **C3** type **Projected Increase**. In cell **D3** type **New Amount**. To copy the formatting of cell **B3** to cells **C3:D3**, click in cell **B3** and click the **Format Painter** button on the toolbar.

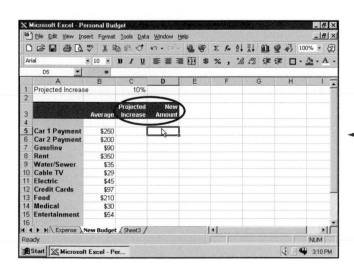

3 Drag the pointer across cells **C3:D3**. Click the **Format Painter** button again to turn the feature off. Wrap the text in these two cells. Click outside the highlighted cells to see the format change.

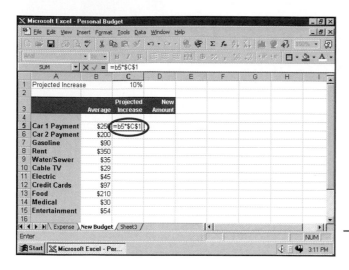

4 In cell **C5** type the formula **=B5*$C$1**. The dollar signs preceding the column C and row 1 addresses tell Excel that this cell address is absolute. In this formula, the variable value of cell B5 (250) is multiplied by the constant value in cell C1 (10%).

In Depth: A formula can contain both relative and absolute cell references. In addition, you can use a *mixed cell reference,* such as A$5. In this cell reference, the A is relative and the 5 is absolute.

5 Press ↵Enter to confirm the entry. Because you have used an absolute reference to the projected increase amount, you can copy the formula to other cells in column C and be sure the copied formulas will still reference the 10% increase number. Use the fill handle to copy the formula in cell C5 to the cell range **C6:C15**.

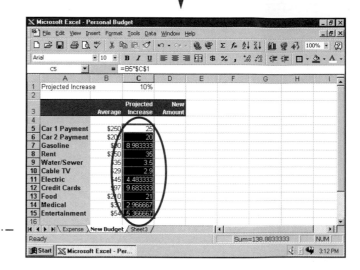

6 To see how the cell references have adjusted during the fill process, click cell **C15**. Notice in the entry bar that the formula in this cell is *=B15*$C$1.* The relative portion of the formula (the reference to the row numbers in column B) has adjusted, while the absolute portion (the reference to cell C1) has not.

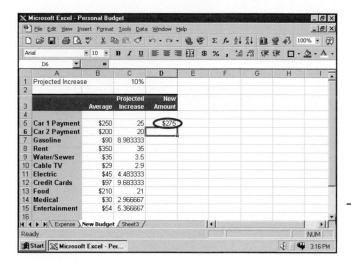

7 Select cell **D5** and type the formula **=B5+C5**. Press ⏎Enter to perform the calculation.

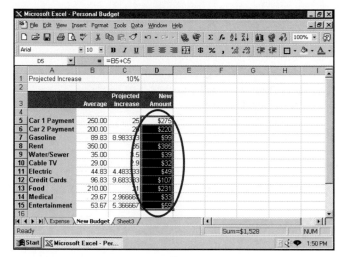

8 Use the fill handle to insert the formula from cell D5 in cells **D6:D15**.

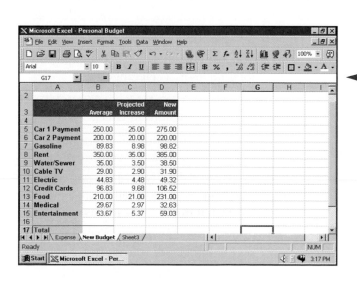

9 Format cell range **B5:D15** for currency with two decimal places and no dollar sign.

10 Double-click in cell **C1** and change the cell value to **4%**. Press ⏎Enter. Note that the change from 10% to 4% changed the projected increase value and new amount totals in rows 5 through 15.

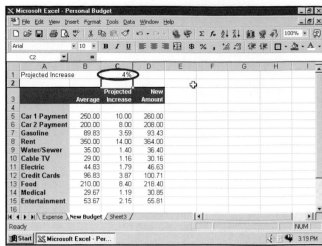

11 To print both worksheets, click **File, Print** on the menu bar and then select **Entire workbook** in the Print dialog box. Click **OK**. Save your changes. Close the workbook.

Student Exercises

True-False

For each of the following, circle either T or F to indicate whether the statement is true or false.

T　F　**1.** To copy a cell's values into other adjacent cells, you can use the Fill button on the toolbar.

T　F　**2.** Excel displays a marquee to indicate an absolute cell reference.

T　F　**3.** You can move data in a worksheet using the drag and drop feature.

T　F　**4.** The function =SUM(b4:b8) gives the same result as the formula +b4+b5+b6+b7+b8.

T　F　**5.** To rename the first sheet in a workbook, double-click the Sheet1 tab and type the new name.

T　F　**6.** The AutoTotal feature lets you quickly total values in a cell range.

T　F　**7.** AVERAGE, MIN, MAX, and COUNT are statistical functions in Excel.

T　F　**8.** The first step in the process of placing a border around data in your worksheet is to select the data.

T　F　**9.** When you insert a row in a worksheet, it appears above the row you selected.

T　F　**10.** A dollar sign ($) used in a formula signifies a relative cell address.

Identifying Parts of the Excel Screen

Refer to the figure and identify the numbered parts of the screen. Write the letter of the correct label in the space next to the number.

1. J
2. C
3. B
4. I
5. A
6. F
7. E
8. D
9. H
10. G

A. Absolute cell address
B. Relative cell address
C. Shading
D. Fill Handle
E. Copy button
F. Current cell location
G. Paste button
H. Border button
I. Name of Sheet1
J. Current worksheet displayed

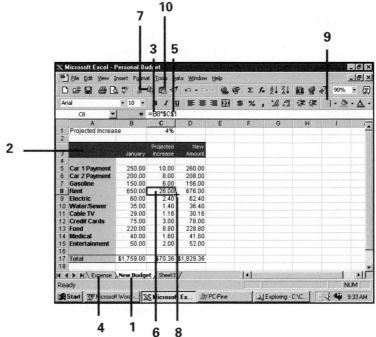

Matching

Match the following statements to the word or phrase that is the best match from the list. Write the letter of the matching word or phrase in the space provided next to the number.

1. H Feature that lets you easily move data
2. K The value in the formula remains a constant
3. E Symbol that indicates the fill handle
4. C Feature that automatically enters a SUM function
5. G Feature that applies borders and shading automatically
6. I Cell references that change to reflect the current row or column
7. A The menu to select when inserting a row or column
8. J Name of the second sheet in a workbook
9. D Color or pattern added to cells in a worksheet
10. F Line that can appear on any side of a cell in a worksheet

A. Insert
B. Edit
C. AutoSum
D. Shading
E. + sign
F. Border
G. AutoFormat
H. Drag and drop
I. Relative cell address
J. Sheet2
K. Absolute cell address

Application Exercises

Exercise 1

1. Open the workbook you created in Lesson 7 called **Fish Farm**. Save the workbook as **Fish Farm 2**.

2. Insert a blank row 5.

3. In cell **A5** enter the word **Price**. Format this heading to match the other row headers.

4. Enter the following prices for each species of fish: Salmon, $.75; Blue Gill, $.30; Trout, $1.25; Catfish, $.75; Perch $.50.

5. Format the prices as currency with two decimal places and dollar signs. Use the same font size, color, alignment, and style as for the other numbers in the worksheet.

6. Enter the words **Total Value** in cell **A12**. Format the heading to match the *Total Count* heading.

7. Enter a formula in cell **B12** that calculates the total value for salmon by multiplying the price per fish by the total number of fish. Use the fill handle to copy the formula for the other species of fish. Format these values as currency with two decimal places and dollar signs. Adjust column widths as necessary to display all data.

8. Type **Total** in cell G4 and format this heading to match the other headings.

9. Use the SUM function in cell **G6** to total the number of fish for the North Shore location. Use the fill handle to copy the function to cell range **G7:G9**.

10. Use AutoSum to create totals in cells **G11** and **G12**.

11. Save your changes. Print the worksheet. Close the workbook.

Exercise 2

1. Open the workbook you created in Lesson 7 named **Creative Computers**. Save the workbook as **Creative Computers 2**.

2. Select the cell range **A4:D10** and move the data down one row.

3. Enter the word **Discount** in cell **A4** and **8%** in cell **B4**.

4. Type **Discount** in cell **E5**. Bold and center the text.

5. Enter a formula in cell **E6** to calculate the discount amount for each item (the price of the item times the discount rate). **Hint:** Use an absolute cell reference. Use the fill handle to copy the formula from cell E6 to cells **E7:E11**.

6. Type **Clearance Price** in cell **F5**. Bold, center, and wrap the text. Adjust the column width if necessary to display the heading correctly.

7. In cell **F6** enter a formula to calculate the computer clearance price. Use the fill handle to copy the formula from cell F6 to cells **F7:F11**.

8. Adjust the title and subtitle to center over all cells containing data. Create a heavy outline border around the title and subtitle. Shade the cell containing the discount rate with Turquoise.

9. Save your changes. Print the worksheet. Close the workbook.

Exercise 3

1. Open the workbook you created in Lesson 7 named **Tree Farm**. Save the workbook as **Tree Farm 2**.

2. This worksheet would be even more useful if it showed the current number of surviving trees. Insert a column between the *Year 2 Loss* column and the *% Loss* column.

3. Type **Current Stock** in cell **E4**. Wrap, center, and bold the text.

4. Insert a formula in cell **E5** to add the values in the *Year 1 Loss* and the *Year 2 Loss* columns and subtract that amount from the *Number Planted* column. Use the fill handle to copy the formula for the other trees.

5. In cell **A11** type **Average Loss**. In cell **F11** use the AVERAGE function to average the values in the cell range F5:F9.

6. Format the cell range **A4:F11** using the 3D Effects 1 AutoFormat.

7. Save your changes. Print the worksheet. Close the workbook.

Exercise 4

1. Open the workbook you created in Lesson 7 named **Student Senate**. Save the workbook as **Student Senate 2**.

2. Copy the Years and Tuition information to the clipboard (A5:B10).

3. Paste this information beginning in cell A5 on Sheet2.

4. In cell **C5** type **Increase**. In cell **D5** type **%Increase**. Format these headings to match the other headings.

5. In cell **C6** calculate the tuition increase for 1996-97 by subtracting cell B7 from cell B6. Use the fill handle to copy the formula to cells **C7:C9**.

6. Calculate the percent increase in cell **D6** by dividing cell C6 by cell B6. Copy the formula to cells **D7:D9**.

7. Format the percents with no decimal places.

8. Name Sheet2 **Increase**.

9. Name Sheet1 **Tuition**.

10. Save your changes. Print the entire workbook. Close the workbook.

Exercise 5

The Eagle Corporation.

As one of the regional sales managers for Eagle Corporation, you are responsible for keeping track of sales for four geographical regions of the country: northeast, southeast, midwest, and west.

Your specific product line responsibility includes copiers, fax machines, telephones, computers, pagers, and all cabinets used to house electronic equipment.

Design a worksheet that keeps track of sales for your product line by the geographical region of the country. In addition, create a second worksheet that shows information on computer sales for these four regions. One specific item in the computer worksheet would include sales by manufacturer (Futura, Generac, Telemark, and Delphous). Use your imagination to come up with other worksheet items.

Name the workbook **SALES**, worksheet 1 **PRODUCTS**, and worksheet 2 **COMPUTERS**.

Lesson 9
Excel Charts

Introduction

One of Excel's most exciting features is its charting capability. You can use worksheet information to create many types of charts that give you a visual representation of the data. You can embed a chart on the same worksheet on which the data appears or create the chart on a separate worksheet.

This lesson is designed to help you become familiar with Excel's charting feature.

Visual Summary

When you have completed Task 6, you will have created charts that look like this:

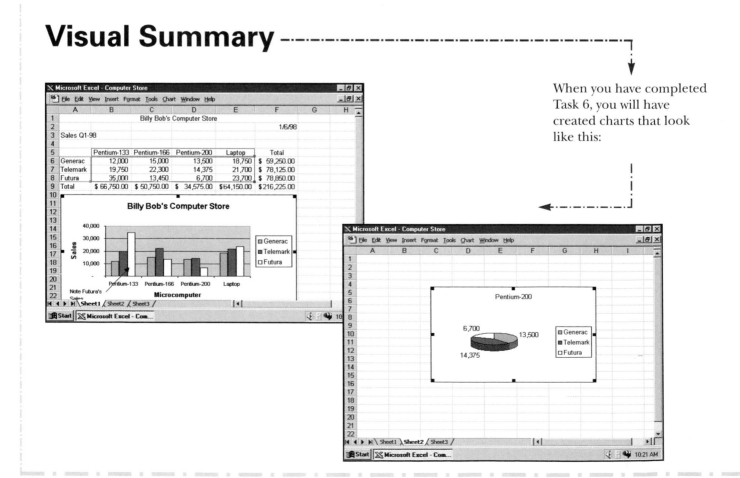

Task 1

Using the Chart Wizard

Why would I do this?

The easiest way to create a chart in Excel is to use a feature called *Chart Wizard*. The Chart Wizard provides a step-by-step methodology to guide you through the process of creating a chart from worksheet data.

In this task, you learn how to create a chart from existing data using the Chart Wizard.

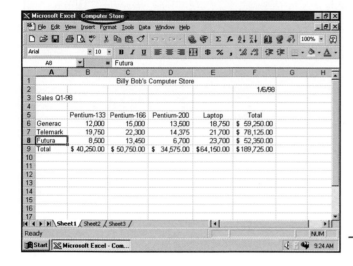

1 Open **Less0901**. Save the workbook on your disk as **Computer Store**.

Chart Wizard button

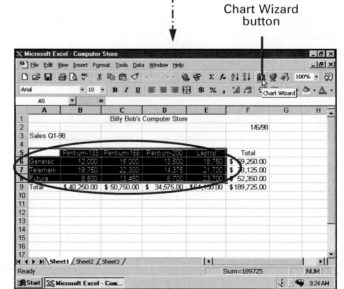

2 To begin creating a chart, select the cell range **A5:E8**. Notice that totals are not a component in the chart. Locate the **Chart Wizard** button on the toolbar.

3 Click the **Chart Wizard** button on the toolbar. The **Chart Wizard** dialog box opens and the Office Assistant displays to ask if you want help. Click the **No, don't provide help now** option button to close the Office Assistant. The default chart type is **Column**. Click the **100% Stacked Column** sub-type (the rightmost option in the first row).

In Depth: The Chart Wizard helps you create a chart in four steps. The first dialog box offers you a choice of 14 different chart types. For each chart type, you can choose among several sub-types that display the charted data in different formats and orientations. To select a chart type, simply click it in the Chart type list. To select a sub-type, click one of the small pictures in the Chart sub-type area of the dialog box. A descriptive paragraph below the sub-types describes the currently selected chart sub-type. After you make your choices in the dialog box, click Next to move to the next step in creating the chart.

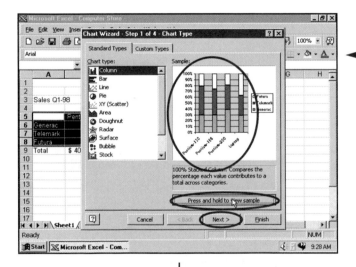

4 To see what the chart type looks like, click the **Press and hold to view sample** button in the dialog box.

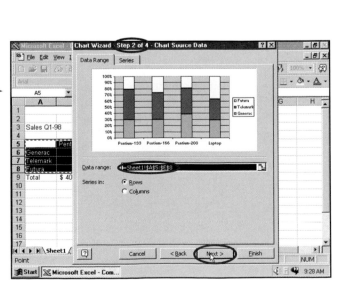

5 Release the mouse button to display the chart sub-types again. To proceed to step 2 in creating the chart, click the **Next** button. The **Step 2 of 4** dialog box displays. Step 2 shows the data range used to supply data for the chart (=Sheet1!$A$5:$E$8). This is the cell range you selected in the worksheet.

6 The data range is correct, so click **Next** to proceed to step 3. The **Step 3 of 4** dialog box displays. Step 3 provides you with a number of options for formatting the chart. If the **Titles** tab is not displayed, click it to display its options.

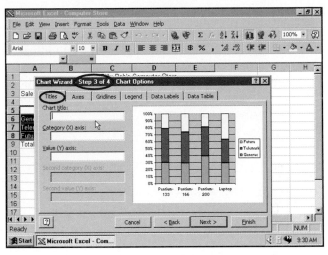

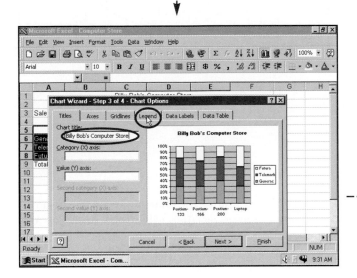

7 In the Chart title box, type **Billy Bob's Computer Store**.

8 Click the **Legend** tab to see the chart options on that tab. Click the **Right** placement option for the legend location in the chart if necessary.

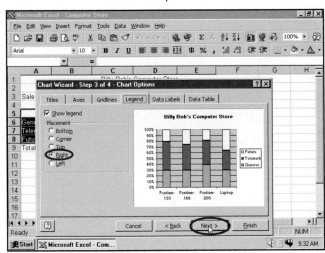

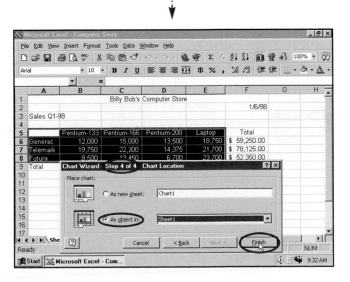

9 Click **Next** to proceed to step 4. The **Step 4 of 4** dialog box lets you specify where the chart is placed when completed. The chart can be embedded in the existing worksheet or placed by itself in another worksheet. To embed the chart in the existing worksheet, click **As object in**.

10 To complete the chart, click the **Finish** button. The completed chart is placed within the worksheet labeled *Sheet1*. Note that the Chart toolbar now appears on your screen showing chart command options. If the Chart toolbar overlays data, drag and move the toolbar to the top of the screen. Save your changes.

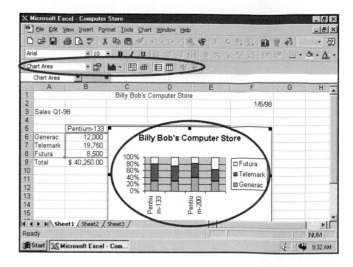

Task 2

Modifying a Chart

Why would I do this?

After you have created a chart, you can modify it in a number of ways. You can move the chart to a new location on the worksheet. You can resize the chart to ensure that the chart legend, heading, or labels will display properly. Any changes you make in the worksheet data referenced in the chart are automatically updated in the chart.

In this task, you learn how to move, resize, and edit chart data.

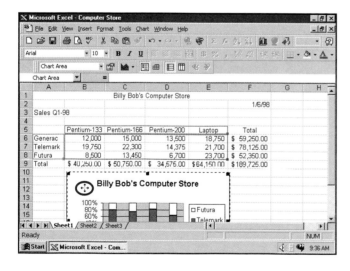

1 If the chart is not surrounded by selection handles, click once on the chart to select it. To move the chart, first position the pointer inside the chart and hold down the mouse button. Notice that the pointer changes to a four-headed arrow. Drag the chart down and to the left until the upper left corner of the chart is in cell B10. Release the mouse button.

In Depth: A chart embedded in a spreadsheet is an object just like the clip art pictures you worked with in Lesson 6. To select a chart, click it once to display selection handles. When you move or resize the chart, Excel shows dashed guidelines to help you determine the final location or size of the chart.

2 Notice that the chart area is not large enough to display the columns adequately, and the column labels do not display correctly. To increase the height of the chart, position the pointer on the bottom center selection handle. The pointer changes to a two-headed arrow. Drag the handle down until the bottom of the chart is at the bottom of row 23.

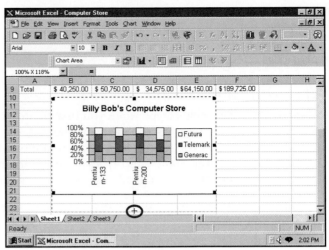

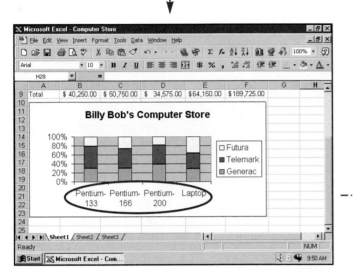

3 To increase the width of the chart, drag the left center selection handle to the left border. Drag the right center selection handle to the right through column F. Notice that the chart column labels now have enough room to display properly.

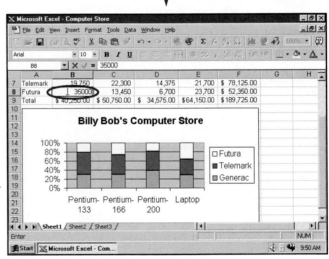

4 Double-click cell **B8** and change the Futura Pentium 133 sales number from 8500 to **35000**.

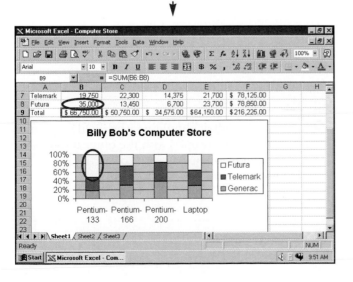

5 Press ⏎Enter to confirm the entry. Excel automatically adjusts the Futura Pentium 133 chart display. Save your changes.

Task 3

Changing the Chart Type

Why would I do this?

Although you select a chart type when you first create a chart, you can change the chart type after the chart has been created. Excel uses the same data you selected for the original chart to create the new chart type. Changing the chart type enables you to select the chart that most effectively represents your data. Be careful when changing the chart type, however. Some chart types are not interchangeable. You cannot create a meaningful column chart, for example, from data you originally used to create a pie chart.

In this task, you learn how to change the chart type.

1 Click once in a blank chart area to select the chart. If the Chart toolbar does not display when you select the chart, click **View**, **Toolbars**, and **Chart** on the menu bar.

In Depth: Select a chart type according to the kind of information you want to display. For example, column charts show variations among a series of similar items. Pie charts show the relationship of parts to a whole. Line charts show trends over time.

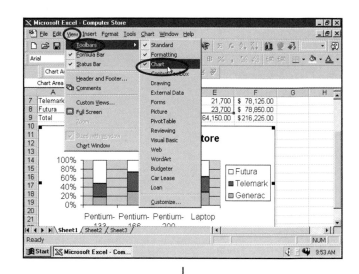

Chart Type button

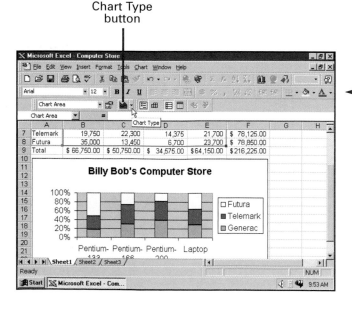

2 The Chart toolbar should now be open on your screen (either grouped with the other toolbars or positioned near your chart). Locate the **Chart Type** button on the Chart toolbar.

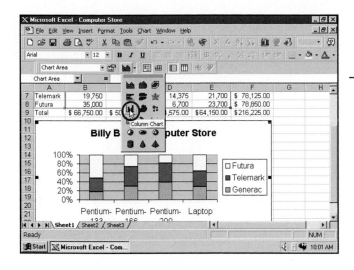

3 Click the **Chart Type** drop-down arrow. A palette of chart choices displays.

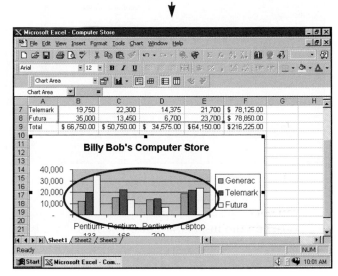

4 Change the chart type by clicking the **Column Chart** option. Excel changes the chart to a column display. Save your changes.

Task 4

Working with Titles and Labels

Why would I do this?

You inserted a title for the entire chart when you created it. As you may have noticed when adding the chart title, you can also insert titles for the *X axis* (the horizontal axis of the chart) and the *Y axis* (the vertical axis of the chart). Axis titles give the viewer more information about the data represented on the chart. If you do not insert these titles when creating the chart, you can insert them later using the Chart Options command. Although Excel chooses default fonts, sizes, and styles for the text labels in a chart, you can easily change text formatting by simply double-clicking the text you want to change.

In this task, you learn how to add axis titles to your chart and format text in the chart.

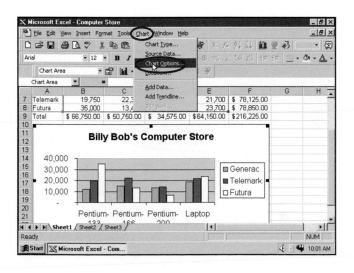

1 Click **Chart, Chart Options** on the menu bar.

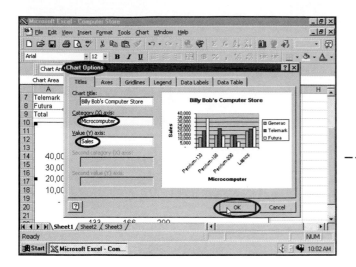

2 The **Chart Options** dialog box opens. Click the **Titles** tab if necessary to display it. Click inside the **Category (X) axis** box and type **Microcomputer**. Click inside the **Value (Y) axis** box and type **Sales**.

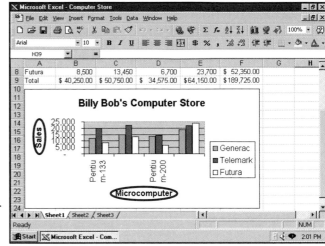

3 Click **OK** to insert the titles. The X and Y axis titles are displayed in the graph.

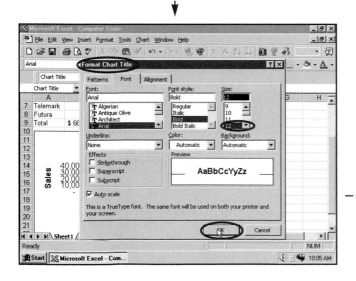

4 Notice that your data area may have become so compressed that you cannot see the columns very well. You can create more room for the columns by reducing the size of various text labels. To reduce the font size of the chart title, double-click the chart title. The **Format Chart Title** dialog box opens. Scroll in the **Size** list box to locate **12** and click it.

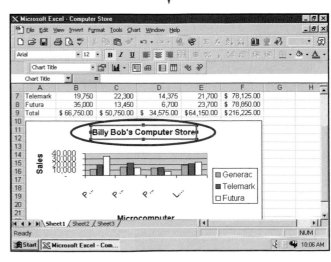

5 Click **OK**. The chart title displays in 12 point size.

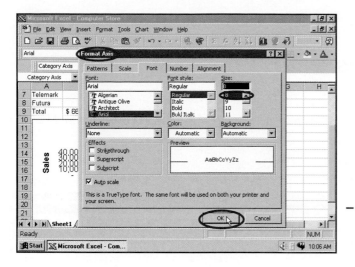

6 Double-click any of the X-axis labels (the computer names below the columns). The **Format Axis** dialog box opens. Select the font tab if necessary. Scroll in the **Size** list box to locate **8** and click.

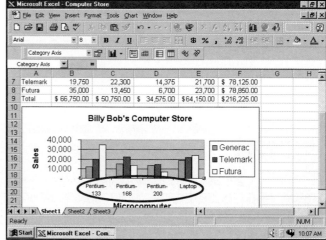

7 Click **OK**. The X-axis labels display in 8 point size.

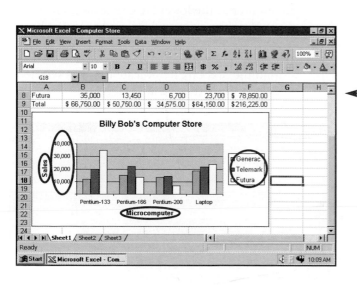

8 Double-click one of the Y-axis labels (the numbers at the left of the columns) and change the size of the labels to **8**. Double-click each of the axis titles and change the title size to **10**. Double-click on text in the legend and change the text size to **10**. Save your changes.

Task 5

Using Chart Drawing Features

Why would I do this?

Excel's drawing feature enables you to add objects to your chart that you can use for emphasis or additional documentation.

In this task, you learn how to create a drawing object on a chart.

Drawing button

1 If necessary, select the chart. Click the **Drawing** button on the toolbar. The Drawing toolbar displays at the bottom of your screen.

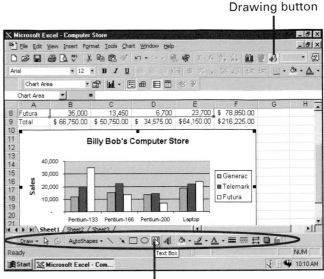

Text Box button

2 Click the **Text Box** button on the Drawing toolbar. The pointer changes to a cross. Position the pointer in the lower left corner under the chart. Drag the pointer down and to the right to create the text box, as shown. When you release the mouse button, the hatched border displays around the text box to indicate that it is selected and ready for text to be inserted.

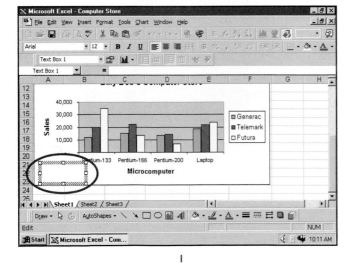

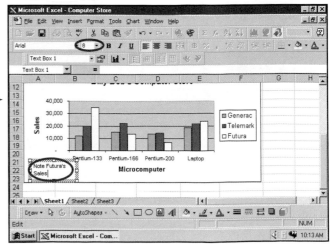

3 Click the **Font Size** down arrow on the toolbar and select a size of **8**. Type **Note Futura's Sales** inside the text box.

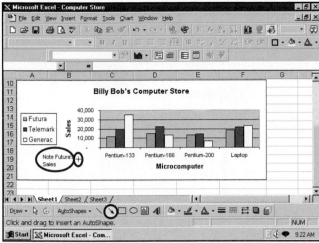

4 Click outside the text box. Click the **Arrow** button on the Drawing toolbar. The pointer changes to crosshairs.

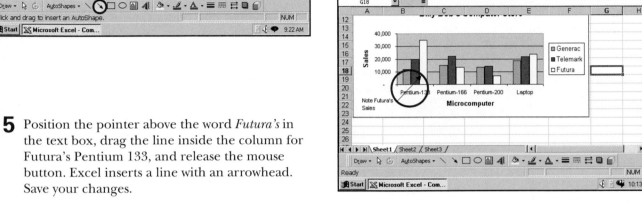

5 Position the pointer above the word *Futura's* in the text box, drag the line inside the column for Futura's Pentium 133, and release the mouse button. Excel inserts a line with an arrowhead. Save your changes.

Task 6

Creating a Special Chart

Why would I do this?

You can create a chart from Excel worksheet data that is nonadjacent. This gives you the ability to choose what data is displayed in the chart.

In this task, you learn how to create a pie chart from nonadjacent data.

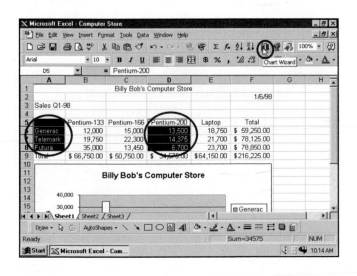

1 Select the cell range **A5:A8**. Hold down Ctrl and select the cell range **D5:D8**.

2 Click the **Chart Wizard** button on the toolbar. The **Chart Wizard** dialog box displays. Click the **Pie** chart type. Click the 3-D pie chart in the first row of chart sub-types.

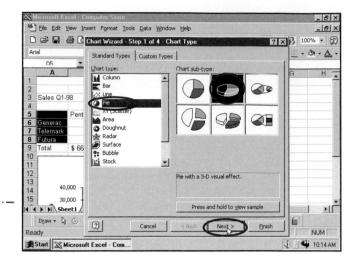

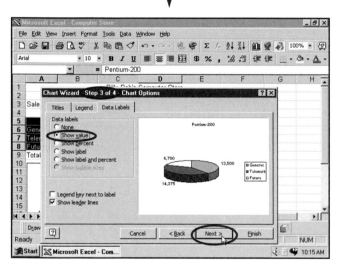

3 Click **Next** twice. The **Step 3 of 4** dialog box displays. Click the **Show value** option button in the Data labels area.

4 Click **Next**. The **Step 4 of 4** dialog box displays. Click the down arrow in the **As object in** box and click **Sheet2**.

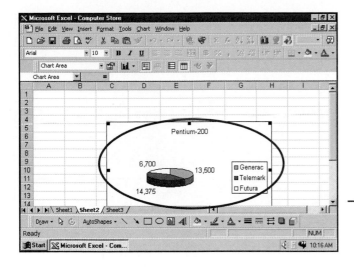

5 Click **Finish** to close the dialog box. Your chart displays by itself in Sheet2 of the workbook.

> **In Depth:** When you have a chart on the same page as the worksheet, you can print the worksheet and the chart together. To print only the chart, select it before issuing the Print command.

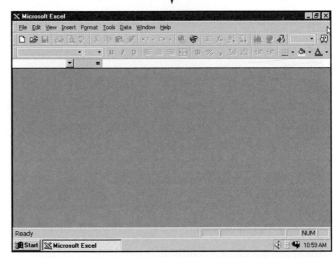

6 Save your changes. Print the entire workbook. Close the workbook.

Student Exercises

True-False

For each of the following, circle either T or F to indicate whether the statement is true or false.

T   F   **1.** The Chart Wizard uses four steps to create a chart.

T   F   **2.** After a chart is completed you cannot make changes to it.

T   F   **3.** After a chart is created, it may be saved on a separate worksheet.

T   F   **4.** After a chart is completed, you can still change the chart type.

T   F   **5.** Changing data in your worksheet automatically changes associated values in your chart.

T   F   **6.** You can move a chart by dragging a selection handle.

T   F   **7.** A dashed guideline shows where a chart used to be before it was moved.

T   F   **8.** The drawing feature in Excel allows you to add text to your chart where you would like it.

T   F   **9.** Excel does not allow you to chart data from a worksheet unless the data is located in adjacent cells.

T   F   **10.** In most instances a legend in not necessary in a chart.

Identifying Parts of the Excel Screen

Refer to the figure and identify the numbered parts of the screen. Write the letter of the correct label in the space next to the number.

1. H
2. E
3. D
4. G
5. A
6. J
7. B
8. D
9. F
10. I

A. Chart Wizard button
B. Legend
C. X-axis label
D. Y-axis label
E. Chart Type button
F. Chart title
G. selection handles
H. Text box
I. Generac's laptop sales
J. Telemark's Pentium 133 sales

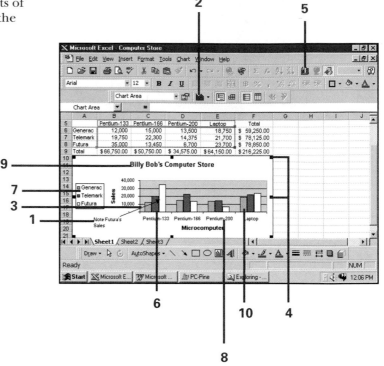

Matching

Match the following statements to the word or phrase that is the best match from the list. Write the letter of the matching word or phrase in the space provided next to the number.

1. H Key used to select nonadjacent cells in a worksheet

2. E The button used to prompt you for information on building a chart

3. B The shape of the pointer when resizing a chart

4. J When you are moving a chart in a worksheet this shows you where the chart will be after you release the mouse button

5. D The location on a chart where you place the pointer to resize a chart

6. A The button used to change the way a chart displays data

7. F The button used to position a box in your chart to add text information

8. K The purpose of step 3 in the Chart Wizard

9. G The best chart type to select to show trends over time

10. C The best chart type to select to show the relationship of parts to a whole

A. Chart Type button
B. Double-headed arrow
C. Pie chart
D. Selection handle
E. Chart Wizard button
F. Text box button
G. Line chart
H. Ctrl
I. X axis
J. Dotted guideline
K. Select chart options

Application Exercises

Exercise 1

1. Open the workbook you created in Lesson 8 called **Fish Farm 2**. Save the workbook as **<u>Fish Farm 3</u>**.

2. Create a 3D pie chart using cells A6:A9 and G6:G9. (**Hint:** Use Ctrl when highlighting the second range of cells.)

3. Type **<u>Population</u>** as the title for the chart.

4. Click the **Data Labels** tab and choose to show values.

5. Place the chart below the worksheet.

6. Resize the chart to cover cells A13:G24.

7. Save your changes. Print the worksheet. Close the workbook.

Exercise 2

1. Open the workbook you created in Lesson 8 named **Creative Computers 2**. Save the workbook as **<u>Creative Computers 3</u>**.

2. Create a clustered column chart using cells A5:A11 and C5:C11.

3. Type **<u>Number on Hand</u>** as the chart title.

4. Type **<u>Item</u>** for the X-axis title.

5. Place the chart on Sheet2 of the current workbook.

6. Resize the chart to cover cells A1:G18.

7. Remove the legend by clicking the legend box and pressing Del.

8. Adjust the sizes of text in the chart to display the columns properly.

9. Change the name of Sheet2 to **<u>Column Chart</u>**.

10. The quantity value for chairs has been updated to **15**. Make this change in the worksheet and then view the change in the chart.

11. Save your changes. Print only the sheet containing the chart. Close the workbook.

Exercise 3

1. Open the workbook you created in Lesson 8 named **Tree Farm 2**. Save the workbook as **Tree Farm 3**.

2. Create a clustered column chart using cells A4:B9 and E4:E9.

3. Type **The Tree Farm** as the chart title.

4. Type **Species** for the X-axis title.

5. Type **Number** for the Y-axis title.

6. Place the chart on Sheet2.

7. Resize the chart to cover cells A1:H15.

8. Adjust text sizes and styles to present the data as clearly as possible.

9. Change the name of Sheet2 to **Tree Loss**.

10. Save your changes. Print only the sheet containing the chart. Close the workbook.

Exercise 4

1. Open the workbook you created in Lesson 8 named **Student Senate 2**. Save the workbook as **Student Senate 3**.

2. Create a line chart using cells A5:A9 and D5:D9 from the sheet named **Increase**.

3. Type **Tuition Increase** as the title for the chart.

4. Type **Year** for the X-axis title.

5. Type **Percent** for the Y-axis title.

6. Place the chart on Sheet3.

7. Resize the chart to cover cells A1.G15.

8. Adjust font sizes and styles to make the chart more attractive and useful.

9. Change the name of Sheet3 to **Chart**.

10. Save your changes. Print the worksheet containing the chart. Close the workbook.

Exercise 5

The Eagle Corporation.

It is your responsibility as an employee in the Human Resources department of Eagle Corporation to conduct quarterly meetings with all employees. At these meetings, you provide a formal presentation to employees about a topic of interest.

The next meeting is in one week, and you are planning to present information on the company's health care package. Design and create a worksheet that shows employees the major cost factors of the health care plan. For example, you may want to include information on dental care, eye care, long-term disability, and prescription drug coverage.

Because you have only 15 minutes to present this information and to answer questions, you use graphs created from Excel to help you quickly display all relevant information concerning Eagle's health care program.

Create two different types of charts that you use at this presentation. After completed, save the spreadsheet to disk. (Name the file **Eagle Health Care**.)

Lesson 10
Integrating Word and Excel

Task 1 Creating the Destination Document

Task 2 Working with the Source Document

Task 3 Using the Paste Special Command

Task 4 Updating Linked Data

Introduction

An integrated application suite such as Office 97 enables you to use the various applications together to create integrated documents. An integrated document uses information from more than one application. There are three main ways to integrate applications. The simplest way to integrate two applications is to copy information from one application and paste it into another. In this case, the copied information becomes a part of the document you paste it into. You can also *embed* data from one application in to another. In this case, the embedded object can be moved and sized like any other object (such as a chart or a clip art picture). To edit an embedded object, double-click it to open its original application. Finally, you can *link* data from one application to another application. If you change the data in the original application, it also changes in the other application.

This lesson shows you how to link Excel worksheet data to a Word document. After you have linked the worksheet and the document, changes you make to the worksheet in Excel are also made in the Word document. In the Application Exercises for this lesson, you will have a chance to practice other ways of integrating Word and Excel documents.

Visual Summary

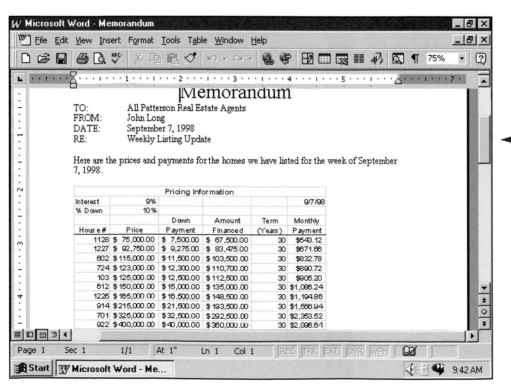

When you have completed Task 4, you will have created a document that looks like this:

Task 1

Creating the Destination Document

Why would I do this?

When you are integrating applications, you work with source documents and destination documents. The *source document* is the document that contains the original data you want to integrate. The *destination document* is the document you want to place the source data in.

In this task, you learn how to create a source document to which you can link Excel data.

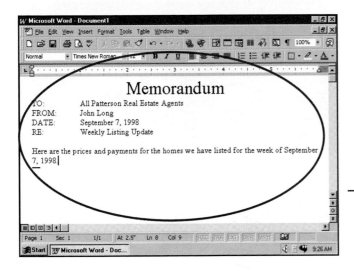

1 Open Microsoft Word and type the memorandum as shown.

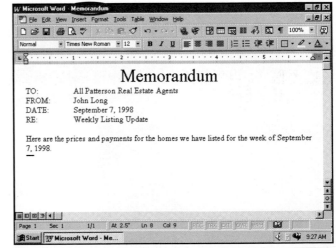

2 Save the document on your disk as **Memorandum**.

Task 2

Working with the Source Document

Why would I do this?

In order to place an Excel worksheet in your Word document, you must first select the data you want to link and place the data on the Clipboard.

In this lesson, you learn how to prepare the source data that is linked to the destination document.

1 Start Excel and open **Less1001**. Save the file on your disk as **Price Data**.

> **In Depth:** When linking data, it is important that all the documents used in the linking process are stored in the same general location. For example, if you store the destination document on your hard drive, you should also store the source document on the hard drive. Office needs to be able to locate all linked documents to maintain the links. Moving or renaming one of the linked documents may make it impossible for Office to correctly update the link.

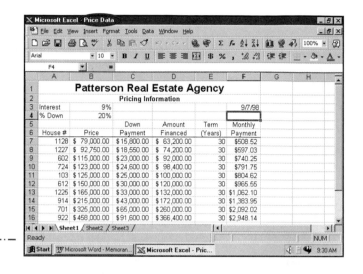

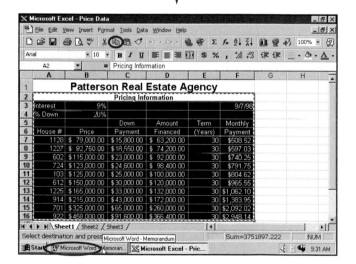

2 Select the cell range **A2:F16**. Click the **Copy** button to place the selected data on the Clipboard.

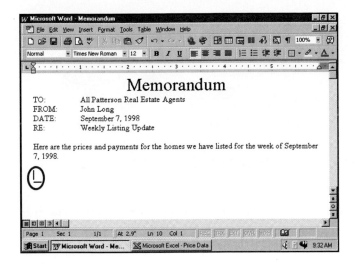

3 Click the **Microsoft Word** button in the taskbar to switch back to the destination document. Position the insertion point after the final period in the memorandum, if necessary, and press ⏎Enter twice.

Task 3

Using the Paste Special Command

Why would I do this?

After you have copied data from the source application to the Clipboard, you have several choices for pasting it into the destination document. Using the Paste button on the toolbar pastes the data into the Word document as a Word table. This table is not linked in any way to the original data. If you want to link the data, you must use the Paste Special command. The Paste Special command opens the Paste Special dialog box, in which you can select options for linking the source and destination documents.

In this task, you learn how to use the Paste Special command to establish a link between the Word document and the Excel worksheet.

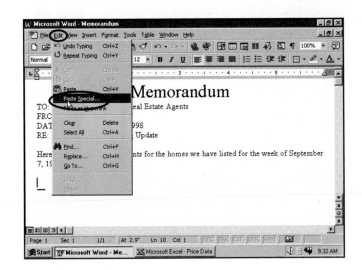

1 Click **Edit, Paste Special** on the menu bar.

2 The **Paste Special** dialog box opens. Select the **Paste link** option. Select **Microsoft Excel Worksheet Object**.

In Depth: The Paste Special dialog box offers several other important options. If you click the Paste option, you embed the data in the destination document. Embedded data is not linked to the source document. You can choose to display the linked or embedded data as an icon in the destination document. To see the data, double-click the icon. You can give the icon a specific name and choose the icon shape. If you deselect the Float over text check box, the data displays at the insertion point as an in-line graphic, which cannot be freely moved on the page.

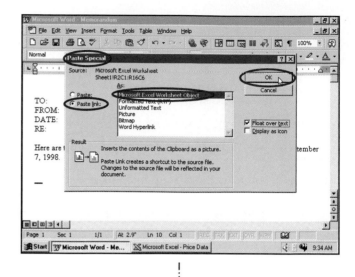

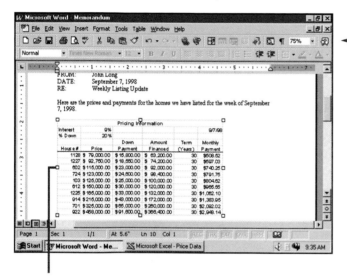

Linked data

3 Click **OK** to paste link the Excel data. The Excel worksheet displays in your Word document surrounded by selection handles like any other object. Save your changes.

Task 4

Updating Linked Data

Why would I do this?

After you have linked a source and destination document, you must make updates in the source document. The destination document is then automatically updated so that you see the new data as soon as you switch back to the destination document.

In this task, you learn how to update linked data.

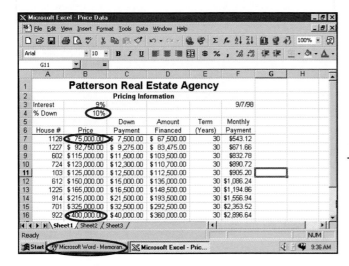

1 Click the **Microsoft Excel** button on the taskbar to switch back to Excel. Make the following changes to the worksheet: Reduce the % Down (cell B4) from 20% to **10%**. Reduce the price of house # 1128 (cell B7) from $79,000.00 to **$75,000.00**. Reduce the price of house # 922 (cell B16) from $458,000.00 to **$400,000.00**. Save your changes.

2 To see the updates in the linked data, click the **Microsoft Word** button in the taskbar. Notice that the changes you made to the Excel worksheet have also been made in this document.

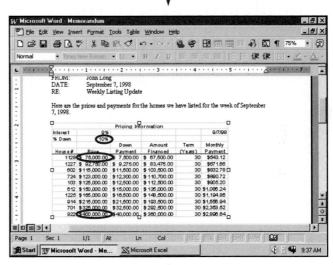

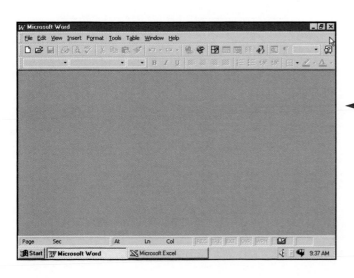

3 Save your changes. Print the document. Close the document and the worksheet.

Student Exercises

True-False

For each of the following, circle either T or F to indicate whether the statement is true or false.

T   F   **1.** In order to link applications in Microsoft Office, you can use the Paste Special command.

T   F   **2.** You can use the Windows taskbar to switch among programs.

T   F   **3.** The source document is the document that contains the original data to be integrated.

T   F   **4.** Embedding is the same as linking.

T   F   **5.** When Excel data is pasted into a Word document, the worksheet data is always placed at the beginning of the document.

Identifying Parts of the Integration Screen

Refer to the figure and identify the numbered parts of the screen. Write the letter of the correct label in the space next to the number.

1. D
2. B
3. A
4. E
5. C

A. Taskbar active application
B. Option that embeds data
C. Option that inserts an icon representing linked or embedded data
D. Taskbar inactive application
E. Option that links data

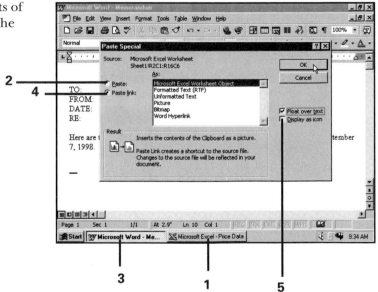

Matching

Match the following statements to the word or phrase that is the best match from the list. Write the letter of the matching word or phrase in the space provided next to the number.

1. _D_ To edit embedded data
2. _A_ To edit linked data
3. _C_ To insert copied data as a Word table
4. _F_ Menu on which Paste Special command is located
5. _B_ Document in which you insert linked data

A. ~~Return to source document~~

B. ~~Destination document~~

C. ~~Paste button~~

D. ~~Double-click embedded object~~

E. ~~Edit~~

F. Paste Special command

Application Exercises

Exercise 1

1. Open the Excel workbook named **Fish Farm 3** that you created in Lesson 9.

2. Start a new Word document and type the information shown in the figure. Save the document as **Fish Letter**.

3. In the Excel worksheet, copy the cell range **A4:F9** to the Clipboard. Close the worksheet without saving.

4. Position the insertion point two lines below the text in the Word document. Click the **Paste** button. Word pastes the data as a Word table.

5. Change the price of Blue Gills to **$0.10** in the appropriate table cell.

6. Save your changes. Print the document. Close the document.

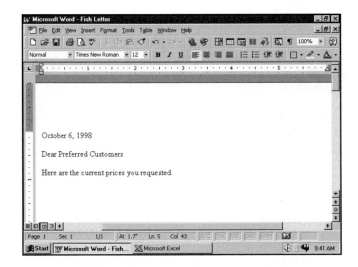

Exercise 2

1. Open the Word document named **Computer Supplies 3** that you created in Lesson 6. Save the document as **Computer Supplies 4**.

2. Open the Excel workbook named **Creative Computers 3** that you created in Lesson 9. Save the workbook as **Creative Computers 4**.

3. Erase the first three paragraphs of the Word document.

4. In the workbook, select the cell range **A4:F11** on Sheet1. Copy the selected cells to the Clipboard.

5. Return to the document. Position the insertion point on a blank line below the bordered paragraph. Click **Edit, Paste Special** to open the Paste Special dialog box. Make sure the **Paste** option is selected and then click **Microsoft Excel Worksheet Object**. Click **OK**. The data is now embedded in the Word document.

6. To edit the embedded data, double-click the worksheet object. Notice that the toolbars of the source application (Excel) display so that you can use them to edit the embedded data. Change the discount amount to **35%**.

7. Click outside the embedded object to update it in Word. You may need to double-click the object again to adjust column widths to display all data. Drag the object to center it under the bordered paragraph.

8. Save your changes. Print the document. Close the document. Close the workbook.

Exercise 3

1. Open the Word document named **Tree 3** that you created in Lesson 6. Save the document as **Tree 4**.

2. Open the Excel workbook called **Tree Farm 3** that you created in Lesson 9. Save the workbook as **Tree Farm 4**.

3. In the Word document, change the name and address of the recipient to: **Dr. Steve Anderson, OSU Extension, The Ohio State University, Columbus, OH 44854**.

4. Erase the contents of the letter and type the following replacement:

   Dear Dr. Anderson:

   As we discussed last week I have been experiencing a high death loss in my fruit trees. The following is a worksheet displaying the latest losses.

5. In the workbook, select cell range A4:F11 from Sheet1. Copy the cells to the Clipboard.

6. Activate the document and use **Paste Special** to link the worksheet after the first (and only) paragraph.

7. In the workbook, change the number of pear trees lost in Year 2 to **1000**. Save your changes and close the workbook.

8. Check the update in the Word document.

9. Save your changes. Print the document. Close the document. (**Hint:** If the linked data replaces your clip art picture, right-click the clip art picture, click **Clip Object, Convert,** and then click **OK** to convert the object to a clip gallery picture. Then print again.)

Exercise 4

1. Open the Word document named **President 2** that you created in Lesson 5. Save the document as **President 3**.

2. Open the Excel workbook named **Student Senate 3** that you created in Lesson 9. Save the workbook as **Student Senate 4**.

3. On Sheet3 of the workbook, click the chart to select it. Click the **Copy** button.

4. Add the following sentence to the end of the second paragraph:

   To see a graphic representation of tuition increases over the past five years, click the icon below.

5. Position the insertion point on a blank line below the paragraph. Open the Paste Special dialog box. Click the **Paste link** option and specify **Microsoft Excel Chart Object**. Click the **Display as icon** check box and click **OK**.

6. Double-click the icon to jump directly to the worksheet chart. Close the workbook.

7. Save changes to the Word document. Print the document. Close the document.

Exercise 5

The Eagle Corporation.

In Lesson 9 you created a worksheet describing the company's health care packages. Create a letter to be sent to all employees describing the findings in the worksheet. Link the worksheet with the new document and print the document.

Change two values in the worksheet and print the document a second time.

Lesson 11
Access 97 Basics

Introduction

Microsoft Access 97 is a database program designed to help you organize and analyze data of many different types. *Databases* store text and number information in individual records. Think of a database as an electronic filing cabinet. After you have stored the information in a database, you can access the data in a number of ways. Queries help you find data that matches specific criteria. Reports let you print only the portions of the database you want to see.

This lesson is designed to help you become comfortable with the basic features of Microsoft Access.

Visual Summary

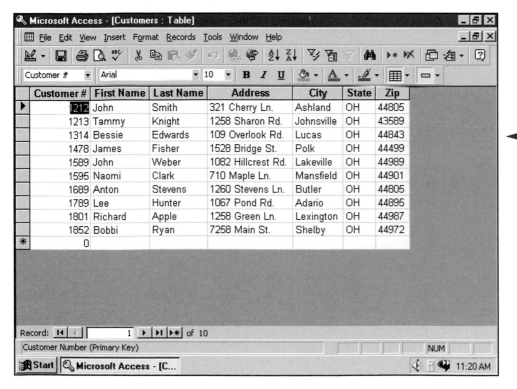

When you have completed Task 7, you will have created a database table that looks like this:

Task 1

Launching Access 97 and Creating a New Database

Why would I do this?

Launching Access starts the Access application so that you can begin creating a database.

In this task, you learn how to launch Access and start a new database.

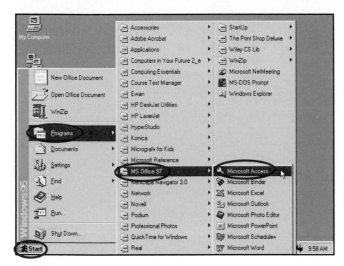

1 To start Access, click the **Start** button, click **Programs, MS Office 97, Microsoft Access**.

2 The Microsoft Access dialog box opens to give you a choice of tasks. You can create a new database, use the Database Wizard to create a database, or work with an existing database. Click the **Blank Database** option button. Click **OK**.

> **In Depth:** Access requires you to name and save a new database before you do any work with the database. You supply a name in the File New Database dialog box.

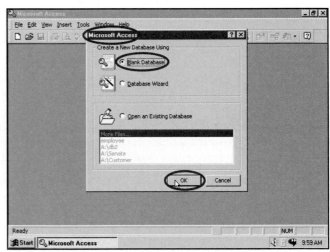

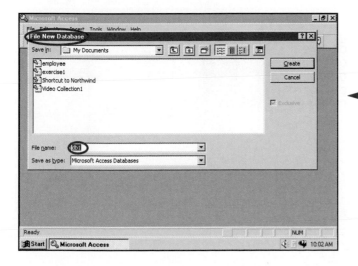

3 The **File New Database** dialog box opens.

4 Select the drive location where you want the database to be saved. Type **Customer** in the **File name** box. Click **Create** to create the new database.

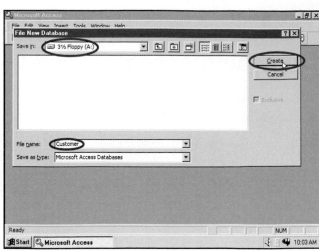

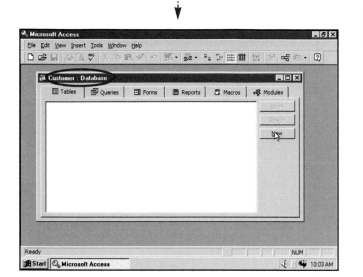

5 The Customer database window opens.

Task 2

Designing a Database Table

Why would I do this?

You have now created a database, but you still have to create the *database objects* within the database to store your data. The most common database object is the *table*. You create tables in Access to store and organize data.

In this task, you learn how to define the structure for the data that you will store in the table.

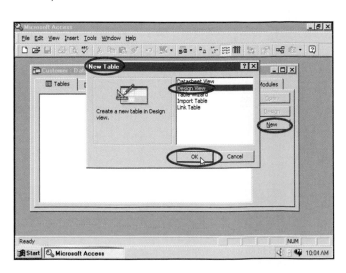

1 The Customer database window is currently open on your screen. To create a new table in the Customer database, click the **New** button. The **New Table** dialog box opens. In this dialog box, you can choose a method for creating the new table.

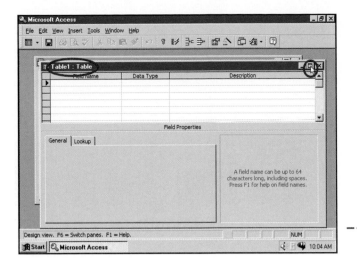

2 Click **Design View** and click **OK**. The Design view window opens. This is the window in which you then create the database table design.

3 Click the **Maximize** button to use the whole screen. The Design view window is maximized to fill the entire screen.

In Depth: Databases are constructed of fields and records. A *field* is a category of data in a database. For example, the Address field contains addresses for each person or company in a database. A *record* is the entire collection of fields for one person or item in a database. For example, a record might contain the Item, Name, Description, Stock, and Price fields in an inventory database. Fields are identified by *field names*. The data inserted in a field is called an *entry*.

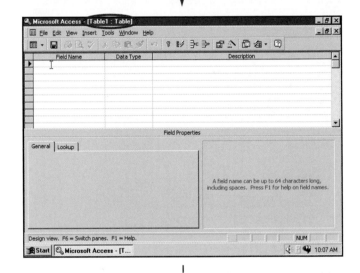

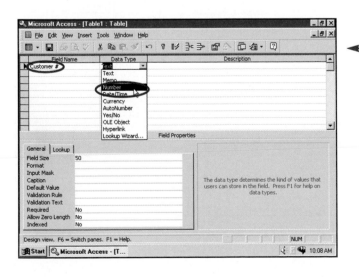

4 To enter the first field name, type **Customer #** at the location of the insertion point. Press ↵Enter to move to the Data Type box. Click the **Data Type** drop-down arrow to see the available data types. Click the **Number** option.

In Depth: The Data Type options help you format the data in your field correctly. By default the Data Type is text, but you can also choose to format your data as a number, date, currency, and so on.

5 Press ⏎Enter to accept the Data Type option and move to the Description box. Here you can add a description of the field if desired. Type **Customer Number (Primary Key)**. Press ⏎Enter to move to the second field in the table.

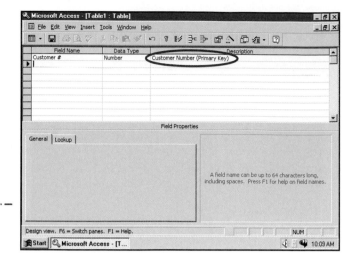

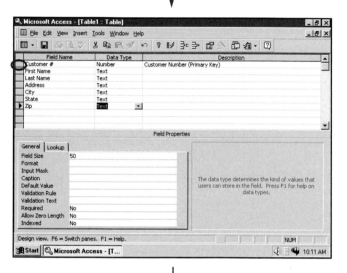

6 Type the remaining six fields as shown.

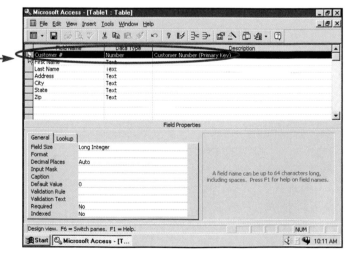

7 When you have finished entering the field names, click the row selector of the **Customer #** field to highlight the field.

Task 3

Setting a Primary Key and Saving the Table

Why would I do this?

Although not required, it is a good idea to specify a primary key field for your table. A *primary key* field contains a value that is unique to a record. No two records can have the same value in their primary key field. This feature is useful when you need to establish a relationship with multiple tables in your database. Setting a primary key also ensures that each record in the table is unique. After you have finished creating the fields for the table, you need to save the table before you enter data into it.

In this task, you learn how to set a primary key for your new database table and save the table.

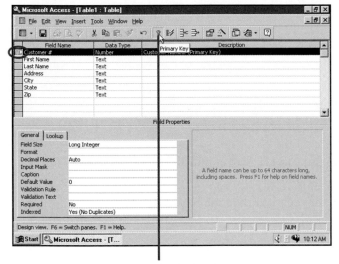

Primary Key button

1 Click the **Primary Key** button on the toolbar. Notice the primary key symbol that displays in the row selector for the Customer # field. The symbol indicates that the Customer # is the primary key for this table.

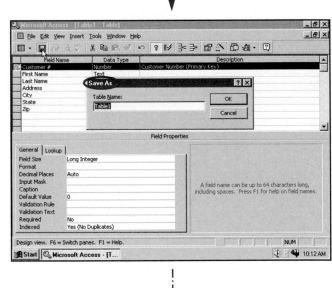

2 Click the **Save** button on the toolbar. The **Save As** dialog box opens.

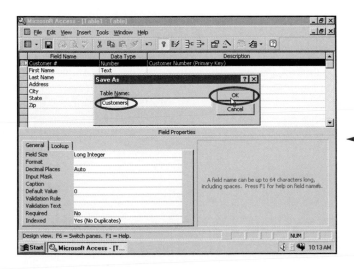

3 In the **Table Name** box, type **Customers**.

4 Click **OK** to save the table with the new name. The Customers table is now saved within the Customers database.

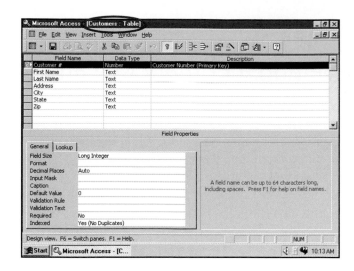

Task 4

Entering Data in Datasheet View

Why would I do this?

Now that you have defined the fields for your database table, you can insert data into the fields. Typically, data entry is done in Datasheet view.

In this task, you learn how to switch to Datasheet view and enter records in the table.

View button

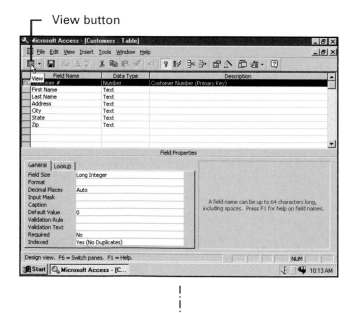

1 Locate the **View** button on the toolbar. Notice that it currently shows an icon similar to a worksheet, with columns and rows. This is the symbol for Datasheet view.

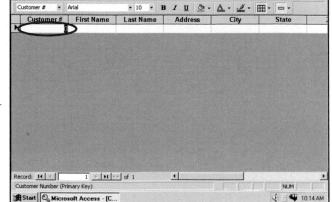

2 Click the **View** button to switch to Datasheet view. The default number entry for the Customer # field is already selected.

3 Type <u>**1212**</u> in the Customer # field and press ⤶Enter. Enter the remaining six fields as shown, pressing ⤶Enter or Tab⇥ after each entry to move to the next field.

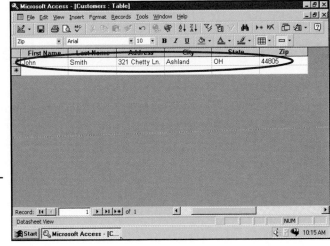

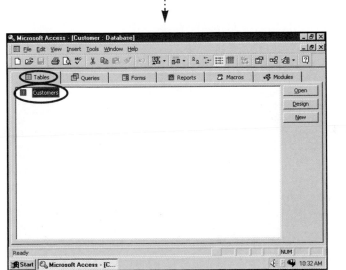

4 Notice that you may not be able to see the entire record on the screen. You can adjust field widths in the database table just as you do column widths in a worksheet by dragging the field's border in the header row. Adjust the widths of all fields so that the entire record displays on the screen.

 Quick Tip: The quickest way to optimize field width is to double-click the field border in the header row.

5 Enter the remaining nine records as shown. Adjust field width to display all data in each record. Click the **Save** button to save your changes.

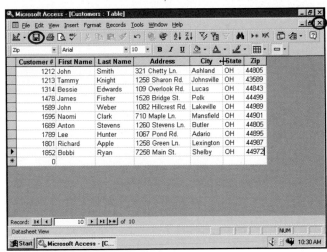

6 To close the database table, click its **Close** button. The Customer database window displays on the screen with your new database table listed on the Tables tab.

Task 5

Creating a Form from a Table

Why would I do this?

As you saw in the previous task, it is sometimes difficult to see all your data for a specific record on the screen at the same time in Datasheet view. One way to solve this problem is to display the table data as a form. A *form* shows all field names and field data on the screen one record at a time. You can create a form by using the field names from a table.

In this task, you learn how to create a form from a table.

1 You need to add another table to the database to track sales data. Create this table first, then you can create the form from it. To create a new table, click the **New** button on the Tables tab in the database window. Then click **Design View** in the **New Table** dialog box and click **OK**. The Design view window opens. Define the fields as shown in the figure.

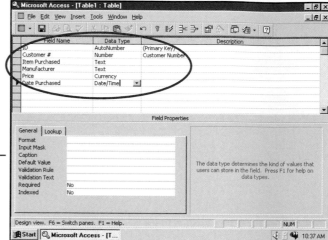

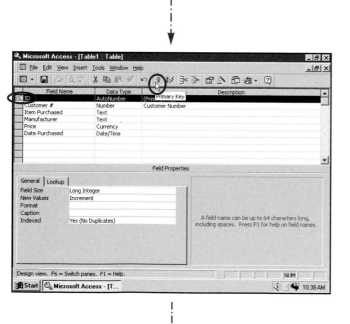

2 Set a primary key using the ID field. Because a customer may order multiple products, the customer number may appear in more than one record in this table. The customer number is not always unique, so it cannot be the primary key field for this table.

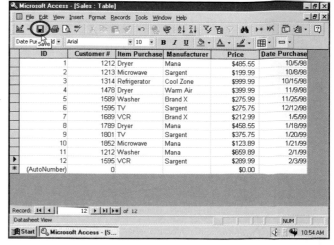

3 Save the table as **Sales**. Switch to Datasheet view and enter the records shown in the figure. You do not have to enter a number in the ID field. Press ↵Enter or Tab↹ to move to the Customer # field, and the ID field displays a number automatically. You do not have to enter the dollar signs in the Price field or the year in the Date Purchased field. Access adds these items automatically.

4 Save your changes and close the table. Click the **Forms** tab in the Customer database window.

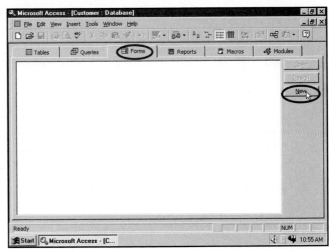

5 To create a new form, click the **New** button. The **New Form** dialog box opens. To let the Form Wizard help you create the form, click **Form Wizard**. To choose a table to base the form on, click the drop-down arrow of the *Choose the table or query* text box and select **Sales**.

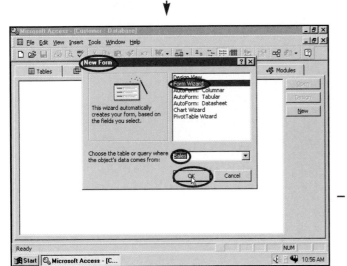

6 Click **OK** to start the Form Wizard. The Form Wizard dialog box opens.

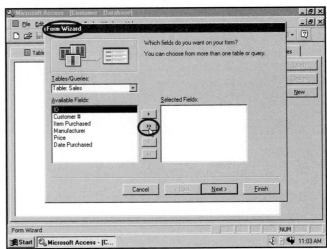

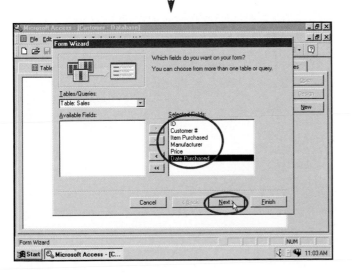

7 To add all the fields to the new form, click the >> button.

8 Click **Next** twice. Select the **Clouds** style.

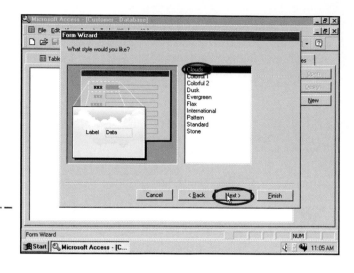

9 Click **Next** to move to the last Wizard dialog box. Access suggests a name for the form and gives you options for displaying it. Type the name **Sales** as the form's title.

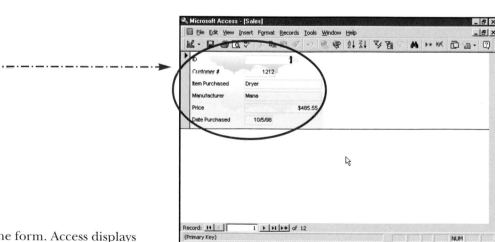

10 Click **Finish** to display the form. Access displays the first record in the table in Form view.

Task 6

Entering Data in Form View

Why would I do this?

Because Form view shows only one record on the screen at a time, entering data can be easier using this view. You can easily see all the data in each field of the record. You move from field to field in the same way as in Datasheet view. To move from record to record, you use the navigation buttons at the bottom of the Form view window.

In this task, you learn how to enter data in Form view and move from record to record.

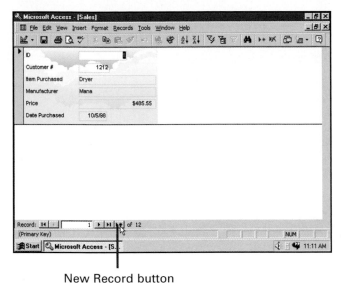

New Record button

1 You should be looking at the first record you entered in Datasheet view in the last task. To enter new data you must move to a new, blank record. Locate the **New Record** button at the bottom of the Form view window.

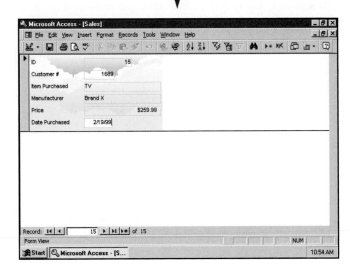

2 Click the **New Record** button to move to a new blank record. Enter the following data, pressing Tab⇆ or ↵Enter after each field to move to the next field (or record).

Customer #	Item Purchased	Manufacturer	Price	Date Purchased
1314	Microwave	Sargent	199.99	2/9/99
1212	Refrigerator	Mana	795.99	2/12/99
1689	TV	Brand X	259.99	2/19/99

3 Save your changes. Close the Form view by clicking the **Close** box. Notice that your form is now stored on the Forms tab in the Customers database window.

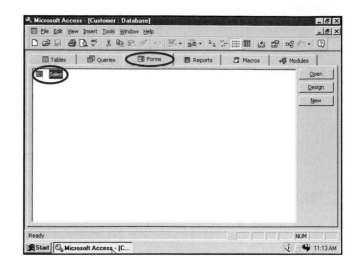

Task 7

Editing Table Data

Why would I do this?

If data in your table is entered incorrectly, or if the data simply needs to be changed, you can easily update or correct fields within records in your table. Besides editing a record, you may find the need to add or delete records in your table.

In this task, you learn how to edit data in an existing table.

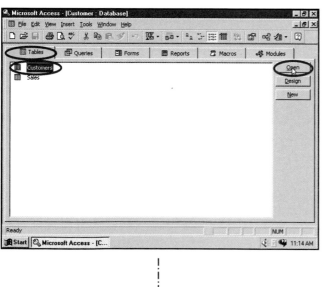

1 You need to make some changes to the Customers table. To open this table, click the **Tables** tab in the database window. Select the table **Customers**.

2 Click **Open** to open the table. Highlight the street field in John Smith's record. Change the street from Chetty to **Cherry**.

3 To add a record to your table, click in the Customer # field to the right of the row selector containing an *. Add record 11 for customer #1900 as shown.

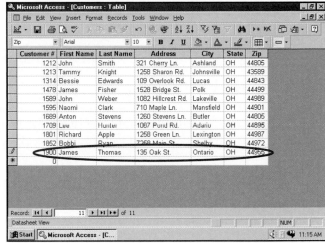

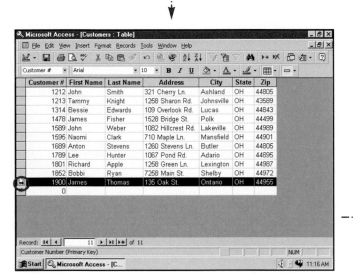

4 To delete a record in your table, first click the row selector for customer #1900 to select the record.

5 Press (Del). You are prompted to confirm the deletion.

Pothole: You cannot undo a record deletion, so be absolutely sure that you want to delete the record and that you have selected the right record to delete before you confirm the deletion.

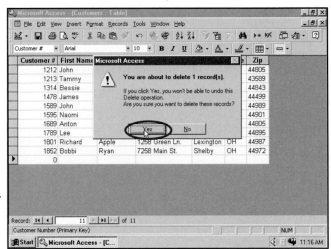

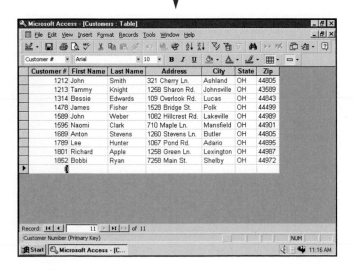

6 Click **Yes** to confirm the deletion. Save your changes.

Task 8

Printing Records and Closing a Database

Why would I do this?

There are times when you want a hard copy of your database in order to view it, write on it, forward it, or file it. You can print an entire database table or all records in Form view. You can also print selected records only in either Datasheet or Form view. When you are finished working with a database, you should close it to free computer memory.

In this task, you learn how to print database records and close a database.

1 To select a specific record to print from Datasheet view, click the row selector for Customer #1478.

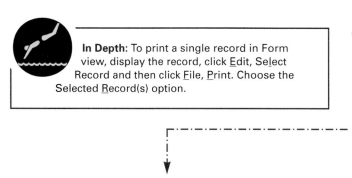

In Depth: To print a single record in Form view, display the record, click Edit, Select Record and then click File, Print. Choose the Selected Record(s) option.

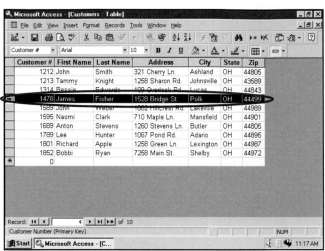

2 Click **File, Print** on the menu bar. The **Print** dialog box opens. Click the **Selected Record(s)** option button.

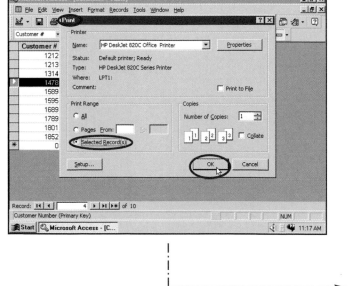

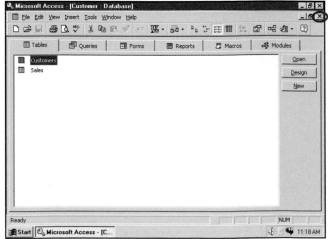

3 Click **OK** to print the selected record. To print all records in the table, click the **Print** button on the toolbar. Close the table by clicking its **Close** box.

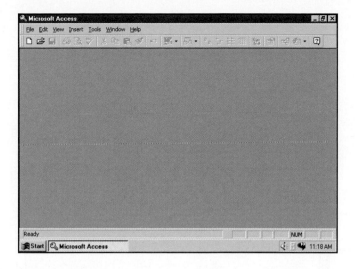

4 Click the Customer database **Close** box to close the database.

Student Exercises

True-False

For each of the following, circle either T or F to indicate whether the statement is true or false.

T   F   **1.** Customer Name would be a good primary key field.

T   F   **2.** An Access database is made up only of tables.

T   F   **3.** Using a database is similar to storing information in a file cabinet.

T   F   **4.** Common data types include numbers, currency, and text.

T   F   **5.** You define fields for a table in Design view.

T   F   **6.** If you type an entry incorrectly, there is no way to correct it.

T   F   **7.** There are two ways to view a table: Design view and Print view.

T   F   **8.** Double-clicking on the border between field names adjusts the width of the field.

T   F   **9.** It is possible to have more than one table in an Access database.

T   F   **10.** A primary key creates a unique identifier for each record in the table.

Identifying Parts of the Access Screen

Refer to the figure and identify the numbered parts of the screen. Write the letter of the correct label in the space next to the number.

1. _____
2. _____
3. _____
4. _____
5. _____
6. _____
7. _____
8. _____
9. _____
10. _____

A. Primary Key button
B. View button
C. Primary key field
D. Customer Number field
E. Data Type column
F. Field Name column
G. State field
H. Close Access button
I. Close Table button
J. Maximize/Restore button

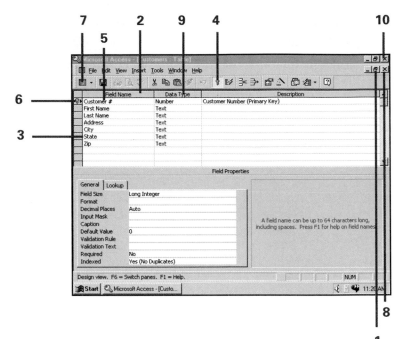

Matching

Match the following statements to the word or phrase that is the best match from the list. Write the letter of the matching word or phrase in the space provided next to the number.

1. ___ Field in which data between records must be unique

2. ___ Data type that allows Access to automatically number each record

3. ___ The view used to see all field names and field data on the screen one record at a time

4. ___ The view used to see the structure of the table

5. ___ The view used to see the data in the table

6. ___ Button used to create a new table

7. ___ Key used to remove a record from a database

8. ___ A field name used if an appropriate primary key field is not available

9. ___ A collection of tables and other objects

10. ___ A method used to help you create a form design

A. AutoNumber

B. ID

C. Database

D. Design view

E. Open

F. New

G. Primary key

H. Del

I. Datasheet view

J. Form view

K. Form Wizard

Application Exercises

Exercise 1

1. Open the Access database named **Agency** from the student disk.

2. Create a form from the **Houses** table. Save the form as <u>Houses</u>.

3. Add the following two new records in Form view. To indicate Yes in the Garage field, press the Spacebar once in that field.

Listing #	Address	City	Bedrooms	Bath	Garage	Sq Footage	Price	Sales Assoc
2350	154 Thomas Dr.	Ashland	3	2	Yes	1750	$84,500	12
2354	487 Carriage Dr.	Lucas	2	1	No	1400	$53,900	11

4. Delete listings 2319 and 2300 in Datasheet view.

5. Change the price for listing 2256 to **$180,000**.

6. Change the number of bedrooms in listing 2321 to **4**.

7. In Form view, print records 3 and 15. Close the Form view.

Exercise 2

1. In the **Agency** database, create a new table to store data about the sales associates. Use the following information to define the five fields of the table. When completed save the table as **Associates**.

Field Name	Data Type	Field Description
Sales Assoc	Text	Primary Key
First Name	Text	
Last Name	Text	
Phone	Text	
Regional Office	Text	

2. Enter the following records for the seven sales associates.

Sales Assoc	First Name	Last Name	Phone	Regional Office
10	Sally	Pine	419-855-9954	Ashland
11	Brenda	Smith	419-694-8547	Mansfield
12	Mike	Jones	419-987-2355	Ashland
13	Diane	Terry	419-747-8594	Ashland
14	George	Peters	419-712-8547	Mansfield
15	Loretta	Tylor	614-654-5874	Mansfield
16	Steve	Glamour	419-741-2584	Ashland

3. Adjust the width of the columns.

4. Print the table from the Datasheet view.

5. Close the table and the database.

Exercise 3

1. Design and create a relational database called **Tree Farm**. Use the following information to define the eight fields of the table. When complete, save the table as **Trees**.

Field Name	Data Type	Field Description
Stock #	Text	Primary Key
Vendor #	Text	
Common Name	Text	
Mature Height	Number	
Shade	Yes/No	
Flowering	Yes/No	
Wholesale Price	Currency	
Current Stock	Number	

2. Enter the following records:

Stock #	Vendor #	Name	Height	Shade	Flowering	Wholesale Price	Stock
15473	12	Red Oak	60	Yes	No	$25.00	500
15658	15	Pin Oak	40	Yes	No	$22.00	320
18525	13	Sugar Maple	45	Yes	No	$18.00	850
19874	14	Red Maple	45	Yes	No	$17.00	500
25411	13	Hybrid Poplar	60	Yes	No	$17.50	600
31111	14	Magnolia	20	No	Yes	$30.00	200
32123	15	Flowering Crab	20	No	Yes	$20.00	350
45854	12	White Pine	50	No	No	$10.00	600
54113	12	Tulip Poplar	80	Yes	Yes	$38.00	200
54144	12	Apple	15	No	Yes	$19.75	700
54545	14	Scotch Pine	35	No	No	$28.00	400
65874	14	Bartlett Pear	30	No	No	$21.00	256
77474	13	Black Locust	50	No	No	$12.00	200
85258	15	Lombard Poplar	50	No	No	$12.00	125
95411	12	Dogwood	20	No	Yes	$35.00	200

3. Adjust the width of the columns.

4. Change the table's orientation for printing to Landscape orientation by clicking **File, Page Setup**; clicking the **Page** tab; and selecting the **Landscape** option. Click **OK**. Then click the **Print** button on the toolbar.

5. Save your changes. Close the table.

Exercise 4

1. Create a second table in the **Tree Farm** database to track wholesale vendors. Use the following information to define the eight fields of the table. When completed save the table as <u>**Vendors**</u>.

Field Name	Data Type	Field Description
Vendor #	Text	Primary Key
Company Name	Text	
Address	Text	
City	Text	
State	Text	
Zip	Text	
Contact	Text	
Phone	Text	

2. Enter the following records for the four tree vendors.

Vendor #	Company Name	Address	City	State	Zip	Contact	Phone
12	Al's Trees	1235 Elm St.	Polk	OH	44859	Al	419-945-2244
13	Sunny Side	745 Church St.	Congress	OH	44958	Sally	419-846-7474
14	A+ Tree, Inc.	45 Gamble Dr.	Ashland	OH	44805	Bob	419-387-5423
15	Berk Brothers	987 Bainey Rd.	Ashland	OH	44805	Mary	419-785-9644

3. Adjust the width of the columns.

4. Print the table of current vendors (use landscape orientation). Save your changes. Close the table and the database.

Exercise 5

The Eagle Corporation.

As the inventory manager for Eagle Corporation, you are responsible for the inventory of all office supplies. You purchase your inventory from three major wholesalers.

Create an Inventory table to store all the inventory for the store, using fields for the item, wholesale price, retail price, quantity on hand, and wholesaler #. This table should contain 15 records.

Create a Wholesaler table that stores data for the wholesalers using fields for the wholesaler #, name, address, city, state, zip, and phone.

Print the two tables.

Lesson 12
Using Filters and Queries

Task 1 Sorting a Database

Task 2 Using a Filter to Display Records

Task 3 Creating a Simple Criteria Query

Task 4 Querying Multiple Tables

Task 5 Using Mathematical Operators in Queries

Task 6 Saving a Query

Task 7 Using a Query to Perform Calculations

Introduction

Now that you are able to create multiple tables in an Access database, you are ready to look at ways to find, sort, and display information contained in a database. Databases can contain hundreds or even thousands of records. To use such a database efficiently, you need to know how to locate specific information. Access provides a number of ways for you to manipulate the data in a database to display only the records you want.

This lesson is designed to help you master Access's most important data manipulation features: sorting, filters, and queries.

Visual Summary

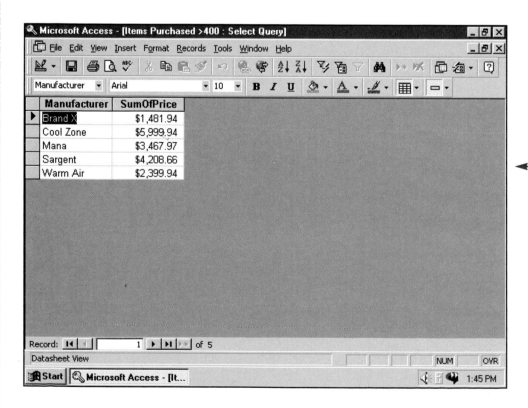

When you have completed this lesson, you will have created a query to calculate totals in a database table. Your query results should look like this:

Task 1

Sorting a Database

Why would I do this?

Access stores records in the order in which you enter them. To help you find specific records, you can sort the database according to the information in any of its fields.

In this task, you learn how to sort records in a database.

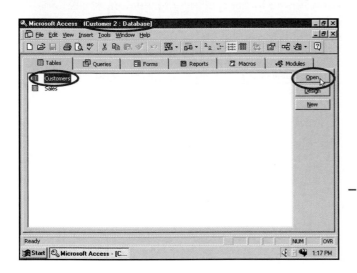

1 Start Access. In the Microsoft Access dialog box, select **Open an Existing Database**. Click **More Files** and then click **OK**. In the **Open** dialog box, locate the **Customer 2** database, click it, and click **Open**.

Sort Ascending button

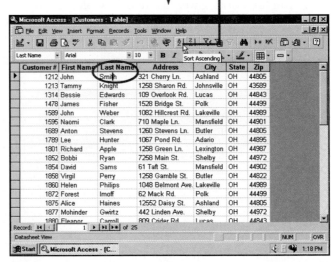

2 Click **Customers** and then click **Open** to open the table. Sort the records by the Last Name field: Click any entry in the Last Name field. Locate the **Sort Ascending** button on the toolbar.

In Depth: You can sort in either ascending (A to Z, 1 to 10) order or descending (Z to A, 10 to 1) order. The Sort buttons on the toolbar enables you to sort only one field at a time. To sort more than one field at a time, you must use a filter.

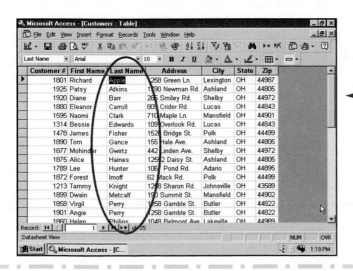

3 Click the **Sort Ascending** button on the toolbar. The records display in ascending alphabetical order according to last name.

4 Now sort the records in descending order according to Zip code. Click any entry in the Zip field and click the **Sort Descending** button on the toolbar.

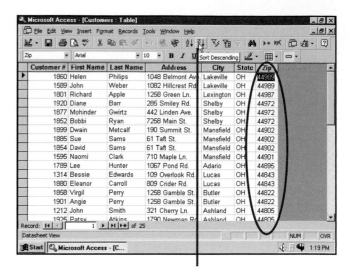

Sort Descending button

Task 2

Using a Filter to Display Records

Why would I do this?

While you are working with a database table, you may occasionally want to display a specific set of records that share a feature; for example, the records of clients who live in a particular city. You can use a *filter* to display records that meet a particular condition. Filters also enable you to sort all records by more than one field at a time.

In this task, you learn how to use a filter to display specific records.

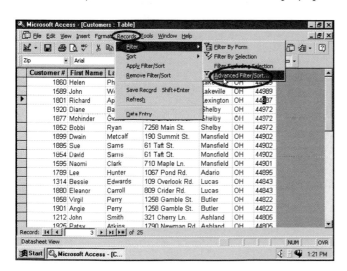

1 You would like to know how many of your customers live in a certain Zip code area. To find this information using a filter, click, if necessary, any entry in the Zip field and then click **Records, Filter, Advanced Filter/Sort** on the menu bar.

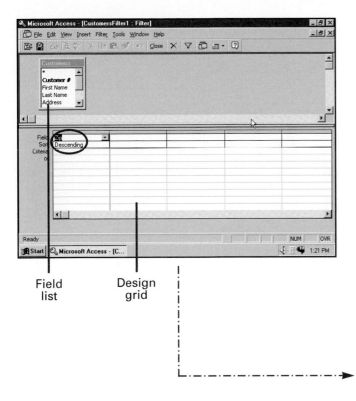

Field list   **Design grid**

2 The filter window opens. The filter window contains a *field list* of fields in the current database and a *design grid* where you can create the filter. Notice that the Zip field already displays in the design grid with a Descending sort specified.

In Depth: You create a filter by placing the fields you want to filter by in the design grid. You can drag fields from the field list to the design grid or double-click on a field in the field list to place it in the grid. Then, you can specify *criteria* that records must match in order to be displayed. For example, if you want to filter records to show only customers named *Ryan*, type **Ryan** in the Criteria box of the Last Name field. You can specify more than one criteria for each field. If you are using a filter to sort, place the fields in the grid in the order in which you want to sort them, for example, Last Name and then First Name. Click the Sort box below the field name and choose the direction to sort (Ascending or Descending).

3 To find all customers in the 44805 Zip code area, type **44805** in the Criteria box under the Zip field.

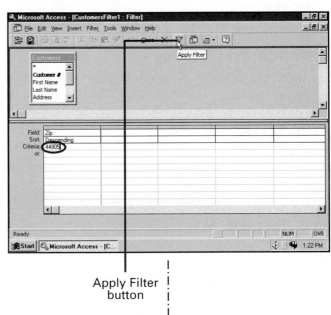

Apply Filter button

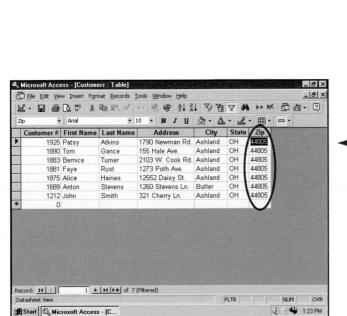

4 Click the **Apply Filter** button on the toolbar to apply the filter. Access displays only the records of customers who live in the 44805 Zip code area.

5 To remove the filter and redisplay all records, click the **Remove Filter** button. Notice that all records display and that they are no longer sorted according to Zip code.

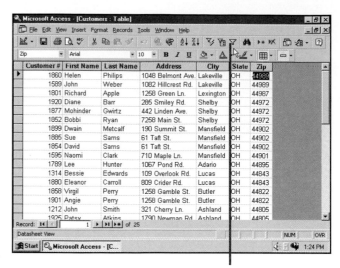

Remove Filter button

Task 3

Creating a Simple Criteria Query

Why would I do this?

Like a filter, a *query* enables you to display records from your database that match specific criteria. When you use a query, however, your results display in a table separate from your database table. Remember that when you used a filter, all fields displayed. When you use a query, you can specify which fields you want to display in the query results table. Access offers a number of different kinds of queries. One of the most popular is the *criteria query*. A criteria query displays records that match one or more criteria.

In this task, you learn how to create a simple criteria query.

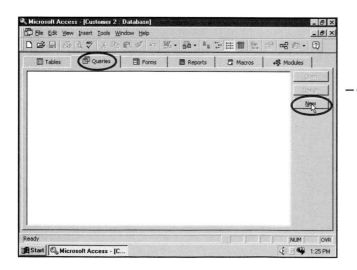

1 Close the database table currently on your screen. Save changes if prompted. The Customer database window displays. Click the **Queries** tab.

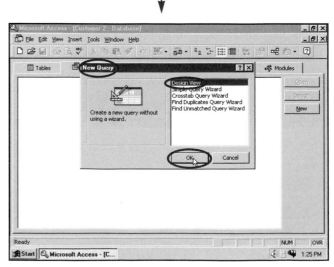

2 To begin creating a new query, click **New**. The **New Query** dialog box opens. Highlight **Design View** to create the query yourself.

3 Click **OK**. The **Show Table** dialog box opens. This dialog box enables you to select the table (or tables) you want to query. Click the **Customers** table.

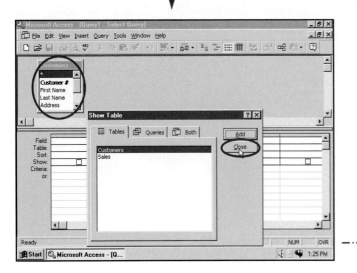

5 Click **Close** in the **Show Table** dialog box. Notice that the query window looks very similar to the filter window you worked with earlier in this lesson. The Show check boxes, which do not display in the filter window, enable you to decide whether to display a field in the query results table.

 In Depth: You can use a field in a query to specify criteria or perform calculations without having to display it in the query results table.

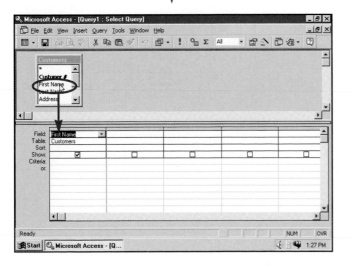

4 Click **Add** to add the table to the query window. Notice that Access adds a field list to the query window behind the **Show Table** dialog box.

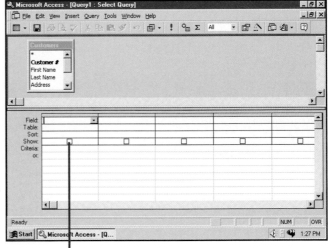

Show check box

6 You want to know the names of any customers who live in Mansfield. For this query, you need to display only the First Name, Last Name, and City fields. Double-click the **First Name** field in the field list to place that field in the design grid.

7 Using the same procedure, place the Last Name and the City fields in the design grid. To instruct Access to display only records of customers who live in the City of Mansfield, type **Mansfield** in the Criteria box under the City field.

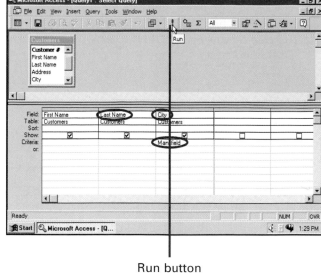

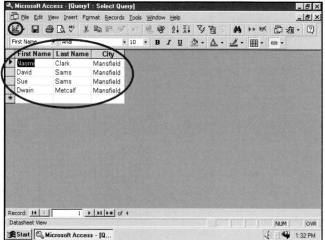

Run button

8 Click the **Run** button on the toolbar to run the query. Access displays a table showing the results of the query. Four customers live in the city of Mansfield.

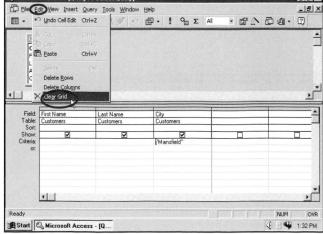

9 To return to the query Design view, click the **View** button. You do not save this query. Clear the design grid by clicking **Edit, Clear Grid** on the menu bar.

Task 4

Querying Multiple Tables

Why would I do this?

In Access you can query multiple tables within the database. This powerful feature enables you to access selected fields from different tables to create a query.

In this task, you learn how to create a query using fields from more than one table.

Show Table button

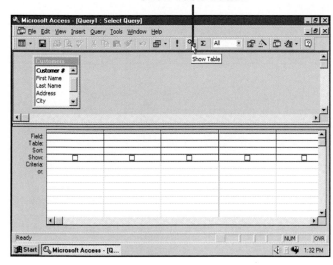

1 To add another table to the query window, you need to display the Show Table dialog box again. Locate the **Show Table** button on the toolbar.

2 Click the **Show Table** button. The **Show Table** dialog box opens. Double-click **Sales** to add the Sales table to your query. Notice that Access automatically establishes a link between the two tables using the Customer # field that appears in both tables.

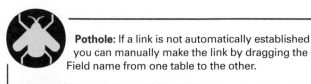

Pothole: If a link is not automatically established you can manually make the link by dragging the Field name from one table to the other.

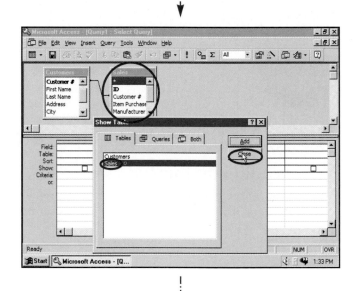

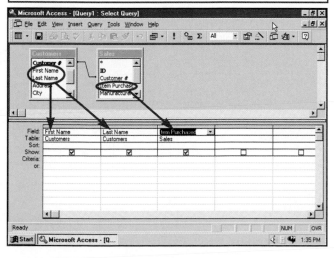

3 Click **Close** in the **Show Table** dialog box. Now let's find out what items a particular customer has purchased lately. For this query, you need the First Name, Last Name, and Item Purchased fields. Double-click the **First Name** and **Last Name** fields from the Customers field list to place those two fields in your query. Double-click the **Item Purchased** field from the Sales field list to place that field in your query.

4 To specify a specific customer name, type **John** in the Criteria box under the First Name field and **Smith** in the Criteria box under the Last Name field.

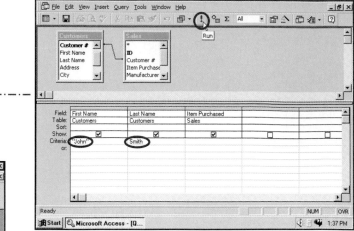

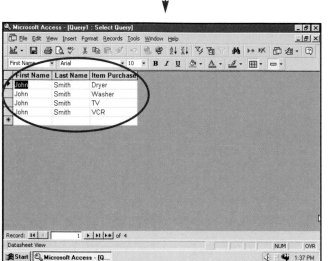

5 Click the **Run** button on the toolbar. The query results table displays, showing the four items that John Smith has purchased.

Task 5

Using Mathematical Operators in Queries

Why would I do this?

You can use mathematical operators such as > (greater than), < (less than), and = (equals) to refine criteria in a query. Mathematical operators are particularly useful when the field you are querying contains numbers.

In this task, you learn how to use mathematical operators to refine a query.

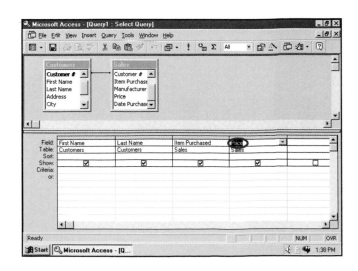

1 Refine your current query to display all customers who have purchased items that cost more than $400. First, click the **View** button to return to the query Design view. Erase the criteria in the First Name and Last Name boxes by selecting each name and pressing Del. To add the Price field to the query, double-click **Price** in the Sales field list.

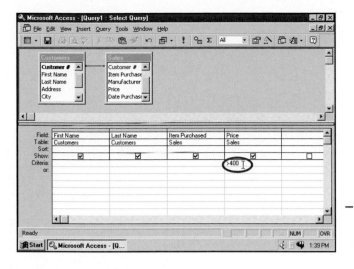

2 To specify that Access should display records when the number in the Price field is greater than $400, type **>400** in the Criteria box under the Price field.

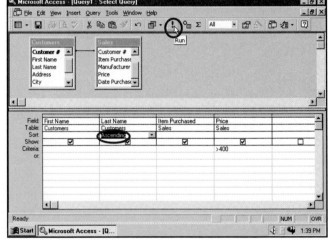

3 To display the query results in alphabetical order by the customers' last names, click in the Sort box under the Last Name field. On the drop-down list, click **Ascending**.

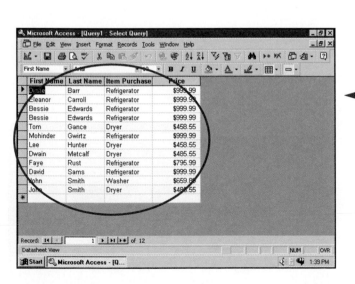

4 Click the **Run** button to run the query. Access displays only the records of customers who have purchased items that cost more than $400. Notice that the customer names appear in alphabetical order by last name.

Task 6

Saving a Query

Why would I do this?

If you work regularly with a database, you find yourself using some queries over and over. To speed your work, you can save queries you use often. Saved queries appear on the Queries tab in the database window. You do not have to open a table to use a saved query. Simply click the query name on the Queries tab and then click the Open button.

In this task, you learn how to save a query for later use.

1 The query you completed in the previous task is one you probably want to use often. To store it for future use, click the **Save** button on the toolbar. The **Save As** dialog box opens to prompt you for a query name.

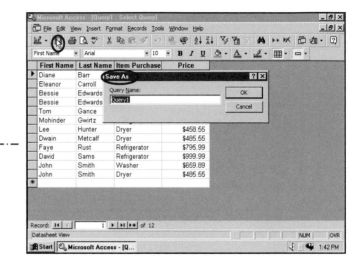

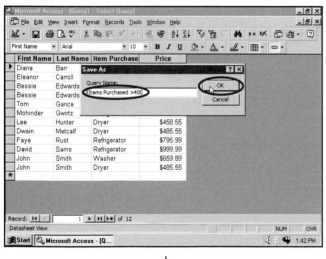

2 Type **Items Purchased >400** in the Query Name box.

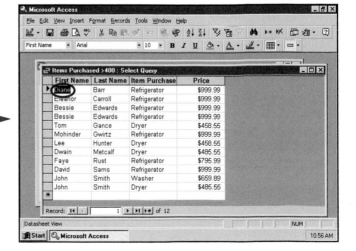

3 Click **OK** to save the query. Notice the new query name in the title bar of the query results table.

Task 7

Using a Query to Perform Calculations

Why would I do this?

Access enables you to perform a number of different kinds of calculations in a query. If you want to determine the total stock value in an inventory database, for example, you can add a field in a query to multiply total stock times price. Access makes the calculation and displays the product in the query results table. Access also enables you to use functions such as those you used in Excel (SUM, COUNT, and so on) to calculate in a query.

In this task, you learn how to sum values in a query.

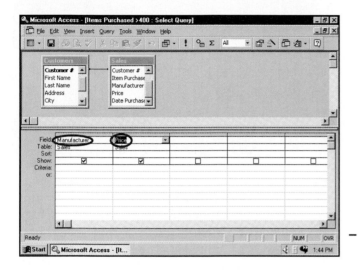

1 Click the **View** button to return to query Design view. Click **Edit, Clear Grid**. In this query, you want to find the total value of items from each manufacturer. First, double-click the **Manufacturer** and **Price** fields from the Sales field list to place those two fields in your query.

In Depth: When you perform calculations in Excel, you use values or cell references in formulas and functions. When you perform calculations in Access, you use field names in the formulas and functions.

2 Next, you need to tell Access how to group the items in the fields you have chosen. You do this using the Totals button on the toolbar. Click the **Totals** button to add the Total box option to your query.

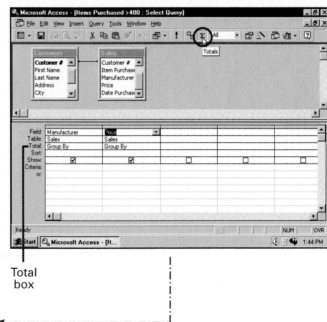

Total box

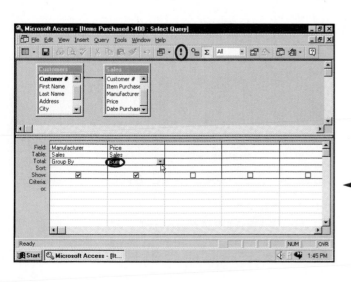

3 To instruct Access to sum the prices of each manufacturer, click the **Group By** drop-down arrow under the Price field. Click **Sum**.

4 Click the **Run** button to run the query. Access displays the query results table. Notice that the Price field name has changed to SumOfPrice.

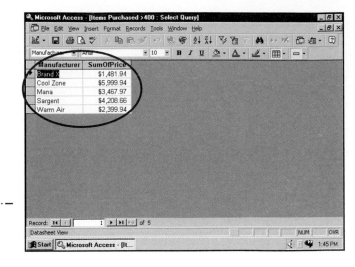

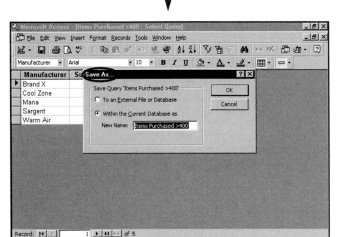

5 Notice that you are still using the query you saved in the last task. To save the calculated query with a new name, click **File, Save As/Export**. The **Save As** dialog box opens.

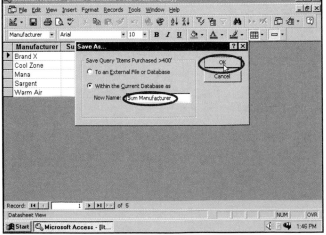

6 If necessary, select the **Within the Current Database as** option. Type the new name **Sum Manufacturer** in the New Name box.

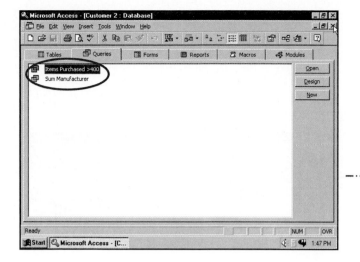

7 Click **OK** to save the query with the new name. Click the **Print** button to print the query results table. Click the **Close** button to close the query results table. Notice that you now have two queries stored on the Queries tab in the database window.

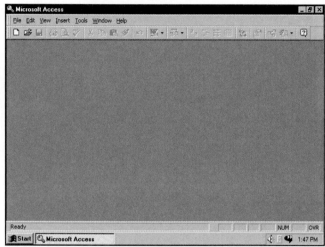

8 Close the database.

Student Exercises

True-False

For each of the following, circle either T or F to indicate whether the statement is true or false.

T   F   **1.** Queries enable you to ask for information from a table in your database.

T   F   **2.** Clicking the field name once selects and moves the field name from the field list to the design grid.

T   F   **3.** You clear the design grid by clicking Clear Grid on the Edit menu.

T   F   **4.** Using multiple tables in a database enables you to access data from different tables to be used in one query.

T   F   **5.** The Sort Ascending button lets you sort up to three fields at a time.

T   F   **6.** When you create a filter, you can choose which fields to display.

T   F   **7.** Using a criteria in a query displays only selected records.

T   F   **8.** A valid criteria is <400.

T   F   **9.** The best way to find records of customers who live in a particular city is to use a sort.

T   F   **10.** You can perform many kinds of calculations in a filter.

Identifying Parts of the Access Screen

Refer to the figure and identify the numbered parts of the screen. Write the letter of the correct label in the space next to the number.

1. _____
2. _____
3. _____
4. _____
5. _____
6. _____
7. _____
8. _____
9. _____

A. Design grid
B. Sorted field
C. Totals button
D. Customers table
E. Sales table
F. Linked fields
G. Run button
H. Show Table button
I. Criteria field

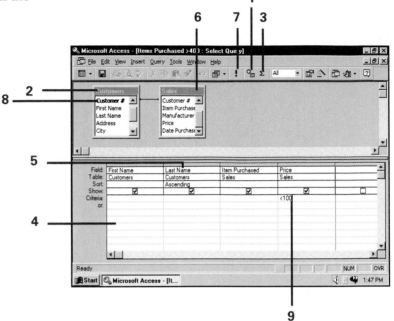

Matching

Match the following statements to the word or phrase that is the best match from the list. Write the letter of the matching word or phrase in the space provided next to the number. Some items may be used more than one time.

1. ___ View used to create a new query

2. ___ Button used to add a table to the query

3. ___ A function used to create totals

4. ___ Sort that lists items in alphabetical order from A to Z

5. ___ Used to display all fields of selected records

6. ___ Button that adds a new row to the design grid to allow for statistical functions

7. ___ Condition that must be met to display a record

8. ___ Menu used to clear the design grid

9. ___ Way to move a field to the design grid

10. ___ Button that displays query results

A. SUM
B. Ascending
C. Double-click
D. Design view
E. Edit
F. Totals
G. Criteria
H. Show Table
I. Run
J. Filter
K. Search

Application Exercises

Exercise 1

1. Open the **Agency** database you worked with in Lesson 11. Sort the **Houses** table by price in descending order. What are the prices of the five most expensive homes?

2. Create a filter to sort by sales associate and price. Which sales associate listed the most expensive home?

3. Create a filter to display records for houses in Lucas to send to a client interested in that city. Print the filtered records in Landscape orientation.

4. Create a filter to display records of all houses with 4 bedrooms and a garage. To specify the criteria for the garage, type **Yes** in the Garage Criteria field. Print the records in Landscape orientation.

Exercise 2

1. Using the **Agency** database and the **Houses** table, create a query to show the address, price, bedrooms, and baths for all homes priced between $100,000 and $150,000. The Criteria for the price range should read **>=100000 And <=150000**. Save the query as **Price Range**. Print the query results table.

2. Create a query to show the regional office, address, price, and sales associates last name. Sort by office and last name. Save the query as **Associate Sales**. Print the records.

3. Create a query to show houses listed by all agents at less than $100,000. Show the associates' names, phone numbers, and regional office. Show the addresses and prices of the houses. Sort by last name and price. Print the records.

4. Create a query to show the total listing prices for each agent using the SUM function. Sort by price in descending order. Print the records. Close the database.

Exercise 3

1. Open the **Tree Farm** database you created in Lesson 11. Sort the **Trees** table by Common Name in ascending order. Print the records.

2. Create a filter to sort the **Trees** table by Mature Height in descending order and Common Name in ascending order. Print the records.

3. Print records for all shade trees that are also flowering.

4. Print records for all shade trees under 50 feet tall.

5. Print records for all shade trees less than 75 feet tall that cost less than $20.00.

Exercise 4

1. Using the **Tree Farm** database, create a query to show the stock number, common name, and current stock of shade trees. Sort by stock number, and do not show the Shade field. (**Hint:** Click in the Show box for the Shade field to remove the check mark.) Print the records.

2. Create a query to show the vendor number, company name, and the common name of all flowering trees. Also include the current stock. Sort by company name. Save the query as **Flowering**. Print the records.

3. Create a query to show the total current stock amounts for each vendor using the SUM function. Include the vendor number, the company name, and the current stock. Sort by company name. Print the records. Close the database.

Exercise 5

The Eagle Corporation.

As the inventory manager of Eagle Corporation, it is your responsibility to provide queried printouts from the inventory database you created in Lesson 11. Your supervisor would like the following printouts:

1. All the fields and records in the Inventory table.

2. All the fields and records in the Wholesaler table.

3. Average wholesale price by wholesaler.

4. Total wholesale price by wholesaler.

5. All items and quantity on hand. Quantity on hand should be in ascending order.

6. Items, quantity on hand, and wholesaler for all items that need to be reordered. (Determine a number for the quantity on hand).

Lesson 13
Creating Reports in Access

Task 1 Creating a Report Using Report Wizard

Task 2 Modifying a Report

Task 3 Using the Label Wizard to Create Mailing Labels

Introduction

Access's *report* feature provides a professional way to present information from a database. A report can be a very basic or sophisticated document that groups and totals information. There may also be times when certain database information may need to be kept confidential, such as payroll salary information. In those cases, you can choose which fields to include in the report to meet your needs, while not compromising confidential information contained in the database.

This lesson is designed to give you a basic understanding of database reports.

Visual Summary

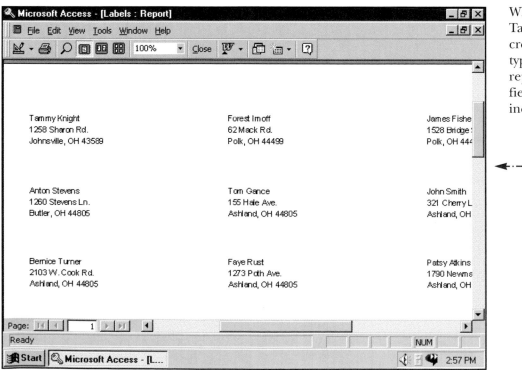

When you have completed Task 3 you will be able to create common report types such as this labels report and select specific fields from the database to include in your report.

Task 1

Creating a Report Using Report Wizard

Why would I do this?

Access provides Report Wizards that make it easy for you to create a report. The Report Wizard guides you through the process of creating a report by providing you options for report layout and ways to group information in the report.

In this task, you learn how to use Report Wizard to create a report.

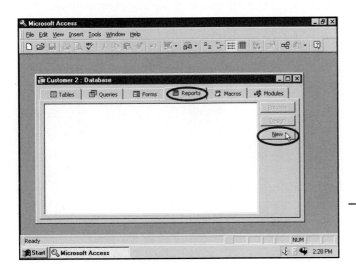

1 Open the **Customer 2** database in Access. You would like to see how sales compare for each manufacturer in your database. You can display this information using a report. Select the **Reports** tab.

2 Click **New** to start a new report. The **New Report** dialog box opens. Select **Report Wizard**. To choose a table to create the report from, click the table drop-down arrow and select **Sales**.

In Depth: The New Report dialog box offers several report options to choose among. Choose Design View to create the report from scratch in Design view. Report Wizard starts a wizard to take you step by step through the process of creating the report. Choose AutoReport: Columnar to automatically create a single-column report. AutoReport: Tabular places all fields of the table in a row and column format similar to a worksheet. Chart Wizard helps you present your data in a graphical format. Label Wizard steps you through the process of creating mailing labels for data in a table. Notice that you can create a report from either a table or a query.

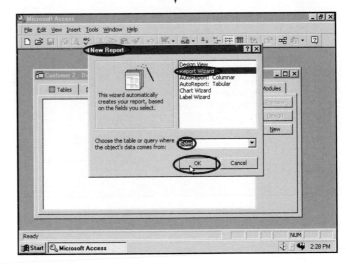

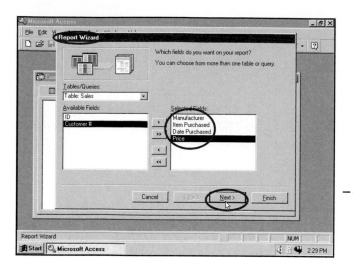

3 Click **OK**. The first **Report Wizard** dialog box opens. In this dialog box, you select the fields that will display in the report. In the **Available Fields** box, double-click on the fields in this order: **Manufacturer, Item Purchased, Date Purchased,** and **Price**. As you double-click each field, it moves to the Selected Fields box.

4 Click **Next** to move to the next **Report Wizard** dialog box. This dialog box lets you choose how to group data in the report. Click the **Manufacturer** field and click the **>** button. The sample page shows *Manufacturer* as the top grouping level for the report.

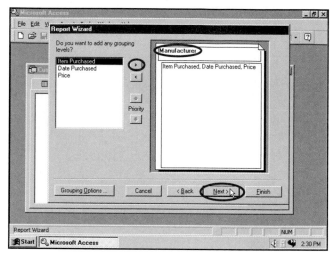

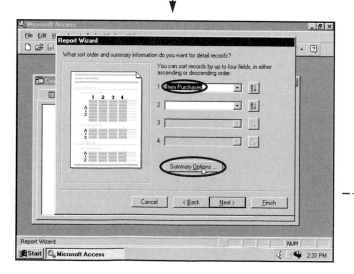

5 Click **Next** to move to the next **Report Wizard** dialog box. This dialog box asks how you want the report sorted. Your report can be sorted on up to four fields. Click the drop-down arrow and select **Item Purchased**.

6 To make the report more meaningful, you can create summaries of the data in fields containing numbers. Click **Summary Options** to open the **Summary Options** dialog box. Access offers a selection of functions that can be applied to numerical data. In this report, the only field applicable is the Price field. To show totals for each manufacturer, click the **Sum** check box.

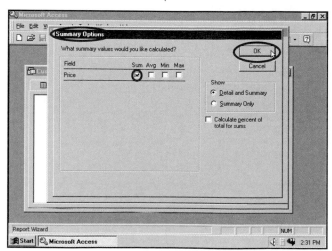

7 Click **OK** to return to the Report Wizard dialog box. Click **Next** to move to the next **Report Wizard** dialog box. The Report Wizard now asks you to describe how you would like the report to look. For this report, you will use the options of **Stepped** and **Portrait**.

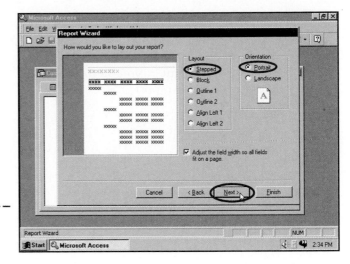

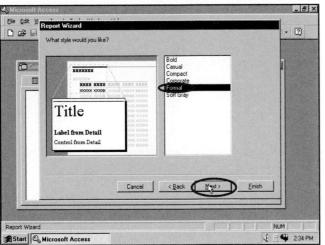

8 Click **Next**. The Report Wizard asks you what style you would like for your report. Click **Formal**.

9 Click **Next**. In the last Report Wizard dialog box type **Total Sales** for the report title.

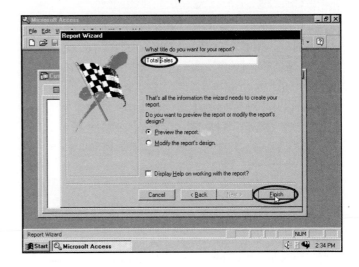

In Depth: Access will automatically save the report. The file name will be the report title name, in this case *Total Sales*. If you make changes to the report and want to keep both reports, you should use the Save As feature to save the modified report with a different file name. It would also be a good idea to change the report header to reflect the purpose of the new report.

10 Click **Finish** to complete the report. Access displays your completed report in a preview screen. You can print the report from this screen if desired using the Print button on the toolbar. Scroll to see the whole report.

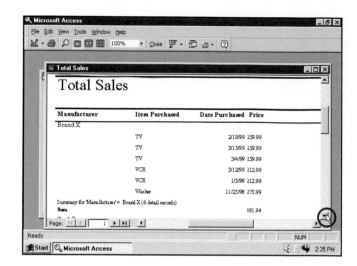

Task 2

Modifying a Report

Why would I do this?

Despite the ease of using Report Wizards, you will sometimes need to make a few changes to the design of your report. You modify a report in Report Design view.

In this task, you learn how to adjust the layout of a report.

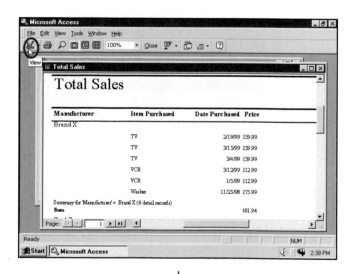

1 Click the **View** button.

2 The Report Design view opens. Report Design view consists of sections that contain specific kinds of report information and a grid of dots to help you align objects in the sections. If the Toolbox opens on your screen, click its **Close** box.

Sections

3 The summary text for each manufacturer clutters your current report. To delete it, first click the =*"Summary for . . .* object in the Manufacturer Footer section to select it.

Selected object

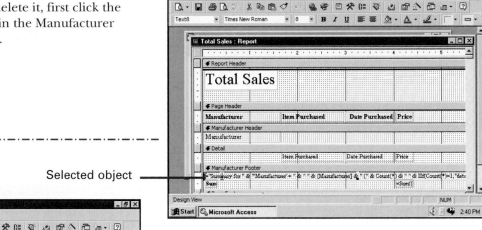

4 Press Del. The object disappears. Select and delete the **Sum** object that was directly below the object you just deleted (at the far left side of the section).

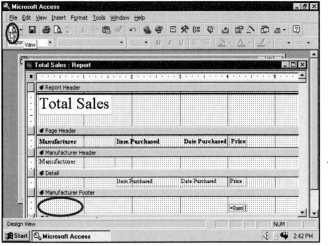

5 To check your modifications so far, click the **View** button. Notice that your report now looks less cluttered. However, the Price data is crowded into the Date Purchased data.

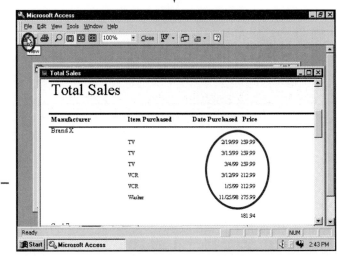

6 Click the **View** button to return to Design view. To move the Price data on the report, you actually have to move three objects in three different sections. Click the **Price** object in the Page Header section. Position the pointer on a selection handle so that the pointer becomes a hand. Drag the object to the right until its left edge is at the 4.5 inch mark on the ruler.

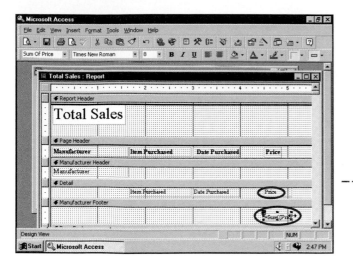

7 Use the same procedure to move the **Price** object in the Detail section and the **=Sum** object in the Manufacturer Footer section. Enlarge these two objects to allow more room for the numbers to display by selecting each object and dragging a handle on the right side to the right.

8 Your report also includes a Grand Total of all prices in the report. Scroll down in Design view to see the Report Footer section. Move the **=Sum** object in this section to the same location you moved the other objects. Adjust the size of the object as shown.

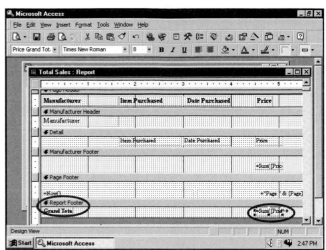

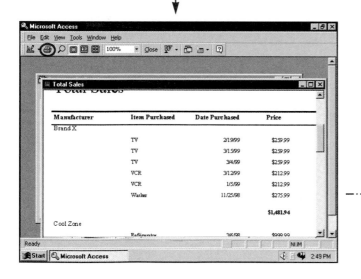

9 To make the subtotals and grand total stand out in the report, click each **=Sum** object and click the **Bold** button on the toolbar. Click the **View** button to check your changes. **Note:** To see the second page of the report, use the navigation buttons at the bottom of the report preview screen.

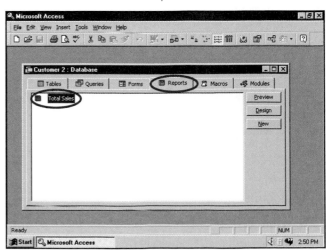

10 Print the report by clicking the **Print** button on the toolbar. Close the report by clicking its **Close** box. Click **Yes** to save changes. Note that Access displays the report name on the Reports tab in the database window.

Task 3

Using the Label Wizard to Create Mailing Labels

Why would I do this?

If you ever have the need to print mailing labels from information contained in your database, you can use the Label Wizard report wizard. Access provides for over 100 different label styles.

In this task, you learn how to use the Label Wizard to create mailing labels.

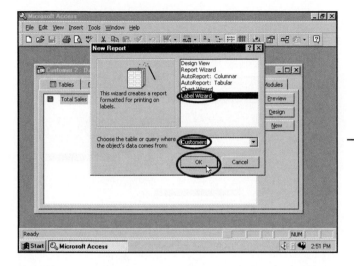

1 On the **Reports** tab, click **New** to start a new report. In the **New Report** dialog box, select **Label Wizard**. Select the **Customers** table.

2 Click **OK**. The first **Label Wizard** dialog box opens. Click Avery number **5160** if necessary.

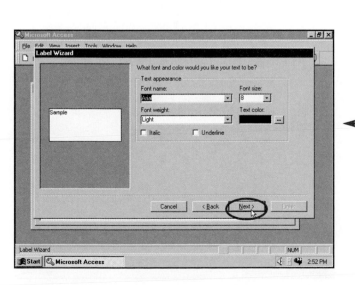

3 Click **Next**. The Label Wizard prompts you for the font and color you would like for the text in your mailing labels. For these labels, use the screen defaults.

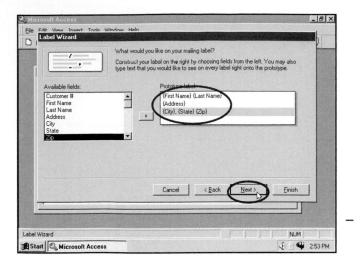

4 Click **Next**. The next dialog box prompts you for the fields you want to include in your mailing labels. Double-click an available field to place the field in the label as shown.

In Depth: Note that you must place spaces and commas where you would want them to appear in your mailing label. To move to a new line, simply press ⏎Enter.

5 Click **Next**. The next Label Wizard dialog box prompts you to select fields you would like to sort by. Double-click the **Zip** field from Available fields to place Zip in the Sort by box.

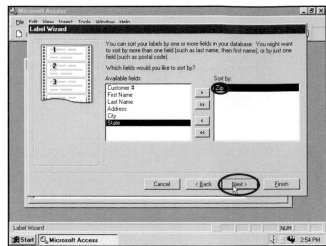

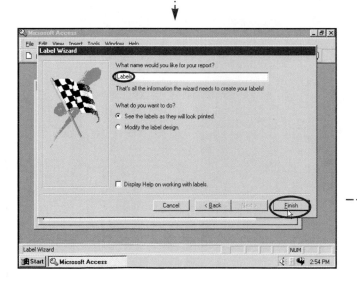

6 Click **Next**. In the last Label Wizard dialog box type **Labels** for the report title.

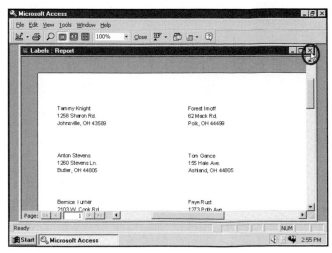

7 Click **Finish**. Access displays your completed labels. To print these labels on label stock, insert the Avery label #5160 mailing label form in your printer and click the Print button. Print the labels now on plain paper by clicking the **Print** button on the toolbar.

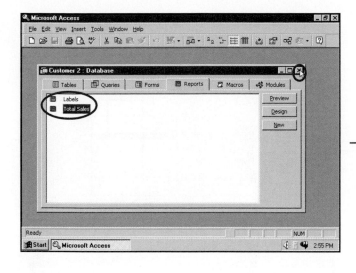

8 Click the report's **Close** box. Note that Access now displays the name of the two reports on the Reports tab.

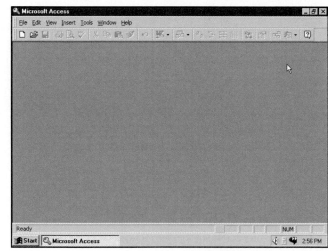

9 Close the database.

Student Exercises

True-False

For each of the following, circle either T or F to indicate whether the statement is true or false.

T   F   **1.** Access's report feature provides a professional way to present information from a database.

T   F   **2.** It is possible to print labels using a variety of fonts.

T   F   **3.** The Report Design view uses a step-by-step approach to guide you through the process of creating a report.

T   F   **4.** Label Wizard places all the fields in a table in a single-column report.

T   F   **5.** Access automatically saves your reports.

T   F   **6.** You can print a report by clicking the Print button.

T   F   **7.** You create a new report by clicking Design.

T   F   **8.** The Label Wizard allows you to choose among three different label sizes.

T   F   **9.** It is possible to print mailing labels with red letters.

T   F   **10.** Report Wizards guide you through the process of creating a report.

Identifying Parts of the Access Screen

Refer to the figure and identify the numbered parts of the screen. Write the letter of the correct label in the space next to the number.

1. _____
2. _____
3. _____
4. _____
5. _____

A. Close box
B. Print button
C. Table used for the report
D. Previously created reports
E. Wizard used to create mailing labels

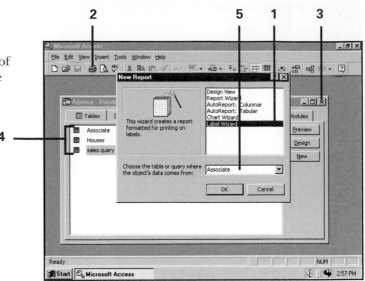

Matching

Match the statements below to the word or phrase that is the best match from the list. Write the letter of the matching word or phrase in the space provided next to the number.

1. ___ Helps create mailing labels
2. ___ Button used to move to the next screen while using a wizard
3. ___ Helps create reports
4. ___ Button used to complete a wizard
5. ___ Button used to create a new report
6. ___ The view that consists of sections showing report information

A. Report Wizard
B. Design View
C. Label Wizard
D. New
E. Next
F. Report Design view
G. Finish

Application Exercises

Exercise 1

1. Open the **Agency** database you worked with in Lesson 12. Use the query called **Associate Sales** that you created in Lesson 12 to create a report. Group the records by Regional Office. Sort by Last Name and Price. Use the title **Associate Sales**.

2. Modify the report as necessary to make it attractive. Print the report. Close the report.

Exercise 2

A client is interested in houses priced between $100,000 and $150,000 in Ashland. The house must have a garage. Create a query named **Ashland Houses** to find the possibilities and then create a report that can be sent to the client to show properties that meet the criteria. Include the name and phone number of the listing agent. Title the report **Ashland Houses**. Modify the report as necessary and print. Close the report. Close the database.

Exercise 3

1. Open the **Tree Farm** database you worked with in Lesson 12. Create a report from the **Tree** table to show current stock. Use the Vendor #, Stock #, Common Name, Wholesale Price, and current Stock fields. Group by Vendor #. Sort by Stock #. Sum the Current Stock field. Title the report **Current Stock**.

2. Modify the report and print it.

3. Create labels to send copies of the report to all of Tree Farm's wholesale suppliers. Print the labels on plain paper.

Exercise 4

1. You want to know the worth of your total inventory of flowering trees, and how much you owe each of your flowering tree suppliers. Open the **Flowering** query you created in Lesson 12 and save it as **Flowering Inventory**.

2. Delete the Vendor # field from the design grid. Specify that the Flowering field not show in the query results. Add the Wholesale Price field and move it to the left of the Current Stock field by clicking at the top of the field to select it and then dragging it to the left.

3. In the next blank field box, type the following **Total Inventory: [Wholesale Price]*[Current Stock]**. Save changes to the query and close it.

4. Create a report using the **Flowering Inventory** query. Group the report by Company Name and sort by Common Name. Sum the Total Inventory field. Title the report **Flowering Tree Inventory**.

5. Modify the report as necessary. If your sum numbers do not show currency formatting, right-click the sum object in Report Design view. Click **Properties** on the shortcut menu. In the Properties box that opens, click the **Format** drop-down arrow and scroll to find the **Currency** format. Then close the Properties box. Print the report. Close the report and the database.

Exercise 5

The Eagle Corporation.

As the inventory manager of Eagle Corporation, it is your responsibility to provide reports from the inventory database you created in Lesson 11. Your supervisor would like the following:

1. Create a report listing the wholesaler name, item, wholesale price, retail price, and quantity on hand. Create a query with the fields before you create the report.

2. Create mailing labels for all the wholesalers.

Lesson 14
Integrating Access, Excel, and Word

Task 1 Copying an Access Query

Task 2 Pasting Access Data in Excel

Task 3 Creating an Excel Chart

Task 4 Inserting an Excel Chart in a Word Document

Task 5 Using Mail Merge

Introduction

This lesson shows you how to use three Office 97 applications to create a document. As you will see, information stored in any one of the applications you have learned so far can be used in other applications to help you deliver a specific message. In this lesson, you will copy an Access database to an Excel worksheet. The data will be used to create a chart. The chart will then be placed in a Word document. You will use mail merge to "send" the document to a list of names stored in an Access database.

This lesson is designed to help you become comfortable using Word, Excel, and Access to create integrated documents.

Visual Summary

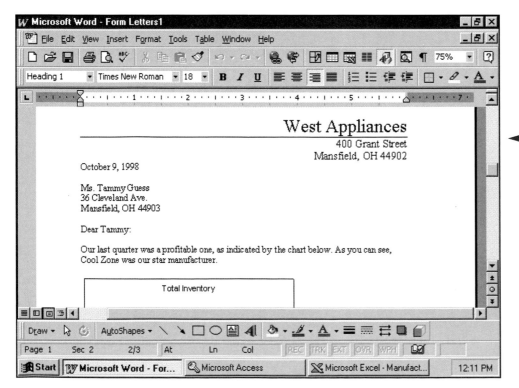

When you have completed Task 4, you will have created a document that looks like this:

Task 1

Copying an Access Query

Why would I do this?

A query you created in the Customer 2 database in the last lesson displays data that would be useful to sales associates of the company. To retrieve the data, you need to open the Access query. You can then copy the query results. This data will be pasted into Excel in the next task.

In this task, you learn how to copy data from a query to the Clipboard.

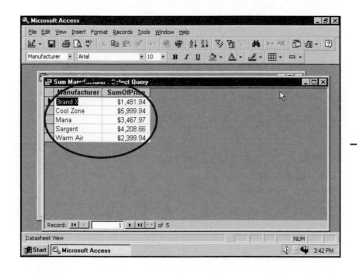

1 Start Access and open the **Customer 2** database you worked with in Lesson 13. Click the **Queries** tab. Select the **Sum Manufacturer** query. Click **Open** to run the query.

Minimize
button

2 The query results table displays on your screen. Select the entire query by dragging the pointer down the record selection row. Click **Copy** to copy the query to the Clipboard.

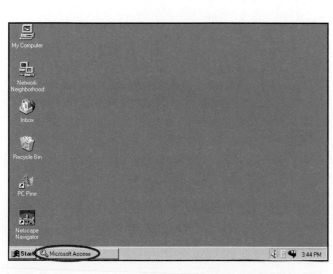

3 Click the application **Minimize** button to reduce Access to a button on the taskbar. Access is reduced to a button on the taskbar.

Task 2

Pasting Access Data in Excel

Why would I do this?

Once you have copied the Access data to the Clipboard, you can paste it in another application in the same way you would paste information from within that application. Office 97 automates the transfer of information so that the pasted data takes on the characteristics of other data in the destination application. Thus, when you paste the data from Access into Excel, it becomes worksheet data.

In this task, you learn how to paste data from Access into Excel.

1 Start Excel. To paste the data you copied to the Clipboard, click the **Paste** button on the toolbar. The Access data appears properly separated into worksheet cells.

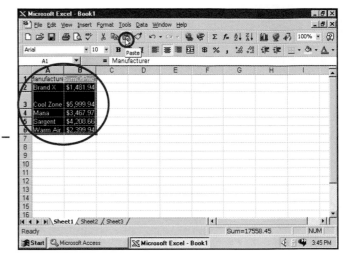

2 Increase the width of column A. Change the column header for column B to **Total Inventory**. Wrap the new heading. (Select **Format, Cells** then **Alignment**.)

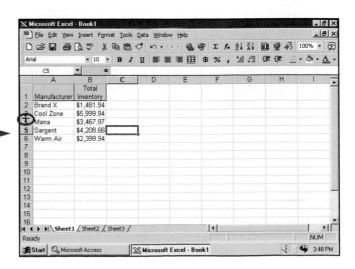

3 Adjust the height of row 3 if necessary to match the heights of other rows by double-clicking at the bottom of the row header (the line below the number 3).

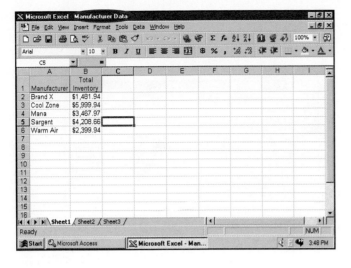

4 Save the worksheet as **Manufacturer Data**.

Task 3

Creating an Excel Chart

Why would I do this?

Now that you have transferred the Access data to Excel, you can use the data to create a chart. Using both applications in this way saves time. If you had not copied the data from Access, you would have had to enter it directly in Excel.

In this lesson, you learn how to create a chart from the Access data you pasted into Excel.

1 Select all data in the worksheet and click the **Chart Wizard** button. The **Chart Wizard Step 1 of 4** dialog box opens.

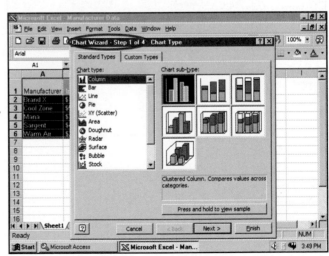

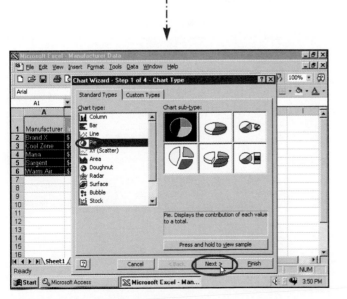

2 To create a pie chart of the selected data, click the **Pie** option. Accept the default chart sub-type.

3 Click **Next** twice. The **Step 3 of 4** dialog box opens. Click the **Data Labels** tab. Select the **Show value** option.

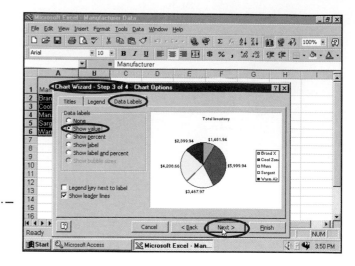

4 Click **Next** to move to the last **Chart Wizard** dialog box. To accept the default options, click **Finish**. Excel displays the chart on the current worksheet.

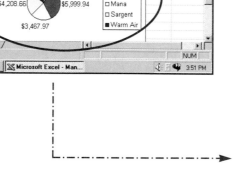

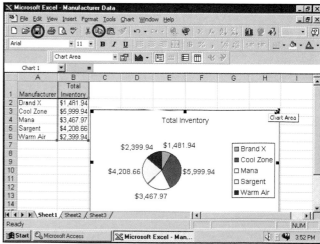

5 Increase the size of the chart and adjust label size so that all data labels display properly.

6 With the chart still selected, click the **Copy** button to place a copy of the chart on the Clipboard. Save your changes and minimize Excel to a button on the taskbar.

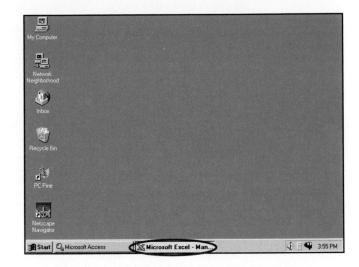

Task 4

Inserting an Excel Chart in a Word Document

Why would I do this?

You are now ready to insert the chart in a Word document, thus completing the conversion of an Access query into a graphic object in a Word document.

In this task, you learn how to insert an Excel chart in a Word document.

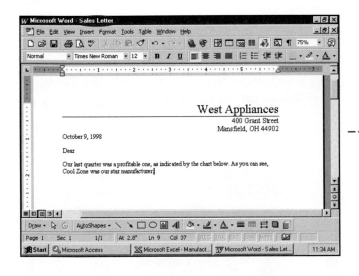

1 Start Microsoft Word. Create the letterhead as shown. Insert the date and the remaining information in the letter. Save the letter as **Sales Letter**.

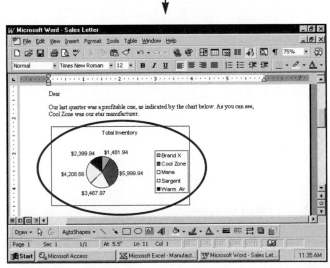

2 With the insertion point at the end of the second sentence, press ↵Enter twice. Click the **Paste** button to place the contents of the Clipboard in your Word document. The contents of the Clipboard are placed in your Word document. Save your changes.

Task 5

Using Mail Merge

Why would I do this?

Mail merge is a feature that allows you to insert data from a data source such as a database into a form letter to create personalized letters. Office 97 allows you to control the merge process from either Word or Access to create form letters.

In this task, you learn how to merge data from an Access database into a Word document.

1 First you must create the database table you will use for the mail merge. Switch to Access and create a new table named **Associates**. You do not need to define a primary key for the table. Insert the fields and data as shown in the figure.

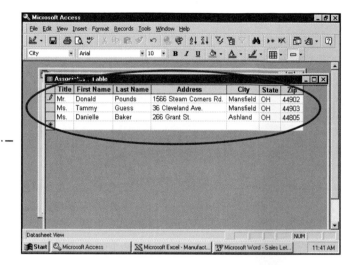

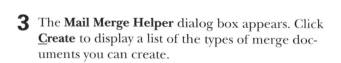

2 Now you need to set up your Word document as a form letter. Switch to Word and click **Tools, Mail Merge** on the menu bar.

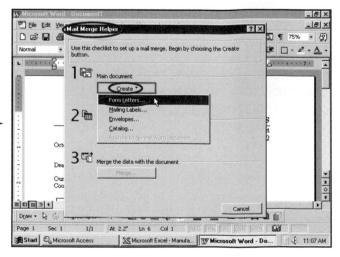

3 The **Mail Merge Helper** dialog box appears. Click **Create** to display a list of the types of merge documents you can create.

4 Click **Form Letters**. Word displays a message box asking if you want to use the current active document for your form letter or start a new main document.

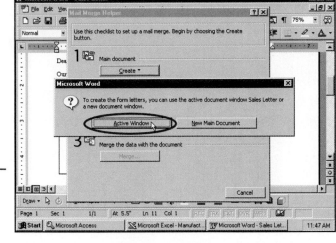

5 Click **Active Window**. Word returns you to the Mail Merge Helper dialog box. You must now locate the data source you will use for the merge. Click **Get Data** to display a list of data sources.

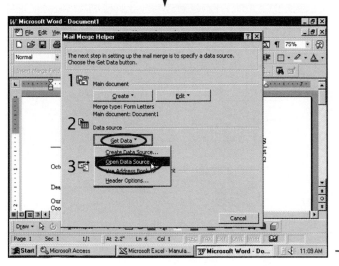

In Depth: Notice on the Get Data drop-down list that you can create a data source in Word or open a data source from Word or another application. If you have names and addresses stored in an Address Book, you can access them from this list to merge into your main document.

6 Click **Open Data Source**. The **Open Data Source** dialog box opens. Click the **Files of type** drop-down list at the bottom of the dialog box and click **MS Access Databases**. Use the **Look in** drop-down list box to locate and select the **Customer 2** database.

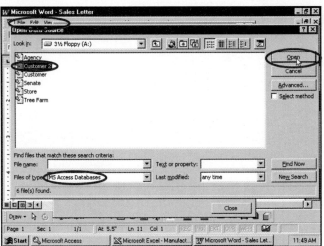

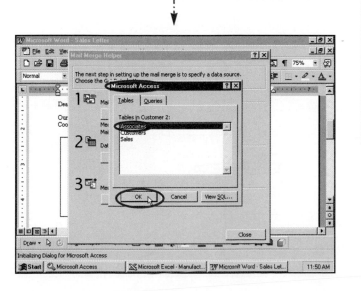

7 Click **Open**. The **Microsoft Access** dialog box opens. Here you can select the table or query you want to use for your merge data. Click **Associates**.

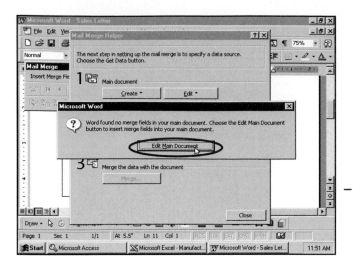

8 Click **OK**. Word displays a message box indicating that you do not have any merge fields in your main document (the form letter Sales Letter).

9 Click **Edit Main Document**. Word returns you to the form letter and displays the Mail Merge toolbar to help you insert merge fields in your document.

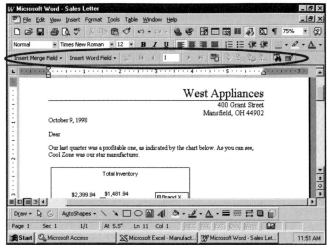

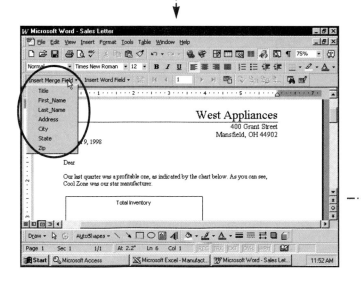

10 Position the insertion point on the second blank line below the date. To insert the first merge field, click the **Insert Merge Field** button on the Mail Merge toolbar. A list of available merge fields displays.

11 Click the **Title** merge field to insert it in the letter. Press the spacebar once and then insert the **First_Name** field. Press the spacebar once and insert the **Last_Name** field. Press ⏎Enter to move to the next line.

12 Insert the remaining merge fields as shown. Don't forget to insert the colon after the First_Name field in the salutation.

Merge to New
Document button

13 Your main document is now ready for the merge. You can merge directly to the printer to print your form letters, or you can merge to a new document that contains all the merged form letters. Locate the **Merge to New Document** button on the Mail Merge toolbar.

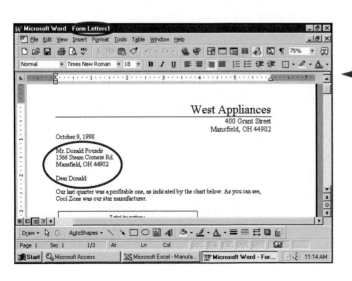

14 Click the **Merge to New Document** button. Word merges the form letter with the Access data and opens a new document named **Form Letters1** containing the merged data. Scroll down in the document to see all three letters. Then return to the first letter.

15 To print only the first letter in the document, click **File, Print** on the menu bar. In the **Print** dialog box, click the **Current page** option, then **OK**. Close the document without saving.

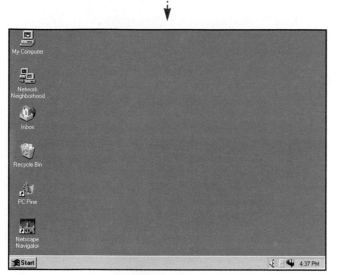

16 Save changes to the **Sales Letter** document and close it. Close all other open applications and save changes if prompted.

Student Exercises

True-False

For each of the following, circle either T or F to indicate whether the statement is true or false.

T F **1.** When an application is minimized it is placed on the taskbar at the bottom of the screen.

T F **2.** You must first close an application before you can open another application.

T F **3.** Open applications are displayed on the menu bar.

T F **4.** When you paste data from one application to another, the data form adjusts so you can edit it in the destination application.

T F **5.** Mail Merge allows you to take names and addresses and merge them with a form letter.

T F **6.** Before information can be transferred from one application to another, it must be pasted to the Clipboard.

T F **7.** You can save up to four different items on the clipboard.

T F **8.** The Mail Merge Helper steps you through the process of creating mail merge applications.

T F **9.** When integrating information it is best if all files are saved together.

T F **10.** Paste and Paste Special both take information from the Clipboard and place it in an application.

Identifying Parts of the Integration Screen

Refer to the figure and identify the numbered parts of the screen. Write the letter of the correct label in the space next to the number.

1. _____
2. _____
3. _____
4. _____
5. _____

A. Mail Merge toolbar

B. Menu to start Mail Merge

C. Button used to add merge fields to the form letter

D. Fields used to determine location for mail merge records

E. Merge to New Document button

Matching

Match the statements below to the word or phrase that is the best match from the list. Write the letter of the matching word or phrase in the space provided next to the number.

1. ___ Button used to move information from the Clipboard to an application

2. ___ Button used to reduce an application to a button

3. ___ To transfer an Excel worksheet to a Word document

4. ___ Button used to move information to the Clipboard

5. ___ Area where all open applications are shown as buttons

6. ___ Button used to begin the four-step chart creation in Excel

7. ___ Button used to add a merge field to a Word document

8. ___ Button used to bring together the data records with the form letter

A. Minimize

B. Taskbar

C. Paste

D. Chart Wizard

E. Copy

F. Insert Merge Field

G. Merge to New Document

H. Integrate

I. Design view

Application Exercises

Exercise 1

1. Open the **Agency** database you worked with in Lesson 13. Open the **Houses** table. Use a filter to display only the houses located in Ashland or Butler. (**Hint:** Type <u>Ashland</u> in the Criteria box, then type <u>Butler</u> in the Or box.) Sort the records by City. Select the displayed records and copy them to the Clipboard.

2. Open Excel. Paste the copied records using the **Paste Special** command. Specify that the records paste as **Text**.

3. Adjust column widths to display all data. Format the Price column for currency with dollar signs and no decimal places. Format the Sq Footage field with commas but no decimal places. Delete the Sales Assoc column.

4. Insert two new rows below the section of data for the Ashland office. In the first blank row, create a formula to total the Price column for the Ashland houses. In the second blank row, use a function to determine the average price of the Ashland houses.

5. Total and average the Butler prices in the same way. Create a grand total to add together the Ashland and Butler totals.

6. Format the worksheet as desired. Select the cells containing data and copy the range to the Clipboard. Save the worksheet as <u>**Homes**</u>.

7. Open Word and write a short memo to the sales agents stating that you are sending a listing of the homes for Ashland and Butler.

8. Use **Paste Special** to paste the worksheet data as a Microsoft Excel Worksheet Object.

9. Save the document as <u>**Agency Integration**</u>. Print the document. Close the document. Close all other open documents.

Exercise 2

1. In Word, create the document shown in the figure.

2. In the **Agency** database, open the **Price Range** query. Copy the records in the query results table.

3. Paste the data in the letter, two lines below the first paragraph.

4. Below the pasted data, type <u>**Thank you for calling the Patterson Real Estate Agency**</u>.

5. Save the letter as <u>**Price Query**</u>. Print the letter. Close the document and the database.

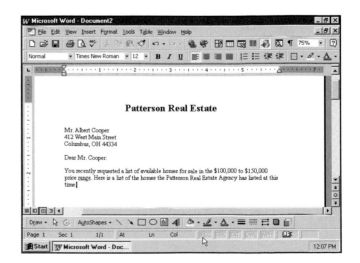

Exercise 3 *Do not Do*

1. In Word, create a form letter to be sent to the vendors for the Tree Farm. Thank the vendors for their support over the last year. (**Hint:** You might want to use the Tree Farm letterhead you worked with in Lesson 10 for this form letter.)

2. Date the letter January 6, 1999. Save the letter as **Tree 5**.

3. Use the mail merge feature to insert merge fields in the form letter. Use the company name, address, city, state, and zip in the inside address. Use the contact name in the salutation.

4. Merge the letters to a new document and print the first two. Close the document without saving.

5. Save changes to **Tree 5** and close it.

Exercise 4

The Eagle Corporation.

1. Open the database you created for Eagle Corporation in Lesson 11. Open Excel and Word to perform the following tasks.

2. Activate Access and open the inventory table.

3. Highlight all records and copy them to the Clipboard.

4. Activate Excel and Paste Special as Text.

5. Change the width of columns if necessary.

6. Add a formula or chart to make a point or clarify data.

7. Highlight cells and copy to the Clipboard.

8. Activate Word.

9. Write a short memo to your supervisor stating that you are sending the listing that was requested.

10. Paste Special as a Microsoft Excel Worksheet Object.

11. Save the document as **Eagle Integration**.

12. Print the document.

Lesson 15
Creating a Slide Show with PowerPoint 97

Introduction

A *presentation* is any communication you make to a group of other people. A presentation graphics program such as Microsoft PowerPoint 97 is designed to help you prepare materials such as slides, overheads, and handouts to use during a presentation. A series of slides you prepare to use during a presentation is called a *slide show*. Slide shows are made up of any number of *slides*. Slides in a slide show can convey different kinds of information to your audience. For example, your slides can present bulleted lists of information, tables, and charts. You can also add clip art images and drawing objects to slides to emphasize key points.

This lesson is designed to provide you with the basic skills you need to create a number of different slides for a presentation.

Visual Summary

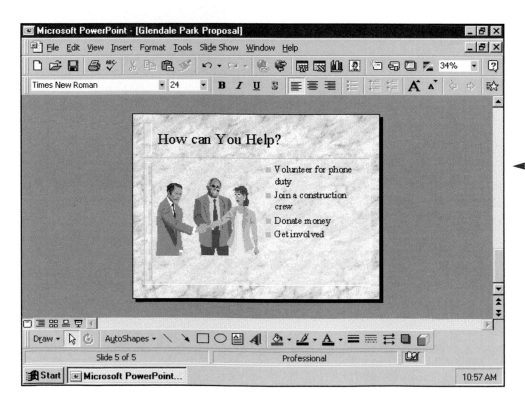

When you have completed Task 7, you will have created a slide show containing five slides. The last slide of the slide show looks like this:

Task 1

Launching PowerPoint 97 and Starting a Slide Show

Why would I do this?

Launching PowerPoint starts the PowerPoint application so that you can begin creating a slide show. As soon as you launch the program, PowerPoint requires you to make several decisions about your new slide show.

In this task, you learn how to launch PowerPoint and start a new slide show.

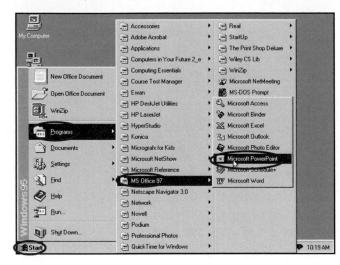

1 To start PowerPoint, click the **Start** button, click **Programs, MS Office 97,** and **Microsoft Power-Point**.

2 The **PowerPoint** dialog box opens to give you a choice of tasks. You can create a slide show using the AutoContent Wizard, use a template to create a slide show, start a new slide show from scratch (Blank presentation), or open an existing slide show. To create a slide show, click the **Blank presentation** option button.

In Depth: The AutoContent Wizard helps you to create a slide show by suggesting sample slides for a number of standard topics, such as meeting agendas, status reports, and so on. Templates supply specific slide backgrounds and formatting for a slide show. You will learn more about using a template later in this lesson.

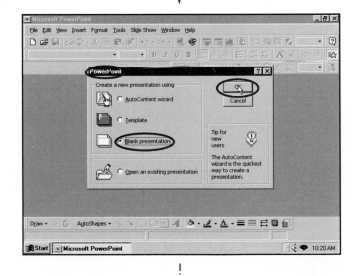

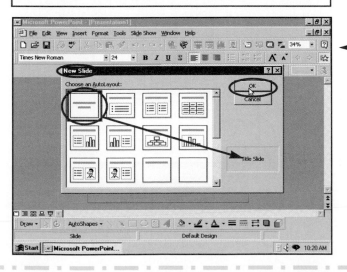

3 Click **OK** to start the new slide show. The **New Slide** dialog box opens. In this dialog box, you can choose what type of layout your first slide will have. PowerPoint offers 24 different slide layouts (you can see only 12 in this dialog box). Slide shows usually begin with a title slide, so PowerPoint selects the Title Slide layout by default. The heavy border around the Title Slide layout indicates it has been selected.

4 Click **OK** to accept the default selection. The first slide of the slide show displays on your screen. Notice the *placeholders* for the title and sub-title.

In Depth: Your PowerPoint screen may or may not contain the Common Task toolbar, depending on your computer's PowerPoint default settings. You can enable or disable this toolbar by using the View menu and Toolbars option feature in PowerPoint. As indicated by its name, the Common Tasks toolbar provides shortcuts to tasks you do repeatedly in PowerPoint.

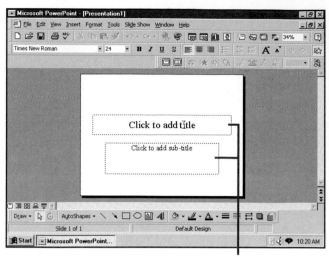

Placeholders

Task 2

Building a Title Slide

Why would I do this?

The Title Slide layout gives you placeholders for a title and sub-title. The title gives your audience important information on your presentation's content. The sub-title can provide additional information or give the name of the person presenting the slide show.

In this task, you learn how to add text to a title slide.

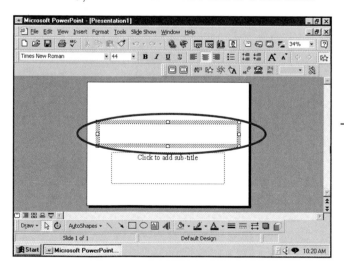

1 Place the pointer inside the title placeholder (labeled *Click to add title*) and click. The placeholder changes to show a hatched border and an insertion point.

2 Type **Glendale Park Proposal**.

In Depth: Notice that PowerPoint specifies a font, font size, and alignment for the text in the title placeholder. The current design template determines the "look" of each slide.

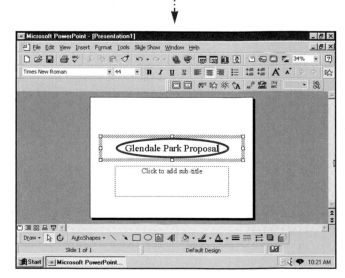

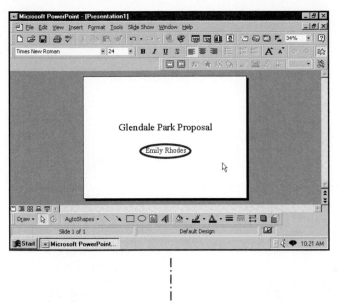

3 Click in the sub-title placeholder to select it. Type your name and then click outside the placeholder.

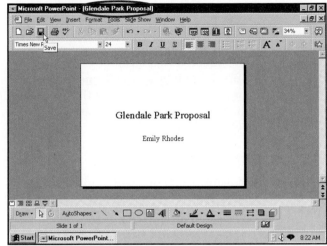

In Depth: Like Microsoft Word, PowerPoint has a built-in spelling checker. If PowerPoint's spelling checker doesn't recognize a word you type in a placeholder, it will mark the word with a wavy red underline. Check your spelling of words marked in this way. To remove the underline, right-click the marked word and click Ignore All on the shortcut menu.

4 Save your new slide show to your disk as **Glendale Park Proposal**.

Task 3
Adding a Bulleted List Slide

Why would I do this?
One of the most frequently used slide layouts is the Bulleted List layout. Bulleted lists help audiences to follow the presenter's points on a step-by-step basis.

In this task, you learn how to add a slide and build a bulleted list on a slide.

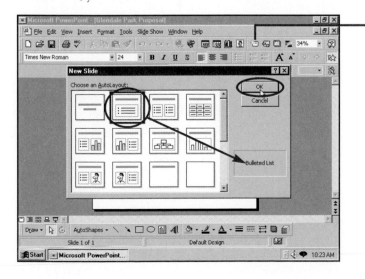

New Slide button

1 To add a slide, click the **New Slide** button on the toolbar. The **New Slide** dialog box opens. Notice that the Bulleted List layout is automatically selected for you.

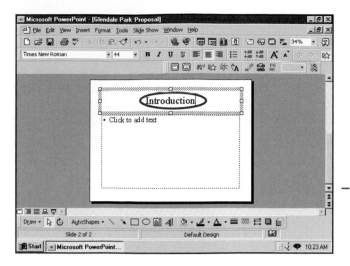

2 Click **OK** to add the Bulleted List slide. Click in the title placeholder and type **Introduction**.

3 Click in the bulleted list placeholder to select it. Type the first item: **Why we need a new park development . . .** Press ⏎Enter to start the next bulleted item. Notice that PowerPoint automatically inserts the bullet symbol for you.

Bullet symbol

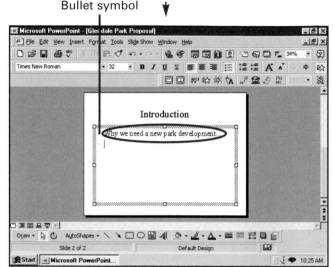

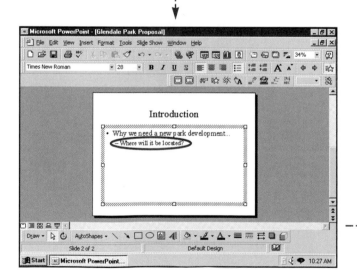

4 To type a subordinate bulleted entry, press Tab↹ to indent the next item. The insertion point moves to the right and PowerPoint displays a new symbol for the subordinate list. Type the entry **Where will it be located?**

5 Type the remaining entries as shown. To return to the main entry level for the last item, press ⏎Enter after the last subordinate entry. Then hold ⇧Shift and press Tab↹ and type the last entry. Save your changes.

In Depth: After you have a few slides in a slide show, you might need to move backward or forward to see a particular slide. Use the scroll bar to navigate among slides in a slide show. When you drag the scroll box, ScreenTips appear with each slide's number and title.

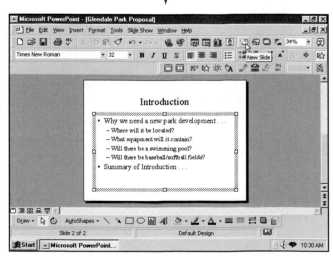

Task 4

Building a Table Slide

Why would I do this?

A table is a good way to show relationships between items of information. Tables can show text, numbers, or a combination of both. When using a table on a slide, you should try to use only a few rows and columns to make sure your presentation is easy to read and understand.

In this task, you learn how to create a table on a slide.

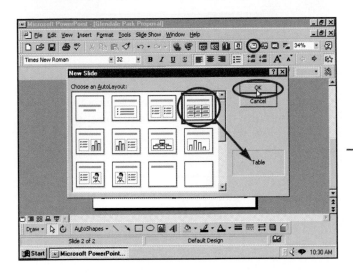

1 First add a slide with the Table layout: click the **New Slide** button on the toolbar. In the **New Slide** dialog box, click the **Table** layout.

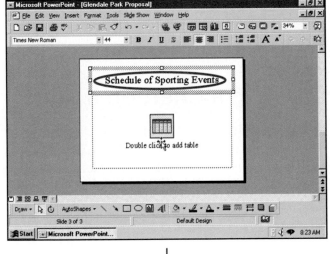

2 Click **OK** to add the slide. Click in the title place-holder and insert the title **Schedule of Sporting Events**.

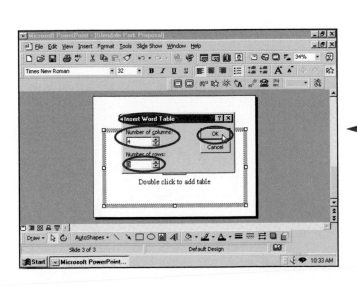

3 Double-click the table placeholder. The **Insert Word Table** dialog box opens. In this dialog box, you choose how many columns and rows your table will have. Change the **Number of columns** field to **4**. Change the **Number of rows** field to **3**.

4 Click **OK**. A table grid displays on the slide, just like a table in Microsoft Word. Type the text in your table as shown using (Tab⇄) to move between cells and to a new line. When you have finished typing the table data, select the heading cells in the table (Spring through Winter).

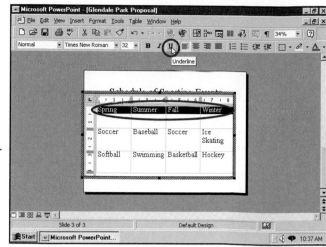

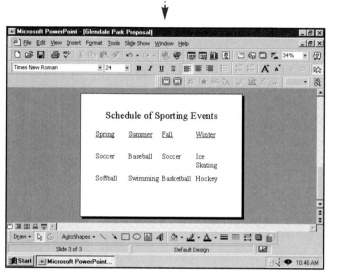

5 Click the **Underline** button on the toolbar. Click outside the table to see the table on the slide. Save your changes.

In Depth: PowerPoint's Table layout actually embeds a Microsoft Word table on your slide. To edit a table, you double-click the table just as you would any embedded object.

Task 5
Creating a Chart on a Slide
Why would I do this?

Charts can help your audience see trends or comparisons of data. PowerPoint contains a sophisticated chart feature that allows you to create many kinds of charts on your slides.

In this task, you learn how to insert a chart on a slide.

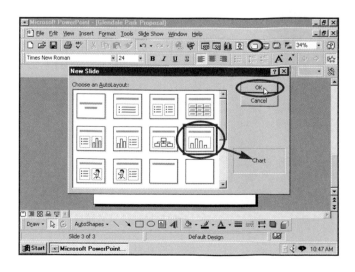

1 Add a slide with the Chart layout: click the **New Slide** button on the toolbar. In the **New Slide** dialog box, click the **Chart** slide layout.

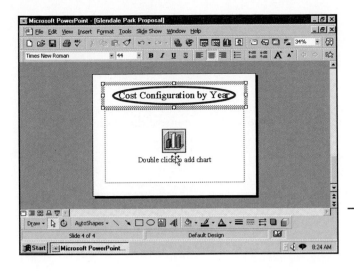

2 Click **OK** to insert the new slide. Type <u>**Cost Con-**</u><u>**figuration by Year**</u> in the title placeholder.

3 Double-click the chart placeholder. PowerPoint displays the *datasheet*, a worksheet-like grid in which you can enter the data to chart. The datasheet currently contains sample information to guide you in adding data. To replace the data, select each cell and type the new data. Use Tab↹ to move from cell to cell. Replace the data in the chart as shown. Notice that PowerPoint plots the new data on the slide as you enter it in the datasheet.

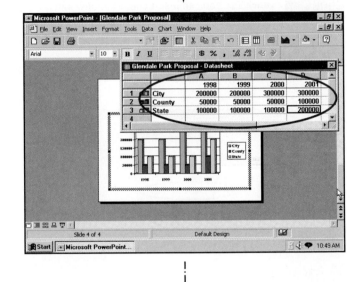

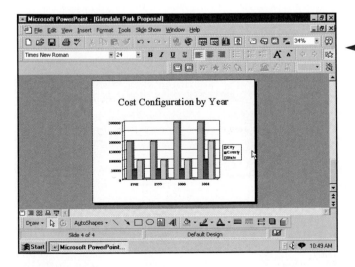

4 Click outside the chart placeholder on the slide to close the datasheet and update the slide. The completed chart is displayed. Save your changes.

Task 6

Inserting a Clip Art Picture on a Slide

Why would I do this?

To add visual effects to your slide, PowerPoint provides a Clip Gallery of hundreds of professionally created images broken down by categories. You can choose among several layouts that automatically control the position of the clip art picture on your slide.

In this task, you learn how to insert a clip art picture on a slide.

1 Add a slide with a layout for a clip art image: click the **New Slide** button on the toolbar. In the **New Slide** dialog box, click the **Clip Art & Text** slide layout.

> **Quick Tip:** You can insert clip art on any slide, even one that does not have a clip art layout, by clicking the Insert Clip Art button on the toolbar.

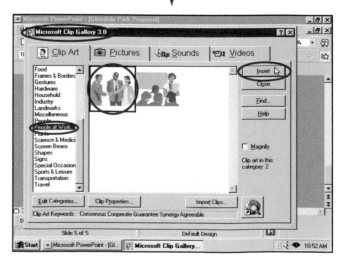

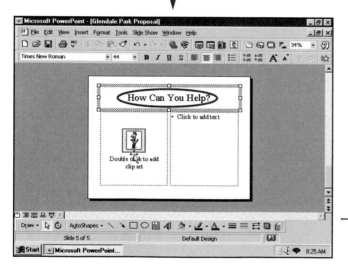

2 Click **OK** to insert the new slide. Type a title in the title placeholder: **How Can You Help?**

3 Double-click the clip art placeholder. The **Microsoft Clip Gallery 3.0** dialog box opens. Click the **People at Work** category to see the clip art pictures available for that category. Use the scroll bar if necessary to locate the picture shown. (You might also find this picture in the People category.) Click the picture to select it.

> **In Depth:** You can resize clip art pictures on slides the same way you did in Word: place the pointer on a selection handle and drag to increase or decrease size. To move a clip art picture on a slide, place the pointer on the picture, hold down the mouse button, and drag the picture.

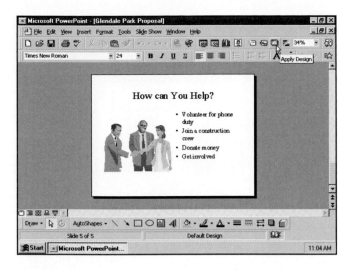

4 Click **Insert** to place the picture in the clip art placeholder on the slide. Add text to the bulleted list placeholder as shown. Click outside the text placeholder. Save your changes.

Task 7
Changing the Design Template

Why would I do this?

So far in this lesson, you have used the default design for your slides. PowerPoint offers many other design templates to choose among. A *design template* controls the background color and pattern of each slide, as well as the text formatting and the colors used for chart elements. Some design templates are very formal in nature, while others are more suitable for casual presentations. When creating a slide show, you must consider how the design template can reinforce your message.

In this task, you learn how to change the design template and see the effect of the new design template on your existing slides.

1 To return to slide 1 in the slide show, drag the scroll box upward to the top of the scroll bar. Slide 1 displays on your screen.

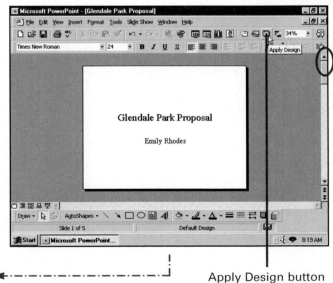

Apply Design button

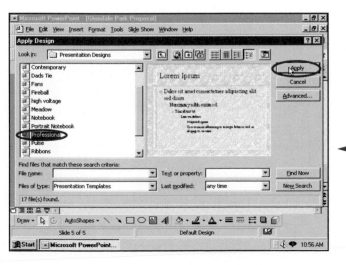

2 Click the **Apply Design** button on the toolbar. The **Apply Design** dialog box opens. The first design is selected by default and a sample of the design is displayed. Click the **Professional** design and see how the sample slide changes.

3 Click the **Apply** button to apply the new design to your slide show. Click the down scroll arrow to see how each slide has changed as a result of the new design template. Save your changes.

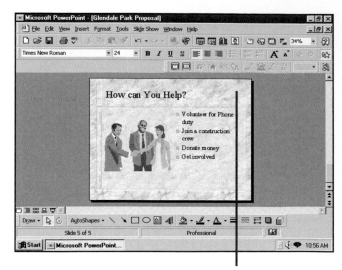

New design
template
in place

Task 8

Running a Slide Show

Why would I do this?

Once you have created your slides, you can run the slides to see what your slide show looks like. When you run the slide show, each slide displays on your screen, taking up the entire screen. After the last slide displays, PowerPoint ends the slide show and returns you to the PowerPoint window.

In this task, you learn how to run a slide show.

Slide Show
button

1 Return to slide 1 if necessary. Locate the **Slide Show** button at the lower left of the slide window.

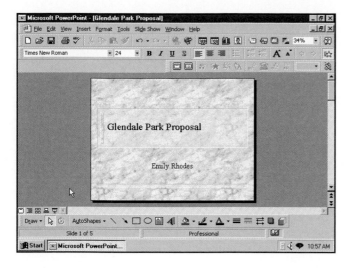

2 Click the **Slide Show** button. Click the left mouse button to view each slide in the slide show. At the end of the slide show, PowerPoint returns you to the PowerPoint window.

> **In Depth:** While running the slide show, click the left mouse button to advance to a new slide. To go back to the previous slide, press (PgUp) or click the right mouse button and click **Previous**.

Task 9

Printing Slides

Why would I do this?

Although slides are chiefly meant to be viewed on a screen, you can also print copies of the slides for your own records or to hand out to your audience. PowerPoint offers you a number of options for printing slides.

In this task, you learn how to print the slides of your slide show as handouts.

1 Click **File, Print** on the menu bar.

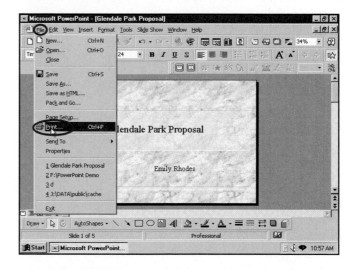

2 The **Print** dialog box opens. To choose a printing option, click the **Print what** down arrow. Click the **Handouts (6 slides per page)** option.

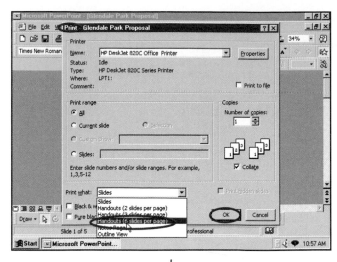

In Depth: Handouts are pages that contain small representations of the slides in your slide show. You can supply these to your audience or use them as file copies of the slides in the slide show. To print one slide at a time, choose the Slides option. If you are printing to a color printer and want color output, do not select the Pure black & white option. This feature is good if you want a hard copy of your output but it does not need to be in color, or if you are printing to a laser printer.

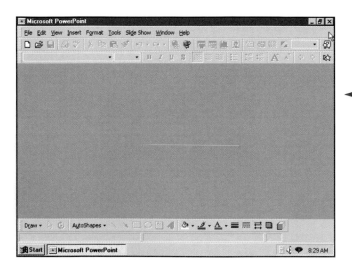

3 Click **OK** to print the slides. Save your changes. Close the slide show by clicking its **Close** box.

Student Exercises

True-False

For each of the following, circle either T or F to indicate whether the statement is true or false.

T   F   **1.** By default, PowerPoint selects a Bulleted List layout as the first slide in a slide show.

T   F   **2.** Adding clip art to a slide show allows the presenter to draw on the screen during the presentation.

T   F   **3.** To add text to a slide, click in a placeholder and begin typing.

T   F   **4.** Subordinate bulleted lists frequently have different bullet symbols.

T   F   **5.** A table in a slide can be used to show text, numbers, or a combination of both.

T   F   **6.** When you create a table in a slide, you are really embedding an Access object on the slide.

T   F   **7.** While running a slide show, you can advance to the next slide by clicking the left mouse button.

T   F   **8.** Clicking the right mouse button automatically takes you to the previous slide.

T   F   **9.** Design templates suggest sample slides for a number of standard topics.

T   F   **10.** You can print up to six slides per page using the Slides print option.

Identifying Parts of the PowerPoint Screen

Refer to the figure and identify the numbered parts of the screen. Write the letter of the correct label in the space next to the number.

1. _D_
2. _C_
3. _E_
4. _B_
5. _A_
6. _F_
7. _G_

A. New Slide button
B. Bulleted List layout
C. Table layout
D. Chart layout
E. Title Slide layout
F. Apply Design button
G. Slide Show button

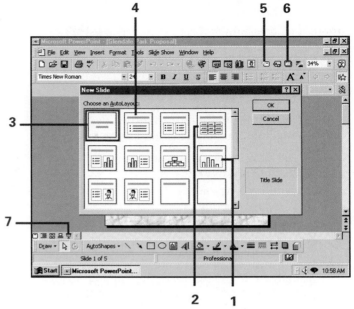

Matching

Match the statements below to the word or phrase that is the best match from the list. Write the letter of the matching word or phrase in the space provided next to the number.

1. _I_ Controls the background and text formats of slides

2. _C_ Object you click on a slide to insert text, a table, or a chart

3. _J_ Slide layout used to present a list of text

4. _A_ Slide layout used to present a picture along with text

5. _B_ Grid in which you type information to create a chart

6. _D_ Moves to the next slide during a presentation

7. _E_ Normally the first slide of a presentation

8. _F_ Button used to add a slide

9. _H_ Key to press to start a subordinate bullet list

10. _G_ Print option to print small representations of slides

A. Clip Art & Text
B. Datasheet
C. Placeholder
D. Left click
E. Title Slide
F. New Slide
G. Handouts
H. Tab
I. Design template
J. Bulleted List
K. Enter

Application Exercises

Exercise 1

1. Start a new slide show and select the **Title Slide** layout. Save your slide show as **Ajax Presentation**.

2. Create a title slide with the title **Ajax University** and your name as the subtitle.

3. Create a bulleted list slide with the title **Features**. Use the following information for the bulleted list:

    NCAA Division II - all sports
    Affordable housing
    Day and evening classes
    15:1 student/faculty ratio
    42 major programs/22 minor programs
    85% of faculty Ph.D.s

4. Create another bulleted list slide with the title **Athletics**. Use the following information to create a bulleted list with main and subordinate entries:

    Football
        60% of players on scholarship
    Baseball
        National ranking in 1996, 1997, 1998
    Soccer
        New program beginning in 1998
    Basketball
        NCAA national runner-up in 1996

5. Create a chart slide with the title **Financial Aid**. Use the following figures in the datasheet:

	1994	1995	1996	1997
No aid	10	10	8	12
30-50% aid	55	60	62	55
Over 50% aid	35	30	30	37

6. Create a Text & Clip Art slide with the title **Environment**. Insert a clip art picture of your choice appropriate to an academic setting. Use the following text for the bulleted list:

    Beautiful 55-acre campus
    New football stadium under construction
    Attractive new student housing
    New student center
    Renovated library

7. Insert a slide with the **Title Only** layout and insert the title **Earn Your Degree at Ajax**. Click the **Insert Clip Art** button on the toolbar and locate the Diploma picture in the **Special Occasions** category (or any other picture appropriate to the slide). Resize the clip art picture as desired and move it if necessary to center it on the slide.

8. Apply the **Notebook** design template. Run the slide show. Save your changes.

9. Print handouts of the slide show, six slides per page and in pure black and white. Close the slide show.

Exercise 2

1. Start a new slide show and select the **Title Slide** layout. Name the slide show **Creative Computers**. Apply the **Contemporary Portrait** design template.

2. On the title slide, insert the title **Contemporary Computers** and the sub-title **Serving All Your Electronic Needs**.

3. Add a bulleted list slide with the title **New Items This Year**. Use the following information for the bulleted list:

   Scanners
   Cellular Phones
   Pagers
   Internet Consulting

4. Add another bulleted list slide with the title **Creative Computers**. Use the following information for the bulleted list:

   For more information:
   Phone: 1-800-555-1234
   Fax: 1-800-555-1244
   E-mail: createcomp@ix.net
   Visit our new Web site at:
   http://www.createcomp.com

5. Insert a clip art picture that relates to one of these forms of communication anywhere on the slide.

6. Add a table slide with the title **Cellular Phones**. Insert the following table data:

Model	Model 836	Model 957
Color	Ivory/Brown	Ivory/Black
Features	.3 Watts	.6 Watts
Price	$147.95	$174.80

7. Save your changes. Run the slide show.

8. Print handouts of the slide show, six slides per page and in pure black and white. Close the slide show.

Exercise 3

Create a PowerPoint slide show on a topic of your choice. The slide show should contain a minimum of six slides using a variety of layouts.

Exercise 4

The Eagle Corporation.

As corporate vice president of Eagle Corporation, you have been asked by the President to prepare a presentation to the board regarding the purchase of Discovery Corporation.

Discovery Corporation is a small (30 employees) manufacturer of specialized wood office furniture products, such as magazine racks, file cabinets, and bookcases. The company is located within 30 miles of your facility and has been in business for over 40 years. The company has a reputation as being a leader in the manufacture of high-quality wood office furniture products. Discovery specializes in oak, maple, cherry, and walnut wood finishes.

Prepare a five-slide presentation that will convince the board that Eagle Corporation should purchase Discovery Corporation.

Lesson 16
Additional PowerPoint Features

Task 1 Changing Text Formats

Task 2 Working in Slide Sorter View

Task 3 Using Slide Transitions

Task 4 Creating Animation and Sound Effects

Introduction

Now that you can create a PowerPoint presentation, you are ready to look at ways to enhance the slides you have created. By using powerful features available in PowerPoint and applying those features to your slides, you can create professional-looking slides.

This lesson is designed to introduce you to additional features in PowerPoint that allow you to enhance slide appearance, reorganize slides in the slide show, and control appearance of the slides during a slide show.

Visual Summary

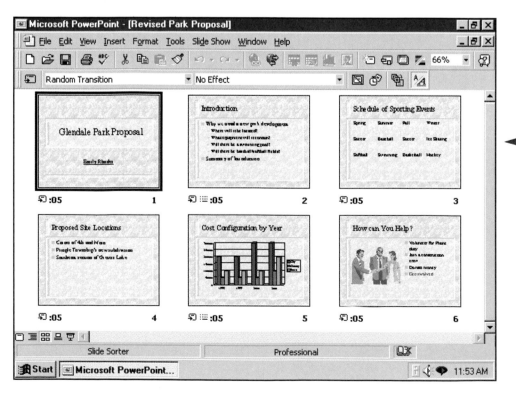

When you have completed Task 4, your slide show will look like this in Slide Sorter view:

Task 1

Changing Text Formats

Why would I do this?

As you have learned, PowerPoint's design templates control not only the background of the slide, but also the font, font size, style, color, and alignment of text in the placeholders on each slide. You can, however, easily change any of these formats to make information within a slide stand out. Formatting options are helpful when you want to drive home an important point.

In this task, you learn how to change default text formatting and alignment.

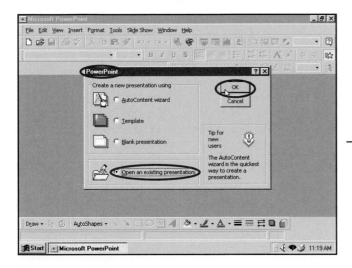

1 Start Microsoft PowerPoint. The **PowerPoint** dialog box opens. Click **Open an existing presentation**.

2 Click **OK**. The **Open** dialog box opens. Locate the file **Glendale Park Proposal** on your disk and click to select it.

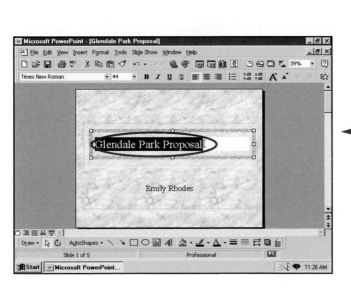

3 Click **Open** to open the slide show. To change the size of the title on slide 1, click the title placeholder and select all the text within the placeholder by dragging the I-beam pointer across the text.

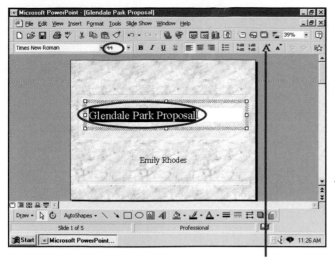

4 Click the **Increase Font Size** button on the toolbar twice to increase the size of the text to 54 point.

Increase Font Size button

5 To change the alignment of the title, click once again in the title placeholder. Click the **Center Alignment** button on the toolbar.

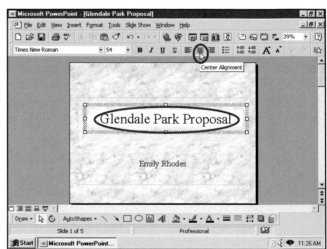

6 To change the style of the sub-title, click in the sub-title placeholder, select both first and last name, and click the **Underline** button on the toolbar.

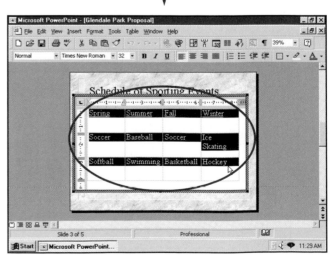

7 Advance to slide 3. The table on this slide would look better if the text were not so crowded. Double-click the table to open its source application. Drag the pointer to select all cells in the table.

8 Click the **Font Size** drop-down arrow to display available font sizes. Click **24**. Click outside the table to update the table on the slide.

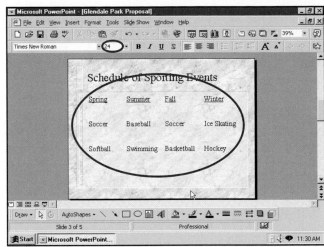

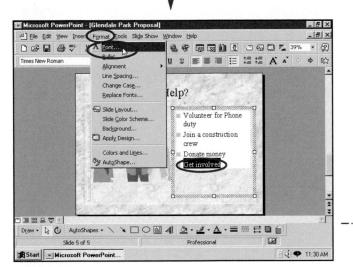

9 Advance to slide 5. To emphasize the last bullet item in the bulleted list, click the bulleted list placeholder and select the words of the last bulleted item. Click **Format, Font** on the menu bar.

10 The **Font** dialog box opens. Click the **Color** drop-down arrow to display a palette of colors selected for the current design template.

In Depth: You can use colors not in the color scheme by clicking the More Colors selection and then selecting a color from the palette on the Colors dialog box. The current design template determines colors for fonts and other elements of the slides. Each design template has a palette of eight complementary colors selected to work well together.

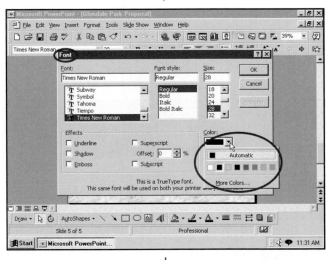

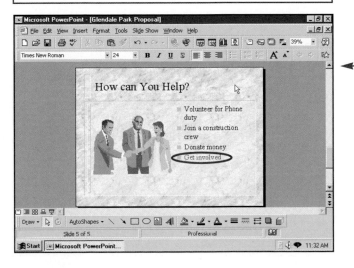

11 Click the purple color on the palette and click **OK**. Click outside the placeholder to see the new color applied to the text.

12 Save the slide show as **Revised Park Proposal**.

Task 2

Working in Slide Sorter View

Why would I do this?

So far in your study of PowerPoint, you have worked exclusively in Slide view. Slide view is used when you are creating and modifying slides. PowerPoint offers several other views, however, that can help you work with your slide show. Slide Sorter view is one of the most useful. In Slide Sorter view, you can easily reorganize a slide show and add additional slides to the show.

In this task, you learn how to use Slide Sorter view to add slides and organize a slide show.

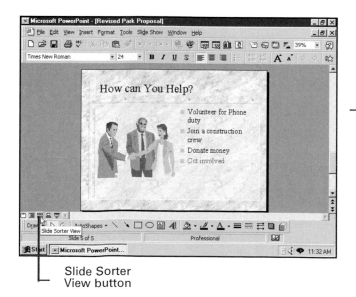

Slide Sorter
View button

2 Click the **Slide Sorter View** button. PowerPoint displays all the slides in the slide show as thumbnails (small representations of the slides). The active slide is surrounded by a heavy dark border.

1 Locate the **Slide Sorter View** button at the lower left of the slide window.

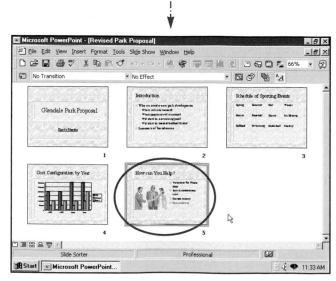

3 To insert a new slide after slide 2 and before slide 3, click inside slide 2 to select it. Click the **New Slide** button on the toolbar. Click the **Bulleted List** layout. PowerPoint automatically inserts the new slide 3.

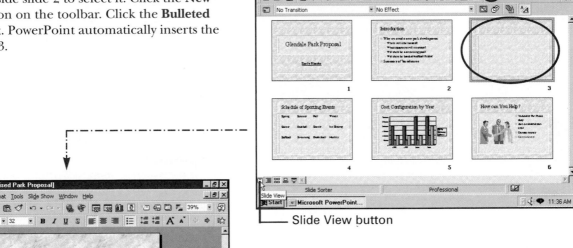

Slide View button

4 To add text to the slide, you must be in Slide view. Click the **Slide View** button at the lower left of the slide window. On the blank slide, type the title **Proposed Site Locations**. Type the three bulleted text items as shown.

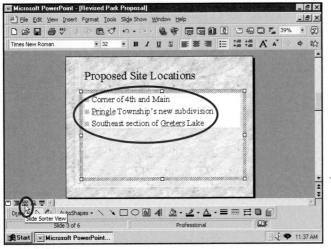

5 Switch back to Slide Sorter view. The new bulleted slide is now shown as slide 3.

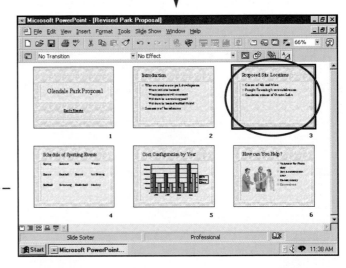

6 You realize that your new slide is not where you want it to be in the slide show. You can easily move it by dragging. Select slide 3, hold down the mouse button, and drag the slide downward and to the left. PowerPoint displays a vertical gray line between slides to indicate where you can move the selected slide. Drag until you see the vertical gray line displayed between slides 4 and 5.

7 Release the mouse button. Notice that slides 3 and 4 have traded places. Save your changes.

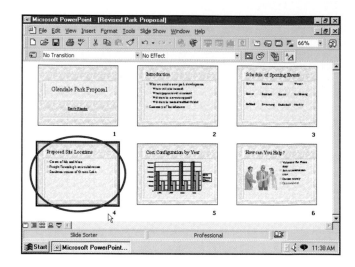

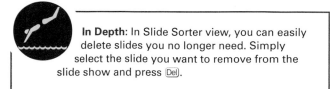

In Depth: In Slide Sorter view, you can easily delete slides you no longer need. Simply select the slide you want to remove from the slide show and press [Del].

Task 3

Using Slide Transitions

Why would I do this?

When you ran slide shows in the previous lesson, you used the left mouse button to advance from slide to slide. Each slide appeared on the screen as soon as you clicked the mouse button. You can make the process of displaying slides in the slide show more interesting using PowerPoint's many slide transition effects. A slide transition controls the way a slide displays as you advance through the slide show. For example, one transition effect causes the next slide in the slide show to drop down from the top of the screen. Another transition causes a new slide to fly in from the left of the screen. Slide transitions also control how you advance slides. You can choose to use the mouse to advance from slide to slide, or select a timing option to have PowerPoint display the slides automatically for you after a specified delay time.

In this task, you learn how to apply slide transition effects to your slide show.

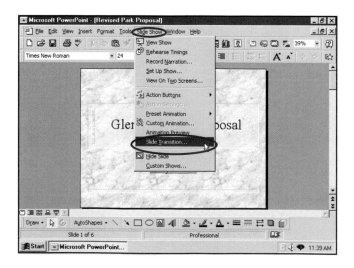

1 Select slide 1 and then switch to Slide view. Click **Slide Show, Slide Transition** from the menu bar.

2 The **Slide Transition** dialog box opens. In this dialog box, you can choose a transition effect, change the advance option, and even choose a sound effect that will play as the slide advances. Notice also that you can choose a transition effect and apply it to the current slide or to all slides in the slide show.

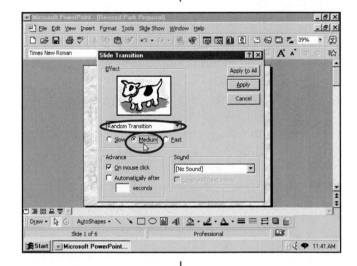

3 For this slide show, you will apply the Random Transition effect to all slides. In the Effect area of the dialog box, click the drop-down arrow of the list box and scroll down to find and select **Random Transition**. Below the Effect list box are three option buttons to determine how quickly the transition occurs. Click the **Medium** option button.

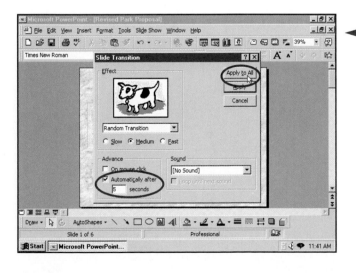

In Depth: You can also add slide transitions in Slide Sorter view. Click a slide you want to add a transition to and then click the Slide Transition Effects drop-down list. Choose a transition from the list. Slide Sorter view displays the effect in this box for the active slide. If you have specified advance settings, the times display under the slides.

4 To specify automatic advance, click the **On mouse click** check box to remove the check mark. Click the **Automatically after** check box. Then type **5** in the **seconds** text box.

5 Click **Apply to All** to use the same transition settings for all slides in the slide show. Now run the slide show. Do not click the mouse button to advance the slides. PowerPoint will advance them automatically for you. Observe the different transition effects as each slide advances. When the slide show ends, switch to Slide Sorter view to see the transition information PowerPoint provides for each slide. Save your changes.

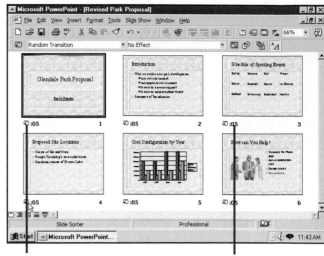

 Quick Tip: To see the transition in effect for a particular slide, click the transition icon below the slide in Slide Sorter view.

Indicates a transition has been applied

Indicates advance timing

Task 4

Creating Animation and Sound Effects

Why would I do this?

PowerPoint offers some special effects that make your slide shows more fun and interesting for your audience. You can animate portions of your slide, such as titles, bulleted lists, and chart elements. You can also add sound effects if your computer is equipped with a sound card and speakers.

In this task, you learn how to add special effects to your slides.

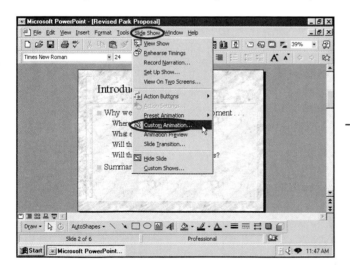

1 Select slide 2. Switch to Slide view. Click **Slide Show, Custom Animation** on the menu bar.

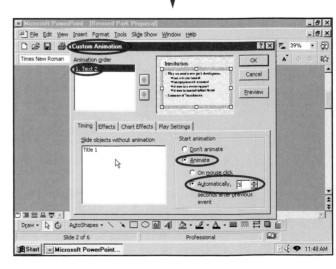

2 The **Custom Animation** dialog box opens. In this dialog box, you can choose what parts of the slide to animate, then choose an animation effect on the Effects tab. To animate the bulleted list on the current slide, click **Text 2**. Click the **Animate** option button. Click the **Automatically** option and set a timing of **3** seconds. These settings tell PowerPoint to animate the bulleted list entries automatically at 3 second intervals.

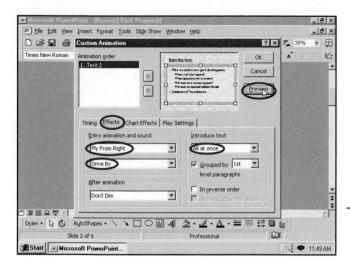

3 Click the **Effects** tab to specify the animation effect. Click the first list box in the **Entry animation and sound** area and select the **Fly From Right** effect. If your computer is equipped for sound, click the second list box in this area and select the **Drive By** sound effect. Click the list box in the **Introduce text** area and select **All at once**.

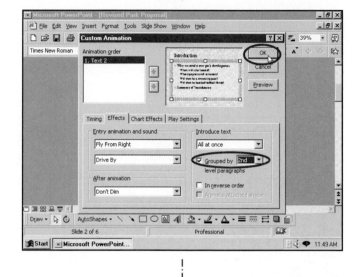

4 To see how your effects will look and sound during the slide show, click the **Preview** button. The sample slide in the dialog box displays your chosen effects. After seeing the preview, you decide the bulleted items should appear one by one, rather than grouped by each main bulleted item. To change the display of the bullet item, click the **Grouped by** list box and select **2nd**.

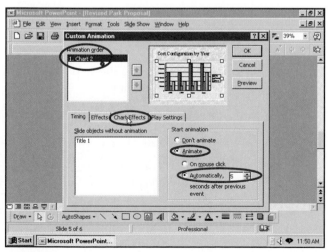

5 Click **OK** to close the dialog box. Move to slide 5. Click **Slide Show, Custom Animation** on the menu bar. The **Custom Animation** dialog box opens. To animate the chart, click **Chart 2**, click the **Animate** button, and choose to start animation automatically **5** seconds after the previous event.

6 Click the **Chart Effects** tab. Click the list box in the **Introduce chart elements** area and select **by Series**. In the first list box in the **Entry animation and sound** area, choose **Wipe Down**. In the second list box, choose the **Laser** sound effect. Preview your selections.

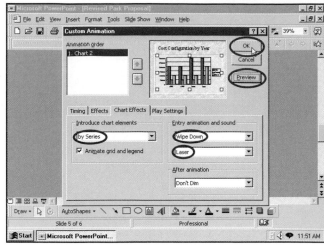

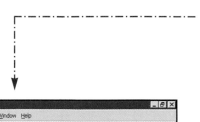

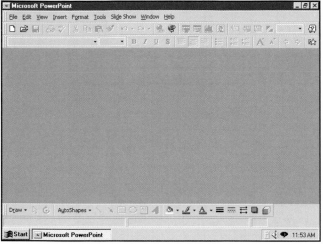

7 Click **OK**. Move to slide 1. Run the slide show and observe the effects you have chosen. Save your changes. Print the slide show as handouts with six slides per page. Close the slide show.

Student Exercises

True-False

For each of the following, circle either T or F to indicate whether the statement is true or false.

T   F   **1.** The Slide Sorter view displays one slide on the screen.

T   F   **2.** A slide transition controls the way the slide is displayed on the screen during a slide show.

T   F   **3.** You can animate only bullet items and chart elements.

T   F   **4.** To modify text, you must open the placeholder and select the text.

T   F   **5.** The font size must be the same for all elements on each slide.

T   F   **6.** Text colors in a slide show are controlled by the design template.

T   F   **7.** When you change text colors on a slide, you must use the colors specified by the design template.

T   F   **8.** Slide timings control the delay before the next slide displays in a slide show.

T   F   **9.** You must be in Slide view to move slides.

T   F   **10.** To have PowerPoint control the display of slides, use the <u>O</u>n mouse click option.

Identifying Parts of the PowerPoint Screen

Refer to the figure and identify the numbered parts of the screen. Write the letter of the correct label in the space next to the number.

1. H
2. A
3. J
4. C
5. E
6. I
7. D
8. B
9. G
10. F

A. Active slide
B. Slide number
C. Transition effect
D. Slide View button
E. Slide Show button
F. Slide Sorter View button
G. New Slide button
H. Title slide
I. Advance timing
J. Slide with clip art

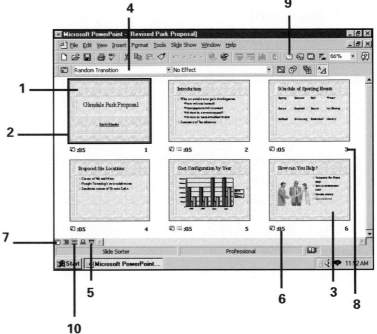

Matching

Match the statements below to the word or phrase that is the best match from the list. Write the letter of the matching word or phrase in the space provided next to the number.

1. C View that displays up to six slides on the screen at once

2. H Button used to run the slide show

3. J Button used to display one slide

4. D Controls movement of text or a chart element during a slide show

5. B Controls how each slide displays during a slide show

6. A Sound effect you can add to a slide

7. E Key used to delete a slide in Slide Sorter view

8. F Indicates where you can place a slide

9. G Tab on which you select options to animate a chart

10. I Button you use to see how animation effects are going to look

A. Laser
B. Transition
C. Slide sorter view
D. Animation effect
E. (Del)
F. Vertical gray line
G. Chart Effects
H. Slide Show button
I. Preview
J. Slide View button
K. Horizontal gray line

Application Exercises

Exercise 1

1. Open the slide show named **Ajax Presentation** that you created in Lesson 15. Save the slide show as <u>**Ajax Revised**</u>.

2. On slide 1 of the slide show, bold and underline the title.

3. Center the titles of slides 2 through 6.

4. On slides 2 and 3, select all the bulleted text and click the **Decrease Font Size** button once to reduce font size.

5. Move the current slide 5 to follow slide 2.

6. Add slide transitions of your choice for each slide. Specify automatic advance after 5 seconds. Use animation effects for the bulleted lists (and titles, if desired) and chart effects for the chart slide.

7. Run the slide show. Save your changes. Print the slide show as handouts with six slides per page. Close the slide show.

Exercise 2

1. Open the slide show named **Creative Computers** that you created in Lesson 15. Save the slide show as <u>**Creative Revised**</u>.

2. On slide 1, change the font of the title to **Times New Roman**, **bold**, **48** point. Change the color of the sub-title to **orange**.

3. On slides 2 through 4, change the titles to **Times New Roman**, **bold**, and **orange**.

4. On slide 4, change the size of text in the table to **28** point. Bold and underline the entries in the first column of the table.

5. Move slide 3 to the end of the slide show. Add a new bulleted list slide at the end of the slide show with the title <u>**Locations**</u>. Format the title to match the other titles in the slide show. Insert the following bulleted items:

   234 West 4th Street
   401 College Avenue
   345 Main Street

6. Add transitions and advance timings as desired. Use animation and sound effects. Run the slide show.

7. Save your changes. Print handouts of the slide show, six slides per page. Close the slide show.

Exercise 3

1. Open the slide show named **My Presentation** that you created in Lesson 15. Save the slide show as <u>**My Final Show**</u>.

2. Modify each slide as desired.

3. Add a new slide and move it if necessary within the slide show.

4. Add transition and animation effects to all slides. Specify advance timings to run the show automatically.

5. Save your changes. Run the slide show.

6. Print handouts of the slide show, six slides per page. Close the slide show.

Exercise 4

The Eagle Corporation.

Your presentation to the board members of Eagle Corporation has convinced them that Eagle Corporation should purchase Discovery Corporation. As a manufacturer of specialized small wood office furniture products, Discovery Corporation would be a good acquisition for Eagle Corporation.

Because of your excellent presentation to the Eagle Corporation board, you have now been asked by the president to prepare and give a presentation to the management team of Discovery Corporation to convince them that it would be in their best interest to be purchased by Eagle Corporation.

Prepare a five-slide presentation that will convince Discovery Corporation that they should accept a buyout offer from Eagle Corporation.

Lesson 17
Integrating Word, Excel, Access, and PowerPoint

Task 1 Preparing the Source Information

Task 2 Preparing the Destination Documents

Task 3 Linking the Chart to the Slide

Task 4 Linking the Chart to the Document

Task 5 Updating the Chart

Introduction

As you have learned by now, the applications in Office 97 have been designed to work together. Despite the different types of information each application handles, you can share the information in a number of ways. This lesson will show you how to link and place an Excel chart into a PowerPoint slide and also into a Word document. Future changes to the Excel worksheet will automatically update both the PowerPoint slide and Word document. Remember, updates must be made to the Excel worksheet, because the link is from Excel to PowerPoint and Excel to Word.

This lesson is designed to show you how you can share data from one application with several other applications.

Visual Summary

After you have completed Task 5, you will have updated a document and a slide with data you copied from Excel.

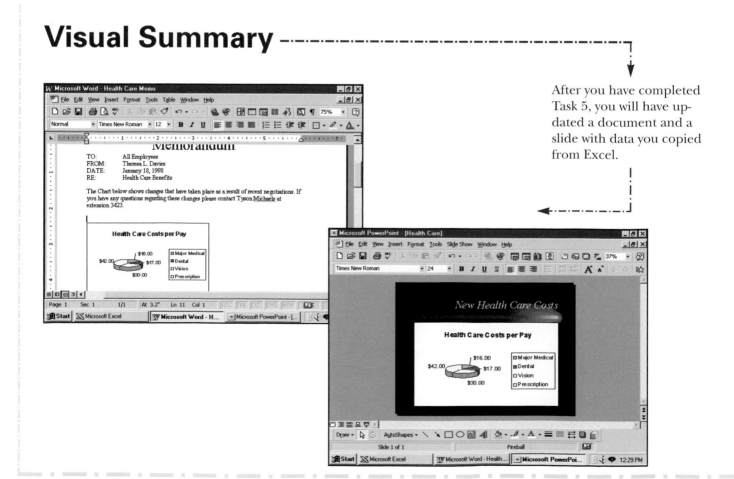

Task 1

Preparing the Source Information

Why would I do this?

As in other integration lessons, you must open the source application and select data you want to link to other applications.

In this task, you copy data from Excel so that you can use it in PowerPoint.

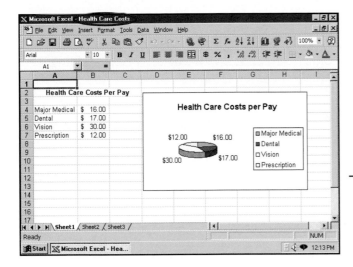

1 Start Excel and open **Less1701** from your student disk. Save the file as **Health Care Costs**.

2 Click inside the chart to select the chart. Click the **Copy** button on the toolbar to place a copy of the chart on the Clipboard.

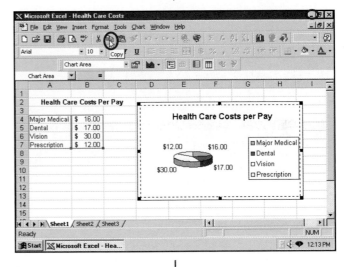

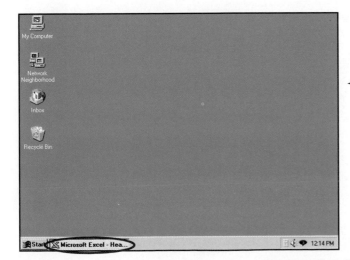

3 Minimize the Excel application.

Task 2

Preparing the Destination Documents

Why would I do this?

You have designated the source information that you will link to two destination documents in different applications. You must now prepare the destination documents for the integration process.

In this task, you learn how to set up two documents to receive the source information.

1 Start Word and open **Less1702** from your student disk. Save the document as **Health Care Memo**.

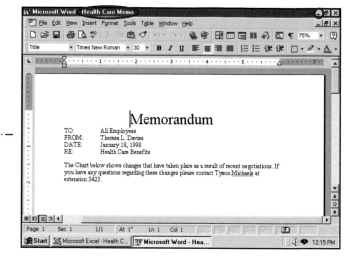

2 Minimize the Word application.

3 Start PowerPoint. Start a new blank presentation and select the **Title Only** layout.

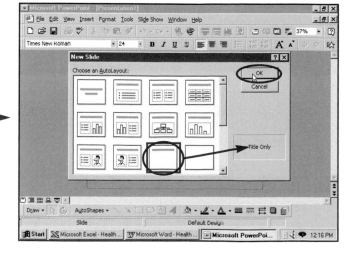

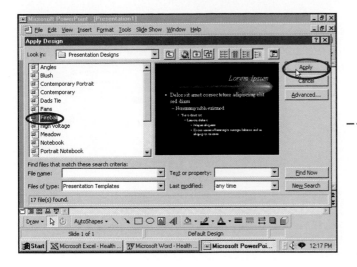

4 Click **OK**. Click the **Apply Design** button on the toolbar. The **Apply Design** dialog box opens. Select the **Fireball** design.

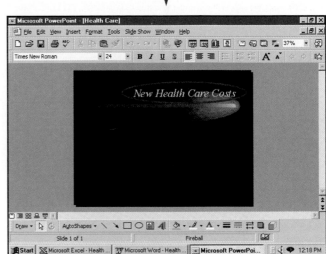

5 Click **Apply** to apply the new design template. Type the title **New Health Care Costs**. Save the slide show as **Health Care**.

Task 3

Linking the Chart to the Slide

Why would I do this?

Because the chart has already been prepared in Excel, you can save time by linking it to the slide rather than creating a similar chart using PowerPoint's chart feature. The link ensures that any updates to the Excel data will also be reflected on the slide.

In this task, you learn how to link the copied chart to the current slide in the slide show.

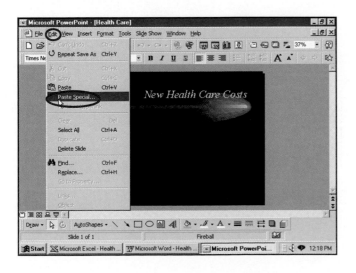

1 You should still be in PowerPoint with slide 1 active. Click **Edit, Paste Special** on the menu bar.

2 The **Paste Special** dialog box opens. Highlight **Microsoft Excel Chart Object**. Click the **Paste link** button.

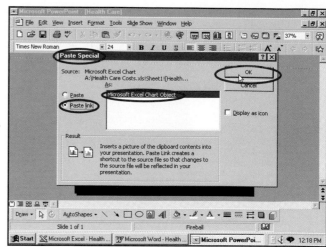

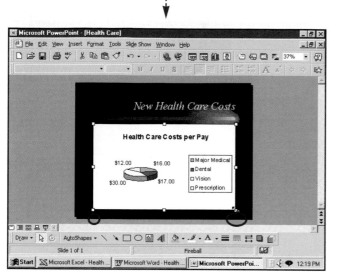

3 Click **OK**. Use the corner selection handles to resize the chart as shown. (Use the corner handles to avoid distorting the text.) Save your changes.

Task 4

Linking the Chart to the Document

Why would I do this?

By linking the Excel chart to the Word document, you ensure that any future changes to the worksheet will automatically be made as well in the Word document.

In this task, you learn how to link the chart to the Word document.

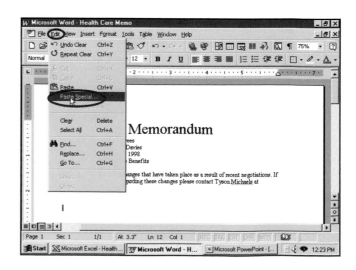

1 Click the **Microsoft Word** button on the taskbar to activate the application. Position the insertion point at the end of the document and press (↵Enter) twice. Click **Edit, Paste Special** on the menu bar.

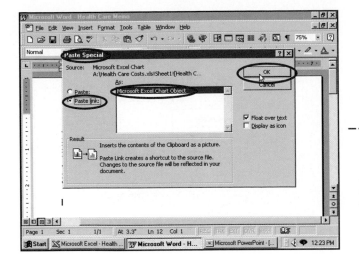

2 The **Paste Special** dialog box opens. Highlight **Microsoft Excel Chart Object**. Click the **Paste link** button.

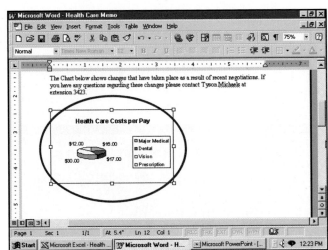

3 Click **OK**. The copied chart displays in the Word document. Save your changes.

Task 5

Updating the Chart

Why would I do this?

Changes you make to the worksheet in Excel will automatically update the Excel chart, the PowerPoint slide containing the Excel chart, and the Word document containing the Excel chart.

In this task, you learn how to update all three charts at one time.

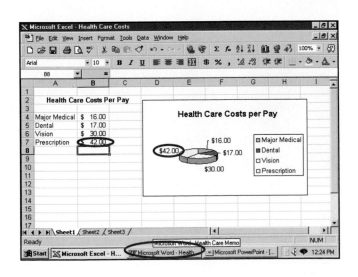

1 Switch to Excel. In cell B7 change the prescription amount from $12.00 to **$42.00** and press **←Enter**. Notice that the Excel chart updates. Save your changes.

2 Switch to the Word document. Note that the Excel chart in the Word document automatically changed to reflect the new prescription amount. Print the document. Save your changes.

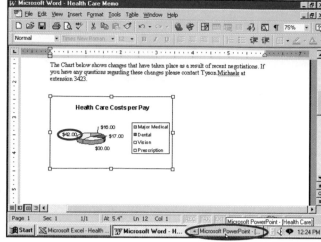

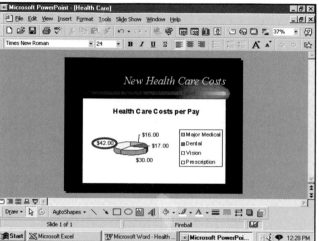

3 Switch to PowerPoint. Note that the Excel chart in the PowerPoint slide automatically changed to reflect the new prescription amount. Print the slide as a handout with two slides per page. Save your changes.

Pothole: If your chart does not automatically update in PowerPoint, right-click inside the PowerPoint chart and click **Update Link**.

4 Close all open documents and applications.

Student Exercises

True-False

For each of the following, circle either T or F to indicate whether the statement is true or false.

T   F   **1.** One reason to use linking is that you can update more than one document at a time with the same information.

T   F   **2.** To open a minimized application, double-click its button on the taskbar.

T   F   **3.** When resizing an object, dragging a side handle helps prevent distortion.

T   F   **4.** You can paste an item from the Clipboard more than once.

T   F   **5.** A linked chart looks the same in a destination document as it does in the source document.

Matching

Match the statements below to the word or phrase that is the best match from the list. Write the letter of the matching word or phrase in the space provided next to the number.

1. ___ Document in which you copy information to integrate

2. ___ Option that creates a shortcut to the source file so changes made in the source file will occur in the destination file

3. ___ Dialog box in which you select linking options

4. ___ PowerPoint slide that displays no placeholder below the title

5. ___ Selection handle that prevents text distortion

A. Paste link

B. Title Only

C. Source

D. Corner

E. Paste Special

F. Side

Application Exercises

Exercise 1

1. Open the document named **Fish Letter** that you created in Lesson 10. Select all cells of the table and copy them to the Clipboard.

2. Start PowerPoint and begin a new slide show. Start with a title slide. Change the design template to **Dads Tie**.

3. Type the title **Joe's Fish Farm** and the sub-title **Fresh Fish at Affordable Prices**.

4. Add a new slide using the **Chart** layout. Type the title **Current Fish Stocks**.

5. Double-click the chart placeholder. In the datasheet, position the pointer in the first cell and then click the **Paste** button. The table data appear in the datasheet. Click the row selector for the first row (it currently contains price data that you don't need). Press Del to remove the row of data from the datasheet.

6. Save the slide show as **Fish Farm Integration**.

7. Print the slide show as handouts with two slides per page. Close all open documents.

Exercise 2

1. Start Access and open the **Agency** database.

2. Create a query using the **Associates** and **Houses** tables to sum the prices of all homes for the two Regional Offices. Save the query as **Sum of Regions**. Copy the query results to the Clipboard.

3. Start a new slide show in PowerPoint. Select the **Title Slide** layout and apply the **Serene** design template. Type the title **Patterson Real Estate**. Save the slide show as **Real Estate**.

4. Add a bulleted list slide and type the title **Regional Listings**. Click the bulleted list placeholder, then click the **Paste** button to paste the contents of the Clipboard to the slide. Delete the first bulleted item (the field names from the query results table). Use Tab⇆ to align the data. Remove the trailing zeroes and decimal points from the price totals.

5. Create a second query using the **Houses** table to show a listing of all four bedroom homes. In the query use Listing #, Bedrooms, Sq Footage, and Price. Save the query as **Four-Bedroom Homes**. Copy the query results to the Clipboard.

6. Add a **Title Only** slide layout and type the title **Four-Bedroom Homes**. Paste the contents of the Clipboard to the slide. Resize the data to fit the slide. Use Tab⇆ to align the data. Remove the decimal points and trailing zeroes from the Sq Footage and Price columns.

7. View the slide show. Save your changes. Print the slide show as handouts with six slides per page. Close the slide show. Close Access.

Exercise 3

1. Start a new slide show in PowerPoint. Apply the **Meadow** design template. On the first slide, type the title **The Tree Farm**. Type the sub-title **Year-End Review**. Save the slide show as **Tree Farm Review**.

2. Add a bulleted list slide and type the title **Fruit Trees**. Click the bulleted list placeholder to open it.

3. In Excel, open the worksheet named **Tree Farm 4** that you created in Lesson 10. Save the worksheet as **Tree Farm 5**. Copy the tree names in cell range A5:A9.

4. Switch back to PowerPoint. The data you copied in Excel is formatted. If you simply paste it into the placeholder, the Excel formats will override the formats of the current design template. To tell PowerPoint to ignore the Excel formatting, click **Edit, Paste Special**. Scroll in the **As** list and select **Unformatted Text**. Click **OK**. Press ⬅Backspace to remove the extra bullet symbol in the placeholder.

5. Add a slide with the **Chart** layout. Type the title **Tree Loss over Two Years**. Double-click the chart placeholder to open the datasheet.

6. Switch back to the worksheet. Select the cell ranges **A4: E9**. Click the **Copy** button on the toolbar.

7. Switch back to PowerPoint. Click in the first datasheet cell. Click **Edit, Paste Link,** and then click **OK**. The worksheet data displays in the datasheet. Click on the slide to close the datasheet.

8. The Year 2 Loss number for cherry trees is incorrect. In the worksheet, change the value to **500**. Save your changes.

9. Check the update on the PowerPoint slide. Save your changes. Print the slide show as handouts with six slides per page.

10. Close all open documents.

Exercise 4

The Eagle Corporation.

As the inventory manager of Eagle Corporation, you are responsible for providing reports from the inventory database.

1. Open the document that you created in Exercise 5 of Lesson 10.

2. Copy the document to the Clipboard.

3. Open PowerPoint.

4. Create a new presentation using a template of your choice.

5. Create a title slide.

6. Add a new slide using the **Title Only** layout.

7. Paste the document on the slide.

8. Use the selection handles to change the size of the document.

9. Add one slide to end the slide show.

10. Save the slide show as **Eagle Integration**.

11. View the slides.

12. Print the slide show as handouts using three slides per page.

Lesson 18
Outlook 97 Basics

Task 1 Launching Outlook 97

Task 2 Exploring the Outlook Folders

Task 3 Working with Calendar

Task 4 Adding Contacts

Task 5 Working with Tasks

Task 6 Using Notes

Introduction

Microsoft Outlook 97 is a personal information manager program that will help you keep track of e-mail, appointments, meetings, tasks, and much more. To use the e-mail capabilities of Outlook, you must have a modem or other communications connection that allows you to send and receive mail. But even if you don't have e-mail capability, you can use Outlook to organize your work and home life.

This lesson is designed to introduce you to some of Outlook's basic features.

Visual Summary

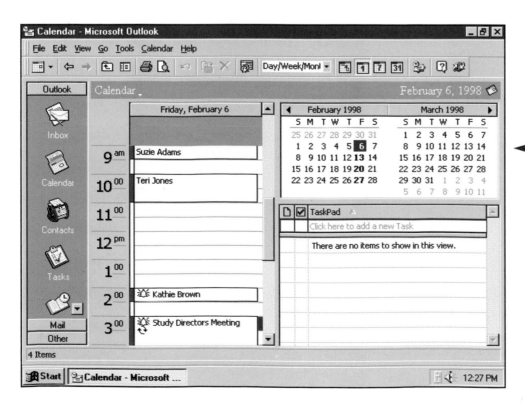

After you have entered appointments in Task 3, you will have created a calendar that looks like this:

Task 1

Launching Outlook 97

Why would I do this?

Launching Outlook starts the Outlook application so that you can begin working with Outlook's many features.

In this task, you learn how to launch Outlook.

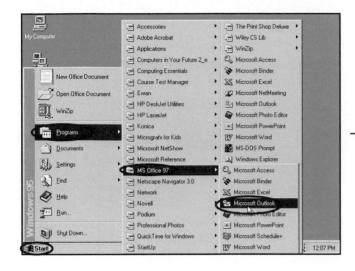

1 To start Outlook, click **Start**, **Programs**, **MS Office 97**, and **Microsoft Outlook**.

2 Outlook opens on your screen. The Office Assistant may also open. The Office Assistant offers a number of options for learning about Outlook. Click **OK** to close the Office Assistant.

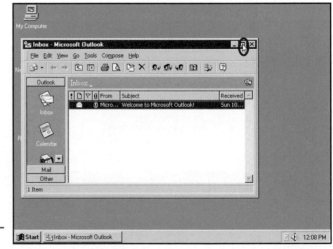

Current folder

Outlook bar

Folder banner

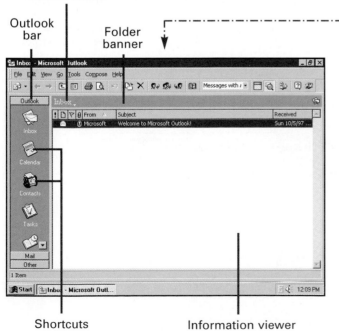

Shortcuts   Information viewer

3 Click the **Maximize** button to make the Outlook window a full screen. Notice that the Outlook screen is partitioned into several panes. By default Outlook opens to the Inbox, the folder you use to organize, create, and store e-mail.

> **In Depth:** Outlook is designed to give you easy access to the information you will be reviewing and storing. The *Outlook bar* contains icons that represent shortcuts to Outlook's folders. The current folder name is displayed in the *folder banner*. The *information viewer* displays the current information in each folder. Outlook offers a number of views for each folder. Your view may differ from the one shown in the figures.

Task 2

Exploring the Outlook Folders

Why would I do this?

Information in Outlook is stored in folders. Each type of information is stored in a specific folder. For example, e-mail messages are stored in the Inbox folder. Appointments are stored in the Calendar folder. The current folder name is displayed in the folder banner at the top of the information viewer. You can move from folder to folder by clicking the shortcuts in the Outlook bar.

In this task, you learn how to display the contents of some Outlook folders.

1 Position your pointer on the **Calendar** shortcut and click. The Calendar folder opens and the information viewer displays the current day with times for appointments. Also displayed are the Date Navigator and the TaskPad.

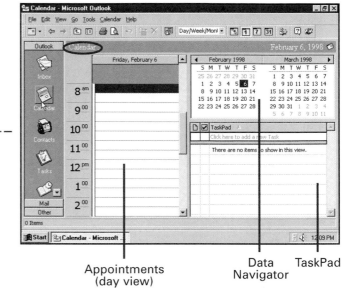

Appointments (day view)   Data Navigator   TaskPad

2 Click the **Contacts** shortcut. The Contacts folder opens. The information viewer displays any contacts that have been added to the folder, or tells you to double-click to add your first new contact.

No tasks have been added to the folder

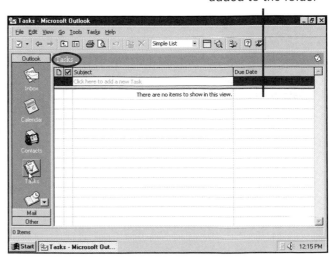

3 Click the **Tasks** shortcut. The Tasks folder opens. The information viewer displays any tasks that have been entered in the folder, or tells you where to click to add a new task.

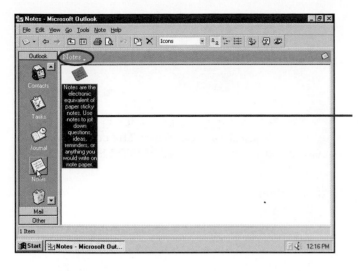

4 Click the **Notes** shortcut. The Notes folder opens. The information viewer displays notes that have been posted to the folder.

Note that has been
stored in the folder

Task 3

Working with Calendar

Why would I do this?

Outlook's Calendar application allows you to schedule events, appointments, and meetings. You can schedule daily, weekly, monthly, or whatever time frame you would like using the Calendar program. You can even assign a reminder to an appointment that sounds an alarm so you will not forget the appointment. If you would like a hard copy of your calendar, you can print the calendar in Daily, Weekly, and Monthly styles.

In this task, you learn how to enter appointments in Calendar, change views, and print the calendar.

1 Click the **Calendar** shortcut to open the Calendar folder. Click inside the 10:00 a.m. time slot.

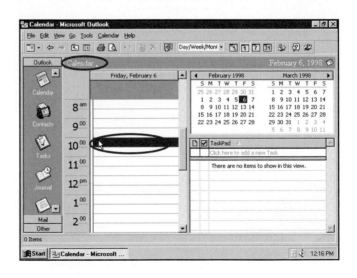

In Depth: To create an appointment on a day other than the current day, click the date in the Date Navigator. To move to a month not currently displayed by the Date Navigator, click the right-pointing arrow at the far right of the Date Navigator's month header.

2 Type **<u>Teri Jones</u>** as the name of the person with whom you have an appointment.

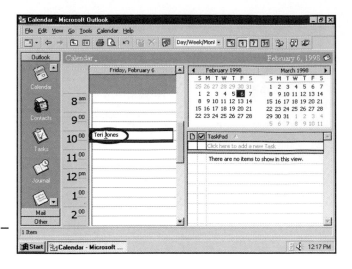

3 Position the pointer on the bottom of the text box until it becomes a two-headed arrow. Drag the arrow down to extend the time for Teri for one hour (10:00 a.m. until 11:00 a.m.).

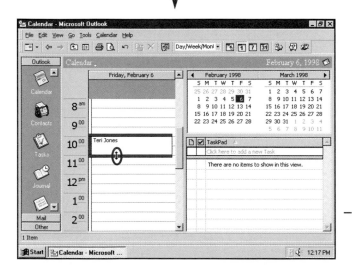

4 Click inside the 9:00 a.m. time slot. Type **<u>Suzie Adams</u>**. Click inside the 2:00 p.m. time slot. Type **<u>Kathie Brown</u>**.

In Depth: Many appointments occur at regular intervals. For example, a class may meet every Tuesday and Thursday from 2:00 p.m. until 3:30 p.m. for an entire quarter or semester. You can schedule a recurring appointment that will automatically display on your calendar at the specified interval and day. When you schedule a recurring appointment, you can indicate the interval of recurrence, such as daily, weekly, or monthly. You can indicate what day of the week the appointment recurs on. You can also specify a date that the recurring appointment stops recurring. For example, you can indicate that the appointment will recur in a particular month and then cease.

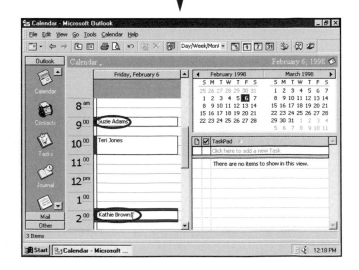

5 Now schedule a recurring appointment. Double-click inside the 3:00 p.m. time slot. The **Untitled - Appointment** dialog box opens. Type **Study Directors Meeting** in the **Subject** text box. In the **End time** box, click the drop-down arrow next to the time and select **4:30 PM** (1.5 hours). Click the **Recurrence** button on the toolbar.

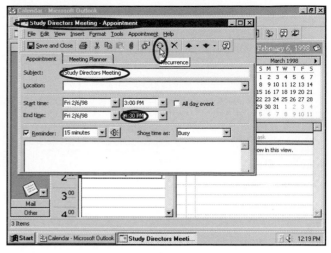

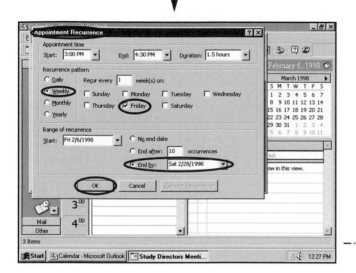

6 The **Appointment Recurrence** dialog box opens. Select the **Weekly** option button to indicate the appointment will occur every week. Click the check box of the current day of the week; that is, if you are doing this task on Tuesday, click the Tuesday check box. To set an ending date for the recurrence, click the **End by** option. Click the date text box and use the Date Navigator to select the last day of the current month (or the next month, if you are in the last week of the current month).

7 Click **OK** to set the recurrence pattern. In the **Study Directors Meeting - Recurring Appointment** dialog box, set a reminder to alert you before the meeting. If there is not already a check mark in the **Reminder** check box, click the check box.

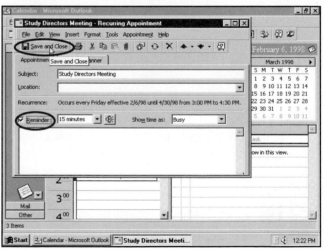

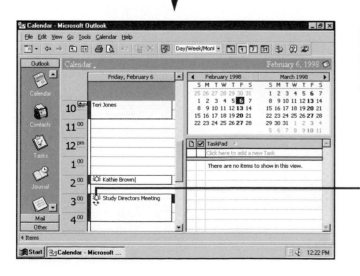

Symbols for reminder and recurring appointment

8 Click the **Save and Close** button. Note the symbols that show the appointment is recurring and that a reminder has been set.

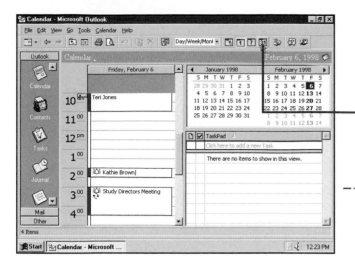

9 To see the recurring appointment, you can change to Month view. Locate the **Month** button on the toolbar.

———— Month button

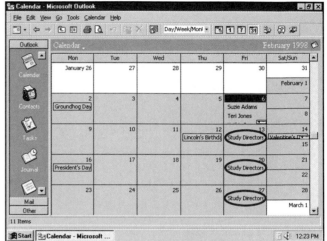

10 Click the **Month** button. The view changes to show the entire month's appointments. Scroll to see how the recurring appointment displays throughout the month.

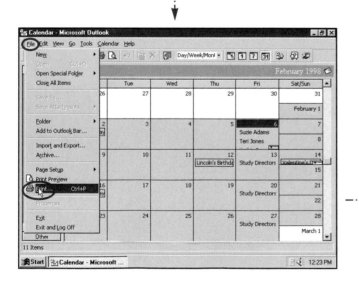

11 To print the current calendar, select **File, Print**.

12 The **Print** dialog box opens. Notice that the **Monthly Style** is chosen by default. Also notice the default dates in the Print range area of the dialog box. You can change these dates if necessary to adjust the number of days printed for the calendar.

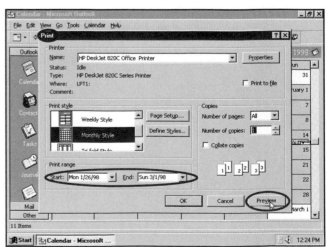

13 To see how your calendar will look when printed, click the **Preview** button. The monthly calendar displays.

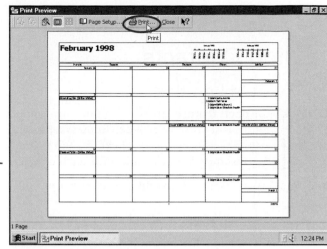

Day button

14 Click the **Print** button in the preview screen, then click **OK** to print a hard copy of the calendar. Click the **Day** button on the toolbar to return to the daily view of your appointments.

In Depth: To delete an appointment, right-click on the colored bar to the left of the appointment. Click **Delete** on the shortcut menu.

15 Delete each appointment by right-clicking on the colored bar to the left of the appointment and then clicking **Delete** on the shortcut menu.

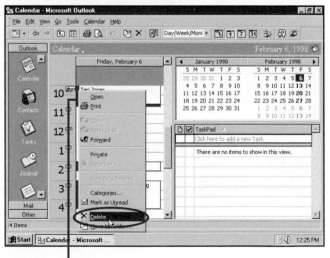

Right-click here to display shortcut menu

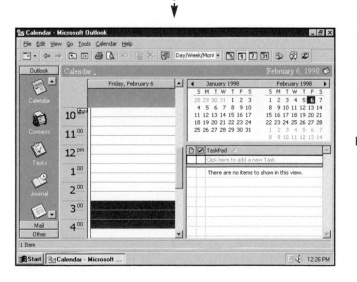

16 When you delete the recurring appointment, a message box displays asking if you want to delete this occurrence of the appointment or all of them. Click the **Delete all occurrences** option and then click **OK**.

Task 4

Adding Contacts

Why would I do this?

Outlook's Contacts feature lets you organize information about people you work or associate with frequently. The Contacts feature is set up like a paper filing system, with tabs that take you to specific letters of the alphabet. You can find a contact easily by simply clicking a tab to see contacts with last names beginning with those letters. You can supply many kinds of information for each contact.

In this task, you learn how to add a contact to Outlook's Contacts folder.

1 Click the **Contacts** shortcut to open the Contacts folder. If anyone has added contacts to the folder, you will see them on the screen, organized in alphabetical order by last name. If no one has added a contact, you will see a blank screen with an instruction to double-click to add a new contact.

2 Double-click in any blank area of the information viewer. The **Untitled - Contact** dialog box opens. In this dialog box, you can insert information about your contact.

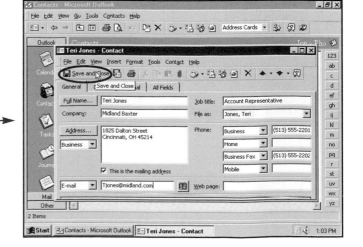

3 Enter the data shown in the figure, using (Tab⇆) to move from field to field in the dialog box.

4 Click the **Save and Close** button to save the information in the Contacts folder. The contact displays in the information viewer.

In Depth: To view all the information stored for a contact, double-click anywhere on the contact information. To delete a contact, click once on the contact's title bar to select it, then press Del.

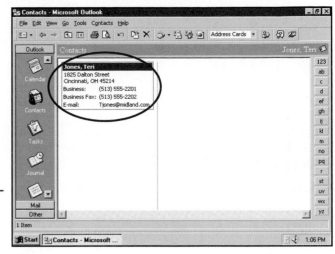

5 Double-click in a blank space to add a new contact. Use your own name or that of a friend and fill in all the information you can. When you have completed the entry, click **Save and Close** to store the new contact.

6 You can print your contact list to have a handy hard copy. Click **File, Print** on the menu bar.

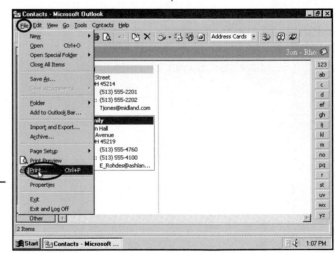

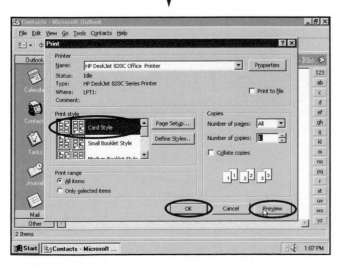

7 The **Print** dialog box opens. Notice the different styles available for printing. Use the **Preview** button to see how each style looks. Click the **Card Style** choice.

8 Click **OK** to print the contacts. Delete both contacts by clicking the title bar of each and pressing (Del).

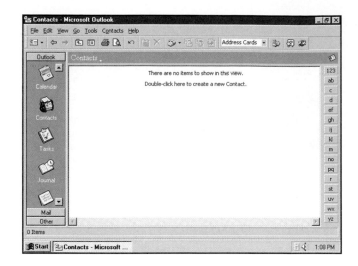

Task 5

Working with Tasks

Why would I do this?

Outlook's Tasks feature lets you create a to-do list that can help you organize your work and home activities. The TaskPad displays your tasks in Calendar view. You enter and modify tasks in the Tasks folder.

In this task, you learn how to create a task list.

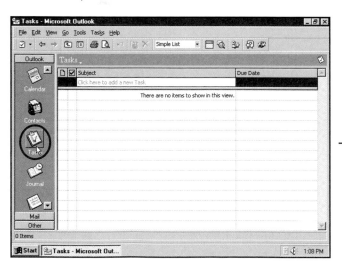

1 Click the **Tasks** shortcut to open the Tasks folder. You should see a screen with no current tasks.

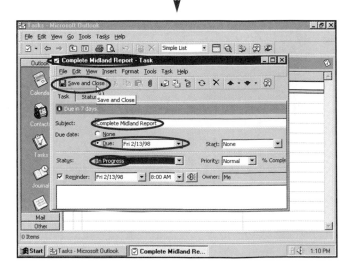

2 To enter a new task, double-click anywhere in the information viewer. The **Untitled - Task** dialog box opens. In this dialog box, you can enter information about the task you are scheduling. Type **Complete Midland Report** in the **Subject** text box. To specify a due date for the task, click the **Due** option and then click the date box. Select a date on the calendar that is one week from the current date. To indicate you have begun working on the task, click the **Status** box and click **In Progress** from the drop-down list.

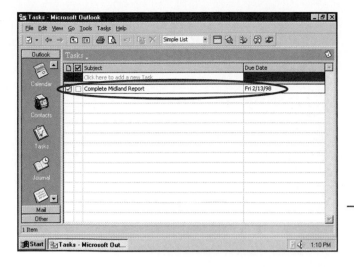

3 Click **Save and Close** to store the task in the Tasks folder.

4 You have been working on sales data for your supervisor. Enter the task shown in the figure. Choose a due date four days from the current date. Make sure to indicate that you have completed 25% of the work.

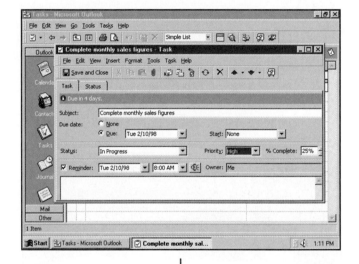

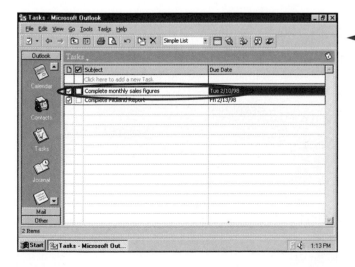

In Depth: You can change data for a task in several ways. You can click in some of the fields, such as Status and Due Date, to see a drop-down list from which you can change or update the field. Double-click the task to see the task's dialog box to make further changes. To delete a task, right-click the task and click **D**elete on the shortcut menu.

5 Click **Save and Close** to store the task. Outlook lists the tasks according to priority, with the high priority task listed first.

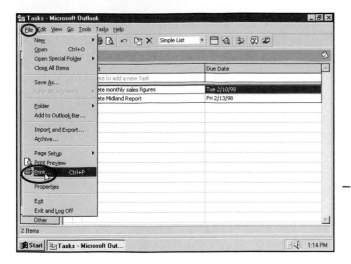

6 You can print your task list to have a handy to-do list. Click **File, Print** on the menu bar.

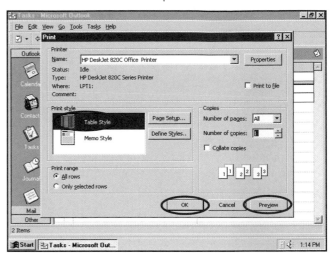

7 The **Print** dialog box opens. Notice the two styles available for printing the task list. Use the **Preview** button to review each. Click the **Table Style**.

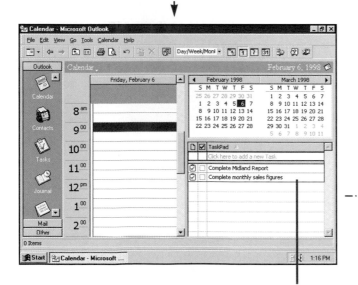

Tasks listed in TaskPad

8 Click **OK** to print the task list. Click the **Calendar** shortcut in the Outlook bar to see the tasks listed in TaskPad.

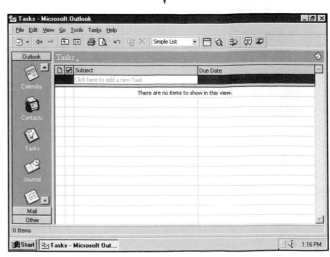

9 Click the **Tasks** shortcut to return to the Tasks folder. Delete each task by right-clicking it and clicking **Delete** on the shortcut menu.

Task 6

Using Notes

Why would I do this?

Outlook's Notes feature gives you an electronic equivalent to the paper sticky notes you use as reminders. You can use notes to jot ideas or to help you remember to do a particular task. While you are creating and using a note, it appears on your screen or on the taskbar like any other application. Once you close a note, it is stored in the Notes folder of Outlook.

In this task, you learn how to create notes.

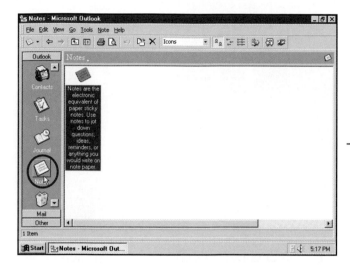

1 Click the **Notes** shortcut to open the Notes folder. If anyone has created notes on your computer, they display in the information viewer. You may see an empty screen.

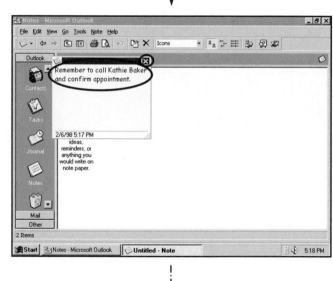

2 Double-click anywhere in the information viewer to open a new note. Type the following note: **Remember to call Kathie Baker and confirm appointment.**

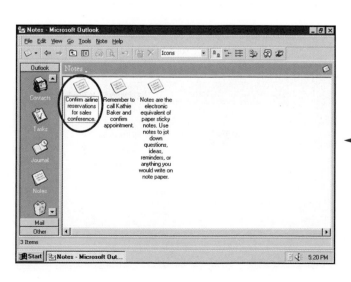

3 To store the note, click its **Close** button. Open another new note and type: **Confirm airline reservations for sales conference.** Store the note.

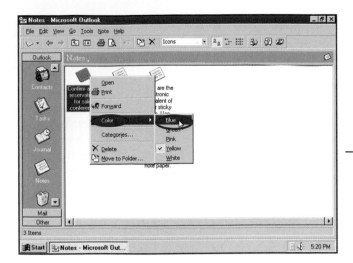

4 To help you keep track of various categories of notes, you can change the note color. Right-click the first note in the information view to display a shortcut menu. Click **Color** to see the color choices on the submenu.

Note icon is now blue

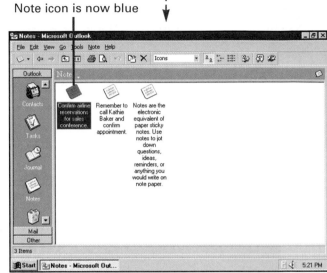

5 Click the **Blue** color. Notice that the note icon has changed color.

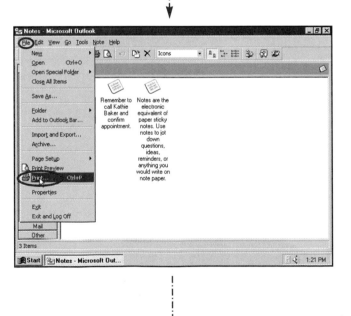

6 You can print your notes to store for future reference or as reminders of tasks you have to complete. With the first note selected, click **File, Print** on the menu bar.

Quick Tip: To print more than one note, click the first to select it, hold Ctrl, and click additional notes.

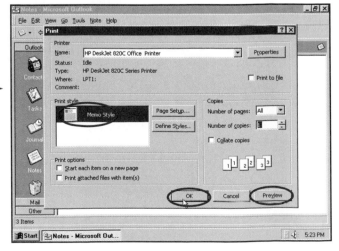

7 The **Print** dialog box opens. Notice the style available for printing the task list. Use the **Preview** button to see what your note will look like when printed. Click the **Print** button to return to the Print dialog box.

8 Click **OK** to print the notes. Delete each note by right-clicking it and then clicking **Delete** on the shortcut menu.

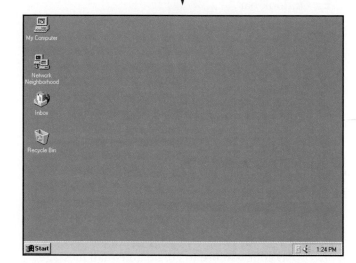

9 Close Outlook by clicking its **Close** box.

Student Exercises

True-False

For each of the following, circle either T or F to indicate whether the statement is true or false.

T   F   **1.** Microsoft Outlook can be used to keep track of your personal schedule.

T   F   **2.** The Notes folder stores information about people you work with frequently.

T   F   **3.** Outlook stores tasks in order of priority.

T   F   **4.** A recurring appointment means the appointment occurs at regular intervals.

T   F   **5.** You can print only calendar information from Outlook.

Identifying Parts of the Outlook Screen

Refer to the figure and identify the numbered parts of the screen. Write the letter of the correct label in the space next to the number.

1. _____
2. _____
3. _____
4. _____
5. _____

A. Shortcut icon
B. Information viewer
C. Folder banner
D. Current folder
E. Outlook bar

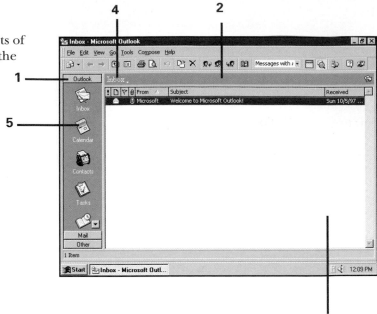

Matching

Match the statements below to the word or phrase that is the best match from the list. Write the letter of the matching word or phrase in the space provided next to the number.

1. ___ Location of shortcut icons

2. ___ Folder you use to create an e-mail message

3. ___ Folder you use to create a to-do list of activities

4. ___ Folder you use to schedule an event or meeting

5. ___ Location of current folder name

6. ___ Item you use to select a month or day not currently displayed

7. ___ Folder you use to organize information about people you work with

8. ___ Feature that lets you schedule appointments that occur at regular intervals

9. ___ Location that shows items currently stored in a folder

10. ___ Folder where you create and store reminders

A. Tasks

B. Appointments bar

C. Recurring appointment

D. Information viewer

E. Calendar

F. Outlook bar

G. Folder banner

H. Inbox

I. Contacts

J. Date Navigator

K. Notes

Application Exercises

Exercise 1

Create and print a monthly calendar showing appointments for Carrie Nelson for the month of October 1998. For the calendar use the following schedule:

1. Monday, October 5. Meeting in Redwood Hall at 4:00 p.m.

2. Every Thursday in October (October 1, 8, 15, 22, 29). Class at the university from 9:00 a.m. until 11:00 a.m. in Clark Hall.

3. Sunday, October 11. 8th Wedding Anniversary. To enter an event such as this one, right-click anywhere on the appointment page and click **New Event** on the shortcut menu.

4. Wednesday, October 21. Kelli's 4th Birthday.

5. Friday, October 23. Meeting with boss at Rover's Restaurant at 12 noon sharp. Be sure to set a reminder for this one.

6. After you have printed the monthly calendar, delete the appointments.

Exercise 2

1. Carrie needs to update her contact list. Add the following contacts:

   Rob Fenner
   CSR
   Taylor Printing
   9010 Central Parkway
   Walnut Hills, OH 45221
   Bus. Phone: 555-1138

   Jack Maggliozzi
   Account Rep
   Robin Color Labs
   5480 Liberty Street
   Cincinnati, OH 45204
   Bus. Phone: 555-2689
   Bus. Fax: 555-6700

2. Print the contacts in a style of your choice.

3. Delete the contacts.

Exercise 3

1. Carrie has several tasks to organize. Add the following tasks to the Tasks folder:

   Review color proofs for Jack
   Complete the task by October 8
   Set the priority as High

   Buy gift for Kelli
   Complete the task by October 21
   Set the priority as High

Finish edit of corporate brochure
Complete the task by October 12
Set the priority as Normal
Indicate that the task is in progress and 50% completed

2. Print the task list in a style of your choice.

3. Delete the tasks.

Glossary

Absolute cell reference   A reference that does not change (is constant) and refers to a specific cell location.

Active cell   The currently selected cell.

Active window   The window ready to accept your commands.

Antonyms   A word having a meaning opposite to a meaning of another word.

Argument   Cell references in parentheses are called an argument. The argument contains cell references or other values that are used in the calculation.

Border   A line you can add to any side of a cell, or to all sides to create an outline. Borders help emphasize areas of the worksheet.

Bullet   A bullet is a graphic character such as a square, diamond, or circle that displays at the beginning of a line to draw attention to that line.

Cell   The intersection of a row and column in the worksheet. A worksheet can contain up to 16,777,216 unique cell locations. Each cell location can contain up to 32,000 characters.

Cell address   Identified by the column letter and the row number that intersect in that cell.

Cell pointer   The heavy outline that indicates the active cell.

Cell range   A group of adjacent cells that have been highlighted.

Chart Wizard   A feature that provides a step-by-step methodology to guide you through the process of creating a chart from worksheet data.

Clicking   Pressing the left mouse button one time. Clicking is normally used to select an object

Clipboard   A temporary storage area in Windows where cut or copied material is stored.

Column   Shown as a letter in the worksheet. A worksheet may contain up to 256 columns.

Criteria   You can use a criteria to display records from a database that meet a particular condition.

Criteria query   A criteria query displays records that match one or more criteria.

Database   Databases store text and number information in individual records. Think of a database as an electronic filing cabinet.

Database objects   The most common database object is the table.

Design grid   Located in the lower pane area of the screen, the design grid is the area where you specify fields to be included, the sort order, and the criteria requirements that must be satisfied to locate a record.

Design template   A design template controls the background color and pattern of each slide, as well as the text formatting and even the colors used for chart elements.

Desktop   The screen that displays when you start Windows 95.

Desktop icons   Picture of a feature or program that gives you easy access to the feature or program.

Destination document   The document you want to place the source data in.

Disk format   Prepares a disk for use, or removes existing files, or checks for disk integrity

Double-clicking   Pressing the left mouse button two times in quick succession. Double-clicking is often used to open or display an object.

Drag and drop   To relocate data in a worksheet to a different area of the worksheet.

Dragging   Pressing and holding the left mouse button while moving the mouse pointer. Dragging is used to move objects from one location to another.

Embed   Data placed in the destination document that is not linked to the source document.

Entry   The data entered in a field is called an entry.

Field   A field is a category of data in a database. For example, the Address field contains addresses for each person or company in a database.

Field list   The field list contains a list of fields in the current database.

Field name   Fields are identified by field names.

Fill handle   Allows you to fill cells adjacent to a selected cell with the same value in that cell. The fill handle can also be used to continue items in a series.

Filter   You can use a filter to display records from a database that meet a particular condition.

Folder   A way to keep files organized.

Font   A font consists of all characters and numbers from a particular typeface in a specific size.

Font style   A change made in the appearance of text, such as bold, underline, or italics.

Footer   Text that displays at the bottom of every page in a document.

Formula

Function   A function is a formula that has already been created for you to perform a specific calculation.

Gridlines   The horizontal and vertical lines on the worksheet.

Handles   Squares surrounding an object to indicate it is selected.

Header   Text that displays at the top of every page in a document.

I-beam   Shape the pointer takes in a text area.

Indent   Space inserted to move a paragraph away from the edge of the text.

Insertion point   The blinking line that indicates where text will appear when you type it.

Label   Text entered in a worksheet cell.

Link   A relationship between a source and a destination document.

Margins   White spaces between the edge of your paper and your text.

Mathematical operator   Common mathematical operators are + (for addition), - (for subtraction), * (for multiplication), and / (for division).

Maximize   Enlarge an application so that the window fills the screen.

Menu bar   Lists the menus available at a particular time in an application.

Minimize   Shrink an application so that it becomes a button on the taskbar.

Mixed cell reference   A reference that contains both a relative and an absolute reference.

Multitasking   Running several applications at the same time.

Office Assistant   Office 97's interactive Help feature that offers context-sensitive help.

Office Shortcut Bar   The group of icons that lets you quickly switch among Office 97 applications.

Page break   Marks the end of each page.

Pointing   Moving the mouse pointer to a specific location on the screen.

Presentation   Any communication you make to a group of other people.

Primary key   A primary key field contains a value that is unique to a record. No two records can have the same value in their primary key field.

Query   A query allows you to display records from your database that match specific criteria.

Record   A record is the entire collection of fields for one person or item in the database. For example, a record might contain the Item, Name, Description, Stock, and Price fields in an inventory database.

Relative cell reference   A reference that changes relative to the location of the formula.

Report   A report can be very basic or a sophisticated document that groups and totals information.

Restore   Returns the window to its original size.

Resize   Changing the width or height of a window..

Right-clicking   Pressing the right mouse button one time. Right-clicking is normally used to display a shortcut menu.

Row   Shown as a number in the worksheet. A worksheet may contain up to 65,536 rows.

Rules of precedence   The order in which calculations are performed in a worksheet formula. Any multiplication operation is performed first, followed by division, addition, and then subtraction. Operations enclosed with parentheses are always calculated first.

Sans serif typeface   Sans serif typefaces do not have small lines at the ends of the strokes.

Scroll arrow   Arrow at either end of the scroll bar that causes the contents of the window to move one line in that direction.

Scroll bar   A bar that automatically appears on the side and/or bottom of the window. when a window is too small to display all the information it contains. This allows the user to scroll through items that do not fit in the window.

Scroll box   Box in the scroll bar.

Serif typeface   Has small lines at the ends of the strokes that make up the characters.

Shading   A color or pattern you add to cells. Shading not only makes your worksheet more attractive, it can also draw attention to specific parts of the worksheet.

Shortcut menus   Display options and commands that relate to the location where you right-clicked.

Slide   The object in a slide show on which you place text, tables, charts, and so on to communicate your ideas to your audience.

Slide show   A series of slides you prepare to use during a presentation.

Source document   The document that contains the original data you want to integrate.

Status bar   Bar at the bottom of the screen that shows information about the current document.

Synonyms   A word having a meaning similar to that of another word.

Table   You create tables in Access to store and organize data.

Taskbar   Usually located at the bottom of the screen, displays the Start button and the names of all open windows.

Title bar   The colored bar at the top of window that gives the application and/or document name.

Typeface   A typeface is a specific design of type.

Value   A number entered in a worksheet cell.

Word wrap   When a word does not fit at the end of a line, it moves to the next line automatically.

Workbook   The entire Excel document is called a workbook. A workbook can consist of a number of worksheets.

Worksheet   One sheet within the workbook. A workbook can contain up to 255 worksheets.

X axis   The horizontal axis of a chart.

Y axis   The vertical axis of a chart.

Index

documents, 37–38
files, 27, 37–38
Office Assistant, 38–39
presentations, 267
tables, 194
Windows Explorer, 21
Word documents, 51
operators. *See* mathematical
operators
outlining. *See* borders
Outlook 97, 292
Calendar, 294, 295–299
closing, 307
Contacts, 294, 300–302
folders, 294–295
Inbox, 293
Notes, 295, 305–307
starting, 293
Tasks, 294, 302–304
window, 293
Outlook bar, 293

P

page breaks, 91, 313
page numbers, in Word documents, 97, 98
Page Numbers dialog box, 97
Page Setup dialog box
Excel, 123, 124
Word, 77
pages, margins, 76–77
Paragraph dialog box, 73, 76
paragraphs
aligning text, 72
borders, 87–88
indents, 73–74
Paste Function button, 138
Paste Special command,
175–176, 283–285
Paste Special dialog box, 176,
284, 285
pasting
charts into Word docu-
ments, 239
data in cells, 111
data from another work-
sheet, 144
query results into work-
sheets, 236–237
text, 52–53
pictures. *See* clip art
pie charts, 165–167, 237–239
placeholders, 250
sub-title, 251
title, 250
pointers, I-beam, 35
pointing, 3, 313
PowerPoint 97
Slide Sorter View, 270–272,
273, 274
Slide view, 270
spelling checker, 251
starting, 249
See also slide shows; slides
PowerPoint dialog box, 249
precedence, rules of, 112, 313
presentations, 248, 313
opening, 267
See also slide shows
previewing
animated slides, 275
calendars, 299

Word documents, 55–56
worksheets, 123–124
primary keys, 187, 313
Print dialog box, 56–57, 125
printing
calendars, 298–299
charts, 167
contacts, 301–302
handouts, 259–260
mailing labels, 228
merged letters, 244
notes, 306
orientation, 123
records, 196
reports, 224
slides, 259–260
tables, 196
tasks, 304
Word documents, 55–57
workbooks, 148
worksheets, 123–125
Programs menu, 35

Q

queries, 206, 313
calculations in, 213–214
copying results to work-
sheets, 235–237
creating, 206–208
criteria, 206–208
mathematical operators,
210–211
modifying, 210–211
on multiple tables, 209–210
names, 212
running, 208
saving, 212
sorting results, 211
query window, 207
quitting. *See* exiting

R

ranges. *See* cell ranges
records, 185, 313
adding, 195
deleting, 195
displaying with filters,
204–205
editing, 194–195
entering, 188–189
entering in Form view,
193–194
printing, 196
selecting, 196
sorting, 203–204
recurring appointments, 296
deleting, 299
entering, 297–298
Recycle Bin, 30–31
relative cell references, 136,
313
reminders
of appointments, 297
in Learn On-Demand, xx
removing
filters, 206
font styles, 71
See also deleting

renaming
files, 29–30
folders, 27, 29–30
worksheets, 143
replacing
misspelled words, 66
text, 53–54
words with synonyms, 68
Report Design view, 224–226
Report Wizard, 221–224
reports, 220, 313
creating, 221–224
grouping data, 222
layouts, 223
mailing labels, 227–229
modifying, 224–226
names, 223
printing, 224
saving, 223, 226
sorting, 222
styles, 223
summary options, 222
resizing
charts, 159
clip art pictures, 86
linked charts, 284
windows, 6–7, 313
Restore button, 6–7
restoring windows, 6–7, 313
right-clicking, 3, 313
rows, in worksheets, 106, 313
adjusting height, 115
inserting, 134
printing headings, 124
selecting, 111
ruler, setting tabs on, 92
rules of precedence, 112, 313
running
queries, 208
slide shows, 258–259

S

sans serif typefaces, 69, 314
Save As dialog box, 25, 49
saving
contacts, 301
queries, 212
reports, 223, 226
tables, 188
tasks, 303
Word documents, 49–50
WordPad documents,
24–25
workbooks, 109
scroll arrows, 8, 314
scroll bars, 8–9, 314
scroll boxes, 8, 107, 314
scrolling
windows, 8–9
worksheets, 106–107
searching. *See* finding
selecting
cells or ranges, 111, 120
charts, 158
clip art pictures, 86
files or folders, 27
records, 196
selection handles, 158
serif typefaces, 69, 314
shading, 141, 314
shortcut menus, 4, 314
shortcuts, in Outlook, 293, 294

Show Table dialog box, 207, 209
Shut Down Windows dialog
box, 16
shutting down Windows, 16
slide shows, 248, 314
automatic advance, 273
changing design templates,
257–258
creating, 249–250
handouts, 259–260
navigating, 252
opening, 267
rearranging slides, 271–272
running, 258–259
special effects, 274–276
Slide Sorter View, 270–272
adding transitions, 273,
274
Slide Transition dialog box, 273
Slide view, 270
slides, 248, 314
aligning text, 268
animation, 274–276
automatic advance, 273
bulleted list, 251–252
charts, 254–255, 275–276
clip art, 256–257
creating, 250–252
deleting, 272
design templates, 250,
257–258, 269
inserting, 271
layouts, 249
linking Excel charts to,
281–284
navigating among, 252
placeholders, 250–251
printing, 259–260
rearranging, 271–272
tables, 253–255
title, 249–251
transition effects, 272–274
sorting
in filters, 204–205
query results, 211
records, 203–204
reports, 222
sound effects, 274
source documents, 173, 314
selecting data in, 174–175
updating, 177, 285–286
worksheets, 281
See also linking
spell checking
in PowerPoint, 251
in Word, 48, 65–67
Spelling and Grammar dialog
box, 65
spreadsheets. *See* worksheets
Start button, 3, 4, 5
Start menu, 4, 5
starting
Access 97, 183
applications, 35, 36
Excel 97, 36, 105
Help, 12
Learn On-Demand, xi–xii
Outlook 97, 293
PowerPoint 97, 249
Windows 95, 3
Word 97, 35, 47
statistical functions, 138–140
status bar, 35, 314
Summary Options dialog box,
222